CRIMINAL JUSTICE, LAW ENFORCEMENT AND CORRECTIONS

INDIGENT DEFENSE

FEDERAL SUPPORT AND INTERNATIONAL PERSPECTIVES

Criminal Justice, Law Enforcement and Corrections

Additional books in this series can be found on Nova's website under the Series tab.

Additional E-books in this series can be found on Nova's website under the E-book tab.

Law, Crime, and Law Enforcement

Additional books in this series can be found on Nova's website under the Series tab.

Additional E-books in this series can be found on Nova's website under the E-book tab.

CRIMINAL JUSTICE, LAW ENFORCEMENT AND CORRECTIONS

INDIGENT DEFENSE

FEDERAL SUPPORT AND INTERNATIONAL PERSPECTIVES

BETTY NICHOLS
AND
JEFF WEAVER
EDITORS

nova publishers
New York

For permission to use material from this book please contact us:
Telephone 631-231-7269; Fax 631-231-8175
Web Site: http://www.novapublishers.com

Additional color graphics may be available in the e-book version of this book.

LIBRARY OF CONGRESS CATALOGING-IN-PUBLICATION DATA

ISBN: 978-1-62257-441-4

Published by Nova Science Publishers, Inc. † New York

CONTENTS

PREFACE

Pursuant to the Sixth Amendment to the U.S. Constitution, every person accused of a crime is afforded the right to have counsel in his or her defense, even if unable to afford such representation. Individuals accused of a crime but unable to afford representation, referred to as indigent defendants, often rely on entities such as public defender offices for the provision of counsel. Several organizations, including the National Legal Aid and Defender Association, conducted national studies of indigent defense, pointing out many challenges in providing counsel across the country, including inadequate funding of defense programs as a whole, inadequate compensation for assigned counsel, lack of investigative resources, inexperienced counsel, and understaffing of public defense offices. In affording indigent defendants their right to counsel, both state and local governments generally decide the type of indigent defense programs to employ and how to fund them. This book provides a look at federal support and international perspectives of indigent defense.

Chapter 1 - The Sixth Amendment to the U.S. Constitution guarantees every person accused of a crime the right to counsel. States and localities generally fund indigent defense services, and the Department of Justice (DOJ) also provides funding that can be used for these services. GAO was asked to review federal support for indigent defendants. This report addresses, for fiscal years 2005 through 2010, the (1) types of support DOJ provided for indigent defense; (2) extent to which eligible DOJ funding was allocated or awarded for indigent defense, the factors affecting these decisions, and DOJ's actions to address them; (3) percentage of DOJ funding allocated for indigent defense and how it was used; (4) extent to which DOJ collects data on indigent defense funding; and (5) extent to which DOJ assesses the impacts of indigent defense grants, indigent defense programs have been evaluated, and DOJ has supported evaluation efforts. GAO surveyed (1) all 4,229 grant recipients about funding allocations and (2) a sample of 253 public defender offices about factors influencing their decisions to apply for funding. Though not all survey results are generalizable, they provide insights. GAO also analyzed grant related documents and interviewed relevant officials.

Chapter 2 – The Legal Services Corporation (LSC) is a private, nonprofit, federally funded corporation that helps provide legal assistance to low-income people in civil (i.e., noncriminal) matters. The primary responsibility of the LSC is to manage and oversee the congressionally appropriated federal funds that it distributes in the form of grants to local legal services providers, which in turn give legal assistance to low-income clients in all 50 states, the District of Columbia, the US territories of Guam and the Virgin Islands, the

Commonwealth of Puerto Rico, and Micronesia (including the Commonwealth of the Northern Mariana Islands, the Republic of the Marshall Islands, and Palau).

Although the authorization of appropriations for the LSC expired at the end of FY1980, the LSC has operated for the past 31 years under annual appropriations laws. On November 17, 2011, the House and the Senate passed the conference report on H.R. 2112 (H.Rept. 112-284). President Obama signed H.R. 2112 into law (P.L. 112-55) on November 18, 2011. P.L. 112-55 (the Consolidated and Further Continuing Appropriations Act, 2012) funded the LSC at $348 million for FY2012. The FY2012 appropriation for the LSC, $348 million, is 13.9% less than the FY2011 LSC appropriation of $404.2 million, 22.7% less than the Administration's budget request, 16% more than the House committee's recommendation, and 12.1% less than the amount passed by the Senate. In addition, since FY1996, all of the LSC appropriations laws have included language that restricts the activities of LSC grantees. The LSC appropriation for FY2012 included existing restrictions on LSC activities.

For FY2013, the Obama Administration requested $402.0 million for the LSC. This amount is $54.0 million (15.5%) above the FY2012 appropriation of $348.0 million for the LSC. The Senate Committee on Appropriations recommended $402 million for the LSC for FY2013. The House-passed appropriations bill (H.R. 5326) for Commerce, Justice, Science, and Related Agencies (CJS) recommended $328 million for the LSC for FY2013. The LSC statute requires that poverty population data from the most recent decennial census be used to distribute LSC funds. Due to changes in the data sets obtained by the 2010 decennial census, information needed by the LSC is no longer available.

On September 19, 2011, the LSC Board recommended several changes to resolve the issue and improve distribution of LSC funds.

Under the LSC's competitive process, legal services providers in every jurisdiction bid to become the LSC grantee for a designated service area in a state. During 2010, the LSC funded 136 local programs/grantees in 919 offices employing 4,350 attorneys. Local programs establish their own eligibility criteria, in which clients served may not have income that exceeds 125% of the federal poverty guidelines. In 2010, 71% of LSC clients were females and 29% were males.

The majority of LSC clients (85%) were between the ages of 18 and 59, 13% were age 60 or older, and 2% were under the age of 18. Almost 47% of LSC clients were non-Hispanic white, 26% were non-Hispanic black, almost 9% were of other races, and about 19% were Hispanic. In 2010, LSC grantees closed 932,406 cases involving issues primarily related to families (divorce, child support, etc.), housing, consumer finance, income maintenance, and health.

Although the LSC is the largest single source of funding for the civil legal services system in the United States, it is not the only source of funding. Local legal services programs supplement their LSC grants with funds from a variety of governmental and private sources. LSC funding accounts for 44% of all funding for civil legal services for the poor in the United States.

Chapter 3 – The vast majority of criminal defendants in the United States are too poor to afford a lawyer, yet adequate funding and resources for defense counsel remains an elusive goal. The U.S. Department of Justice (the Department) seeks effective, evidence-based solutions to problems in indigent defense so that the nation can deliver on its constitutionally guaranteed promise to provide legal representation to people accused of crime who cannot afford it.

In January 2011, the Department's Access to Justice Initiative (ATJ) and National Institute of Justice's (NIJ) International Center jointly convened an Expert Working Group (EWG) on *International Perspectives on Indigent Defense* to explore domestic and international practices in indigent defense.

That the convening started on the same day that the Governor of Massachusetts announced his plans to overhaul the commonwealth's public defender system was only further evidence of the importance of identifying the best approaches to the delivery of defender services.

The 40-person EWG consisted of leading experts drawn from multidisciplinary communities, including domestic and international practitioners, researchers, government officials and advocates from nine countries. The goals of the workshop were to:

- Help suggest federal priorities on indigent defense;
- Help identify research in the field of indigent defense;
- Learn about alternative and best practices in the provision of defender services for the poor from the United States and around the globe;
- Consider the transferability of successful international practices to the United States; and
- Forge sustained American and international collaborations in the field of criminal legal aid.

Over a day and a half, participants were led in a facilitated discussion around the following six panels:

- The state of indigent defense in the United States generally;
- Costs associated with being indigent in the criminal justice system;
- Improvements to the provision of defender services for the poor;
- Improvements to the provision of defender services for juveniles;
- The intersection of indigent defense and immigration; and
- Indigent defense in indigenous communities.

At the conclusion of the facilitated discussions, participants were divided into five breakout groups to identify specific, actionable recommendations for ATJ and NIJ. These breakout groups aligned with the panel topics of the convening and were organized to consider *costs* of being indigent, *general improvements* to the criminal justice system, improvements for *juveniles*, special considerations for *immigrants* and special considerations for *indigenous communities*.

The breakout groups were asked to create recommendations to advance ATJ's and NIJ's efforts to set federal priorities in indigent defense, identify research gaps in the field and identify international practices that should be assessed for transferability to the United States.

This chapter provides an overview of the EWG's discussions and includes the breakout groups' recommendations following the summary of the corresponding panel presentations.

ATJ and NIJ were pleased they could foster a new level of cooperation between domestic and international researchers and practitioners in the field of criminal legal aid. Although the level of participation in the EWG is a measure of this new cooperation, so too are the many contacts that have continued after the meeting.

This chapter provides the federal government and the indigent defense community with recommendations that can help steer the direction of indigent defense research and potential reform strategies for years to come.

The authors have included an appendix summarizing the international practices identified in the workshop. No effort has been made to assess whether these practices can or should be transferred to the United States. It is the hope of the authors that assessments of the transferability of some of these practices can be produced in the months ahead.

In: Indigent Defense
Editors: Betty Nichols and Jeff Weaver

ISBN: 978-1-62257-441-4

Chapter 1

INDIGENT DEFENSE: DOJ COULD INCREASE AWARENESS OF ELIGIBLE FUNDING AND BETTER DETERMINE THE EXTENT TO WHICH FUNDS HELP SUPPORT THIS PURPOSE*

United States Government Accountability Office

ABBREVIATIONS

ABA	American Bar Association
AOUSC	Administrative Office of the U.S. Courts
ARRA	American Recovery and Reinvestment Act
ATJ	Access to Justice Initiative
BIA	Bureau of Indian Affairs
BJA	Bureau of Justice Assistance
BJS	Bureau of Justice Statistics
CCLI	Capital Case Litigation Initiative
DOI	Department of the Interior
DOJ	Department of Justice
ICRA	Indian Civil Rights Act
JABG	Juvenile Accountability Block Grant
JAG	Edward Byrne Memorial Justice Assistance Grant
JIDNC	Juvenile Indigent Defense National Clearinghouse
JJDP	Juvenile Justice and Delinquency Prevention Grant Title II
JRJ	John R. Justice Program
NIJ	National Institute of Justice
NTTAC	National Training and Technical Assistance Center
OJJDP	Office of Juvenile Justice and Delinquency Prevention

* This is an edited, reformatted and augmented version of United States Government Accountability Office publication GAO-12-569, dated May 2012.

OMB	Office of Management and Budget
OJP	Office of Justice Programs
SAA	state administering agency
TCCLA	Tribal Civil and Criminal Legal Assistance
TJADG	Tribal Juvenile Accountability Discretionary Grants Program
TPA	Tribal Priority Allocations
WCR	Wrongful Conviction Review Program

WHY GAO DID THIS STUDY

The Sixth Amendment to the U.S. Constitution guarantees every person accused of a crime the right to counsel. States and localities generally fund indigent defense services, and the Department of Justice (DOJ) also provides funding that can be used for these services. GAO was asked to review federal support for indigent defendants. This report addresses, for fiscal years 2005 through 2010, the (1) types of support DOJ provided for indigent defense; (2) extent to which eligible DOJ funding was allocated or awarded for indigent defense, the factors affecting these decisions, and DOJ's actions to address them; (3) percentage of DOJ funding allocated for indigent defense and how it was used; (4) extent to which DOJ collects data on indigent defense funding; and (5) extent to which DOJ assesses the impacts of indigent defense grants, indigent defense programs have been evaluated, and DOJ has supported evaluation efforts. GAO surveyed (1) all 4,229 grant recipients about funding allocations and (2) a sample of 253 public defender offices about factors influencing their decisions to apply for funding. Though not all survey results are generalizable, they provide insights. GAO also analyzed grant related documents and interviewed relevant officials.

WHAT GAO RECOMMENDS

GAO recommends that DOJ increase grantees' awareness that funding can be allocated for indigent defense and collect data on such funding.

DOJ concurred with the recommendations.

WHAT GAO FOUND

The Department of Justice (DOJ) administered 13 grant programs from fiscal years 2005 through 2010 that recipients could use to support indigent defense, 4 of which required recipients to use all or part of the funding for this purpose. DOJ also provides training to indigent defense providers, among other things.

From fiscal years 2005 through 2010, recipients of the 4 grants that required spending for indigent defense allocated or planned to use \$13.3 million out of \$21.2 million in current dollars for indigent defense. However, among the 9 grants that did not require allocations or awards for indigent defense, two-thirds or more of state, local, and tribal respondents to GAO's surveys reported that they did not use funds for this purpose, partly due to competing priorities. DOJ has listed the grants on its website. However, no more than 54 percent of grantees or public defender offices responding to GAO's surveys were aware that such funding could be used to support indigent defense. Taking steps to increase awareness would better position DOJ to help ensure that eligible grantees are aware that they can access federal funding to help address their needs. DOJ officials acknowledged that opportunities exist to enhance grantees' awareness.

When recipients allocated funding for indigent defense, the amount was generally small relative to the total award and most commonly used for personnel and training. For instance, among grant recipients who reported in GAO's surveys that they had allocated funding for indigent defense, allocations as a percentage of total awards ranged from 2 percent to 14 percent.

DOJ generally collects data on funding allocated for indigent defense when the grant program requires such funding or identifies it as a grant priority, but does not do so in two juvenile-focused grants. According to DOJ, it does not collect such data in these two programs because indigent defense is 1 of 17 purposes for which grant funds can be used. GAO has previously reported that agencies should collect data to support decision making, and the Attorney General has committed to focusing on indigent defense issues. Collecting data on the amount of funding from these two grants that is used to support indigent defense would position DOJ to better assess if it is meeting the Attorney General's commitment.

DOJ assesses the impact of indigent defense grant funding and has mechanisms to help indigent defense providers evaluate services. All 9 of the DOJ grant programs that required or prioritized funding to be used for indigent defense included output measures that described the level of grant activity, such as the number of defenders hired, and 7 of the 9 included outcome measures that described the intended results of the funds, such as the percent increase in defendants served. Nine of the 118 public defender offices or agencies that responded to GAO's survey provided GAO with a copy of an evaluation that had been conducted of their office; those that did not most frequently cited lack of personnel (28 of 62) and lack of expertise or the need for technical assistance (26 of 62) as the reasons. DOJ has mechanisms that could address these challenges. For instance, DOJ provides technical assistance through a website.

May 9, 2012

Congressional Requesters

Pursuant to the Sixth Amendment to the U.S. Constitution, every person accused of a crime is afforded the right to have counsel in his or her defense, even if unable to afford such representation.[1] Individuals accused of a crime but unable to afford representation—referred to as indigent defendants—often rely on entities such as public defender offices for the provision of counsel. Several organizations, including the National Legal Aid and Defender Association, conducted national studies of indigent defense, pointing out many challenges in providing counsel across the country, including inadequate funding of defense programs as a whole, inadequate compensation for assigned counsel, lack of investigative resources, inexperienced counsel, and understaffing of public defense offices. In affording indigent defendants their right to counsel, both state and local governments generally decide the type of indigent defense programs to employ and how to fund them.

States, localities, and, in some cases, tribes fund indigent defense services, and the federal government—through the Department of Justice (DOJ) and the Department of the Interior's (DOI) Bureau of Indian Affairs (BIA), for tribes—also provides funding that can be used to support indigent defense services. [2] However, in this country's current fiscal crisis, several states have reported that when determining how to allocate scarce budget resources, they have reduced or eliminated state funding for state and local indigent defense services. Further, although tribes—which retain limited, inherent sovereignty—are not bound by restraints placed upon the federal or state governments through the Bill of Rights or other amendments to the U.S. Constitution, many tribal governments choose to provide indigent defense services and face similar challenges as state and local governments in doing so.[3]

You requested that we assess federal funding and other federal support to state, local, and tribal governments to assist them in providing counsel to indigent defendants. Specifically, this report addresses the following questions:

1. What type of support, if any, have DOJ and BIA provided for state, local, and tribal indigent defense?
2. For fiscal years 2005 through 2010, to what extent was eligible DOJ and BIA funding allocated and awarded for indigent defense, what factors affected decisions to allocate and award funding for this purpose, and what actions have DOJ and BIA taken, if any, to address these factors?
3. When fiscal year 2005 through 2010 federal funding was allocated or awarded for indigent defense, how did it compare to the total allocations or awards made, and how did recipients use the funding?
4. To what extent does DOJ collect data on indigent defense funding when the grant program specifies that funds be allocated or awarded for this purpose or highlights it as a priority?
5. When a grant program specifies that funds be spent for indigent defense or highlights it as a priority, to what extent does DOJ assess the impacts of this grant funding, and to what extent have there been evaluations of indigent defense programs and has DOJ supported these evaluation efforts?

To determine what DOJ grant programs and BIA funding could be used for indigent defense from fiscal years 2005 through 2010, we analyzed the Catalog of Federal Domestic Assistance and DOJ's website, and consulted DOJ and BIA officials responsible for administering state, local, and tribal grant and funding programs.[4] We obtained records of all recipients of relevant DOJ grants, and identified recipients of relevant BIA funding through BIA's annual budget justifications. Further, we interviewed knowledgeable agency officials about the source of the grant data and the controls in place to maintain the integrity of the data and determined that the data were sufficiently reliable for our purposes. In addition, we interviewed DOJ and BIA officials with knowledge of other assistance the agencies provide to support indigent defense.

To determine the extent to which state, local, and tribal government recipients allocated federal funding for indigent defense, the factors that influenced their decisions, and the amounts allocated, we conducted separate web-based surveys of all recipients of fiscal year 2005 through 2010 DOJ formula grants that could be allocated for indigent defense— the Edward Byrne Memorial Justice Assistance Grant (JAG), [5] Juvenile Justice and Delinquency

Prevention Grant Title II (JJDP) and the Juvenile Accountability Block Grant (JABG)—and tribal governments that received funding through BIA Tribal Courts tribal priority allocation (TPA) distributions from fiscal years 2005 through 2010.[6] Forty-six percent of JAG recipients (1,818 of 3,963; including 89 percent of state agencies and 45 percent of localities and tribes) completed the JAG survey; 89 percent of JJDP recipients (50 of 56) completed the JJDP survey; 82 percent of JABG recipients (46 of 56) completed the JABG survey; and 68 percent (105 of 154) of recipients completed the Tribal Courts TPA survey.[7] Because all recipients of JABG and JJDP funding were included in our population and we received response rates of 82 and 89 percent, we consider our results generalizable to the population of JABG and JJDP recipients. While all eligible members of our target population of JAG recipients and recipients of BIA Tribal Courts TPA distributions were included in our survey, due to the relatively low response rates and the possibility of other errors all questionnaire surveys face, our results represent only those respondents who participated in our survey and should not be generalized to the population of JAG recipients or recipients of BIA Tribal Courts TPA distributions.[8] Moreover, dollar amounts reported by JAG respondents have limitations and should be treated as estimates. See appendix I for additional discussion of these limitations and the reasons they occurred, and additional details of our survey methods. However, the responses provide insights into the extent to which JAG funding and BIA Tribal Courts TPA distributions have been allocated for indigent defense. Moreover, to determine the purposes for which this funding was used and to identify the most frequently reported uses, we conducted follow-up interviews with selected survey respondents who reported allocating funding for indigent defense.[9]

Further, to determine the extent to which DOJ awarded eligible discretionary grants for indigent defense, we obtained project descriptions of grants available for indigent defense from DOJ.[10] We reviewed these descriptions to identify the number and amount of grants used either all or in part for indigent defense and the uses of these funds.

To determine what actions, if any, DOJ and BIA have taken to address factors influencing recipients' decisions to allocate funding for indigent defense, we interviewed DOJ and BIA officials responsible for each type of funding. We also reviewed DOJ's guidance to recipients to determine the extent to which DOJ communicated that funding could be used for indigent defense programs. We compared this guidance against relevant statutes, and DOJ's stated commitment to support indigent defense.

In addition, we reviewed DOJ grant documentation to identify grants for which indigent defense was identified as a priority or purpose of the grant. For these grants, we reviewed grant performance measures outlined in DOJ grant solicitations. We also conducted interviews with relevant DOJ officials about the extent to which DOJ collects data on whether grants were allocated or awarded for indigent defense and measures the impact resulting from grant funds for indigent defense. We analyzed this information to determine the status of DOJ's efforts and the mechanisms available to collect such data and assess the impact. We compared DOJ's measures against criteria in Office of Management and Budget (OMB) guidance[11] and our prior work on performance measures, which states that leading organizations promote accountability by establishing results-oriented, outcome goals and corresponding performance measures by which to gauge progress towards attaining these goals.[12] To determine whether performance measures were outcome-oriented, two analysts also independently reviewed performance measures DOJ established to assess whether the measures focused on the intended result of the program. The analysts then met to discuss and resolve any differences in the results of their analyses.

Further, to determine the extent to which evaluations had been conducted of indigent defense programs, we conducted a web-based survey of a random sample of 253 public defender offices or agencies from among 841 identified nationwide; 118 offices or agencies completed the questionnaire for an unweighted response rate of 47 percent. Respondents to this survey were generally a county or city public defender office, state-run public defender office, or firm or nonprofit organization under contract to provide indigent defense services. Due to the relatively low response rate and the possibility of other errors all questionnaire surveys face, our results represent only respondents who participated in our survey and should not be generalized to the population of public defender offices or agencies. However, the results provide insights into the evaluation conducted of public defender offices and the challenges associated with conducting such an evaluation. In addition, we conducted a literature search of peer-reviewed journals. In December 2011, we held a listening session at a National Legal Aid and Defender Association conference where public defenders described challenges to conducting evaluations, among other topics.[13] Finally, to identify actions DOJ has taken to evaluate indigent defense systems, we reviewed studies funded or conducted by DOJ and interviewed DOJ officials about its efforts to evaluate indigent defense systems. Additional details on our scope and methodology are contained in appendix I.

We conducted this performance audit from February 2011 to May 2012 in accordance with generally accepted government auditing standards. Those standards require that we plan and perform the audit to obtain sufficient, appropriate evidence to provide a reasonable basis for our analysis based on our audit objectives. We believe that the evidence obtained provides a reasonable basis for our analysis based on our audit objectives.

BACKGROUND

States and localities have developed and largely funded their own indigent defense systems. To do so, they have generally adopted one or more of the following methods for providing indigent defense—employing full or part-time public defenders to handle the bulk of cases requiring counsel; entering into contracts with private attorneys, often after a bidding contest, to provide counsel; or developing a list, or "panel," of private attorneys who accept a predetermined fixed rate and from which the court appoints as defense counsel when needed. Further, depending on the state, funding for the indigent defense system is provided by the state, localities within the state, or a combination of state and local funding.

According to DOJ, as of its most recent census of public defender offices issued in 2007, 22 states have established statewide—and state funded—public defender agencies to provide indigent defense in which a central office oversees the operations, policies, and practices of all public defender offices located in the state.[14] In another 27 states, local jurisdictions—largely counties—are responsible for providing and, in whole or in part, funding, indigent defense services. The remaining state funds 100 percent of its indigent defense services, which are provided by assigned counsel, but does not have city, county, or state public defender offices.

Unlike states, tribes—which retain limited, inherent sovereignty—are not bound by restraints placed upon the federal or state governments through the Bill of Rights or other amendments to the U.S. Constitution, including the Sixth Amendment's right to counsel provision. [15] However, the Indian Civil Rights Act of 1968 (ICRA), as amended, limits the extent to which tribes may exercise their powers of self-government by imposing conditions on tribal governments similar to those found in the Bill of Rights to the U.S. Constitution.[16] For example, ICRA extends the protections of free speech, free exercise of religion, and due process and equal protection under tribal laws.[17] Among other protections afforded under ICRA, tribes must also afford a defendant the right to be represented by counsel at his or her own expense, and, as amended, the right to be provided counsel at the tribe's expense if a sentence of imprisonment for more than 1 year is sought.[18]

DOJ and, in the case of tribes, DOI are the primary federal agencies that play a role in supporting indigent defense.

First, DOJ, as the agency responsible for ensuring the fair and impartial administration of justice for all Americans, works to provide support to all participants in the justice system. Further, in a June 2010 speech before a nonprofit organization dedicated to protecting the rights of individuals in North Carolina, the Attorney General identified a crisis in the criminal defense system, and stated the department's commitment to focusing on indigent defense issues and developing and implementing solutions. Within DOJ, two components provide services that could support indigent defense providers, the Access to Justice Initiative (ATJ) and the Office of Justice Programs (OJP).

- Established in March 2010 to address criminal and civil access to justice issues, ATJ is charged with helping the justice system efficiently deliver outcomes that are fair and accessible to all, irrespective of wealth and status. ATJ staff work within DOJ, across federal agencies, and with state, local, and tribal justice system stakeholders to increase access to counsel and legal assistance and to improve the justice delivery systems that serve people who are unable to afford lawyers. According to DOJ, ATJ is comprised of seven staff and, in fiscal year 2011, had a budget of $1.27 million. ATJ staff focused their efforts on indigent defense as well as a range of pressing criminal and civil access to justice issues, including foreclosure and veterans' affairs.
- OJP works in partnership with the federal, state, local, and tribal justice communities—which include indigent defense providers—to identify the most pressing crime-related challenges confronting the justice system; to provide training, coordination, and innovative strategies and approaches for addressing these challenges; and to provide grant funding for implementing these strategies. Within OJP, several bureaus provide research, technical assistance, and funding that could support indigent defense providers. Specifically, the National Institute of Justice (NIJ) seeks to provide objective, independent, evidence-based knowledge and tools to meet criminal justice challenges, particularly at the state and local levels. Among other things, NIJ funds research and development, assesses programs and policies, and publicizes its findings. In addition, the Bureau of Justice Statistics (BJS) serves as DOJ's primary statistical agency, collecting, analyzing, publishing, and disseminating information on criminal justice systems. Finally, both the Bureau of Justice Assistance (BJA) and the Office of Juvenile Justice and Delinquency Prevention (OJJDP) provide training, technical assistance, and grant funding

designed to enhance and support the criminal and juvenile justice systems, respectively. Such funding may be awarded through formula grants, which are awarded on a noncompetitive basis generally using statutorily defined calculations, or discretionary grants, for which applicants generally compete for funding.[19]

Second, within DOI, BIA is responsible for supporting tribes in their efforts to ensure public safety and administer justice as well as to provide related services directly to, or through contracts or compacts with, federally- recognized tribes.[20] To that end, BIA's Office of Justice Services supports law enforcement, detention, and tribal court programs. In addition, the Division of Tribal Justice Support for Courts within BIA's Office of Justice Services works with tribes to establish and maintain tribal judicial systems. This includes conducting assessments of tribal courts and providing training and technical assistance on a range of topics, including establishing or updating law and order codes. Further, tribal courts may receive funding through BIA's TPA.

All federally-recognized tribes are eligible to receive TPA funds—either through contracts or compacts—for operating tribal programs and, in general, these funds are available for use to provide basic tribal services, such as social services, child welfare, natural resources management, and tribal courts.

DOJ and BIA Make Funding, Training, and Technical Assistance Available to Support Indigent Defense

DOJ and BIA provide funding, training, and technical assistance that could support indigent defense, which may help to address challenges that public defenders face.

Specifically, public defender offices or agencies that responded to our survey most frequently reported that obtaining adequate funding (75 of 106, or 71 percent) and providing appropriate compensation for their attorneys (77 of 107 or 72 percent) were extremely or very challenging to the ability of their office or agency to provide indigent defense services.[21] For instance, one survey respondent explained that their office's best attorneys leave to pursue positions offering higher compensation.

DOJ makes funding available through formula and discretionary grants that could be used for indigent defense. Specifically, we identified 13 grant programs that DOJ administered from fiscal years 2005 through 2010 that recipients could use for this purpose.

Three of these programs—the John R. Justice Program (JRJ), Capital Case Litigation Initiative (CCLI), and Juvenile Indigent Defense National Clearinghouse Grant (JIDNC)—required recipients to allocate or use funding for indigent defense, either because of its authorizing statute or requirements that DOJ set in its grant solicitation. In addition, a fourth program—the Wrongful Conviction Review Program (WCR)—limits eligibility for funding to nonprofit organizations, as well as public defender offices, that represent convicted defendants (who are, according to DOJ, indigent) in claims of innocence. As a result, for the purposes of our review, we consider the WRC grant to require that funding be used for indigent defense. See table 1 for a description of the DOJ grant programs that require that funding be used for indigent defense.

DOJ also administered nine grant programs from fiscal years 2005 through 2010 that recipients could choose to allocate or award to indigent defense, but were not required to do so. In five of these nine programs— the JAG, JABG, Tribal Juvenile Accountability Discretionary Grant (TJADG), Byrne Competitive Grant Program, and the Tribal Civil and Criminal Legal Assistance Grant (TCCLA)—DOJ identified indigent defense as a priority or specific purpose of the grant. It did so by identifying indigent defense either as a purpose area, a stated priority in its grant solicitation, a specific category in the grant, or as a national initiative.

According to DOJ, it established indigent defense as a priority to encourage spending in this area.22 See tables 2 and 3 for a description of the DOJ grant programs that do not require funding to be used for indigent defense, although recipients can use funds for such purposes.

Table 1. DOJ Grant Programs that Require Funding to Be Allocated for Indigent Defense

Name of grant program	Purpose	Type	Appropriatedamounts, fiscalyears 2005-2010
John R. Justice	Provides loan repayment assistance for local, state, and federal public defenders and state and local prosecutors. Requires funding be split between defense and prosecution	Formula[a]	2010: $10 million
Capital Case Litigation Initiative	Provides training on death penalty issues to improve legal representation to indigent defendants and enhance the capability of prosecutors to represent the public. Since fiscal year 2009 requires funding in one grant category be split between defense and prosecution	Discretionary	2007: $1 million 2008: $2.5 million 2009: $2.5 million 2010: $2.5 million
Wrongful Conviction Review	Helps ensure high-quality representation for potentially wrongfully-convicted defendants in cases of post-conviction claims of innocence.	Discretionary	2009: $3 million 2010: $3 million
Juvenile Indigent Defense National Clearinghouse	Supports the improvement of juvenile indigent defense.	Discretionary	2010: $500,000

Source: GAO analysis of DOJ grant documents and data.

Note: DOJ did not receive appropriations for JRJ grants in fiscal years 2005 through 2009, CCLI grants in fiscal years 2005 and 2006, WCR grants in fiscal years 2005 through 2008, and JIDNC grants in fiscal years 2005 through 2009.

[a] DOJ uses a formula to allocate JRJ, but the statute establishing JRJ neither establishes a formula nor requires that a formula be followed in administering the grant.

In addition, we determined that BIA funding could be used for indigent defense. According to BIA officials, if tribes choose to use BIA funding for this purpose, this funding would come from the tribes'

Table 2. DOJ Grant Programs for which Allocating Funding for Indigent Defense Is a Priority or Stated Purpose

Name of grant program	Purpose	Type	Appropriated amounts,fiscal years 2005-2010
Justice Assistance Grant	Is the leading source of federal justice funding to state, local, and tribal governments to support purpose areas including law enforcement; prosecution and courts; prevention and education; corrections and community corrections; drug treatment and enforcement; planning, evaluation, and technology improvements; and crime victim and witness initiatives. Indigent defense has been identified as a priority in the grant solicitation since fiscal year 2010.	Formula	2005: $634 million 2006: $416.4 million 2007: $525.2 million 2008: $170.4 million 2009: $546 million ARRA: $2 billion 2010: $519 million
Juvenile Accountability Block Grant	Supports states and units of local government in their efforts to strengthen their juvenile justice systems. One purpose area includes hiring court-appointed defenders.	Formula	2005: $55 million 2006: $50 million 2007: $49.4 million 2008: $51.7 million 2009: $55 million 2010: $55 million
Tribal Juvenile Accountability Discretionary Grant	Provides funds to federally recognized tribes to combat delinquency and improve the quality of life in American Indian/Alaska Native communities. One purpose area includes hiring court-appointed defenders.	Discretionary	2005: $1 million 2006: $1 million 2007: $1 million 2008: $1 million 2009: $1.1million 2010: $1.1 million
Byrne Competitive	Helps improve the functioning of the criminal justice system, prevent or combat juvenile delinquency, and assist victims of crime (other than compensation) within specific identified areas. Indigent defense was prioritized as a national initiative in fiscal year 2009.	Discretionary	2007: $0 2008: $16 million 2009: $30 million 2010: $40 million
Tribal Civil and Criminal Legal Assistance	Provides funding to nonprofits and organizations for quality legal assistance targeting members of Indian tribes and tribal justice systems, pursuant to the federal poverty guidelines. The program also provides quality technical assistance to support development and enhancement of tribal justice systems. Indigent defense is one grant category in the program.	Discretionary	2010: $3 million

Source: GAO analysis of DOJ grant documents and data.

Note: Allocating funding to indigent defense was not a requirement for any of these grant programs. DOJ did not receive appropriations for Byrne Competitive grants in fiscal years 2005 and 2006, and for TCCLA grants in fiscal years 2005 through 2009. According to DOJ, it awarded competitive grants for national initiatives in fiscal year 2007 using funds that had been appropriated for Byrne Discretionary grants (Byrne Congressional Earmarks) for which no specific earmark had been specified.

Tribal Courts TPA, which are distributed pursuant to contracts or compacts.[23] Through contracts and compacts, tribes, rather than BIA, determine the best use of their funds. BIA does not specify requirements for spending levels on particular tribal court services, including indigent defense, because the nature of tribal sovereignty precludes BIA from placing requirements on how tribes spend their TPA funding. Tribes allocated a total of approximately $22 million through their Tribal Court TPA in each fiscal year from 2005 through 2010.

Further, within DOJ, BJA announced a new solicitation in April 2012 that focuses on helping indigent defense systems adhere to principles established by the American Bar Association (ABA) for public defense delivery systems.[24]

These principles, approved in 2002, were created as a practical guide for those creating and funding new, or improving existing, public defense delivery systems. The principles include the fundamental criteria necessary to design a system that provides effective, efficient, high-quality, ethical legal representation for indigent defendants in which defenders have no conflicts of interest, such as representing two defendants in the same case. According to DOJ, BJA will award $1.4 million of new discretionary grant funding to support projects that help make achievement of these principles a reality.

According to officials from BJA and ATJ involved in developing the solicitation, BJA and ATJ staff worked closely together to develop the grant, and also conducted outreach to indigent defense advocates to determine the type of assistance that would benefit public defenders. The officials explained that the grant will be flexible enough that a diverse group of public defender offices will be eligible to apply for funding because it will allow both less developed and more developed offices to identify areas for improvement in adhering to the ABA principles.

In addition to funding, DOJ, BIA, and the Administrative Office of the U.S. Courts (AOUSC) provide training and technical assistance to indigent defense providers. [25]

For instance, BJA's National Training and Technical Assistance Center (NTTAC) accepts requests for and provides training and technical assistance to state, local, and tribal criminal justice stakeholders.26 DOJ has also awarded funding to the ABA to convene a focus group of 18 successful reformers from across the country to develop strategies for reforming indigent defense systems.

In its January 2012 report to DOJ, the group suggested measures DOJ could take to improve indigent defense, including providing funding for programs that bring training and resources to regions that are most in need, among other things.[27] In addition, BJA has a cooperative agreement with American University to provide technical assistance to criminal courts, including indigent defense providers.

For instance, American University conducted a workshop on improving the criminal case process with the Texas Indigent Defense Board. Furthermore, DOJ (through ATJ and the U.S. Attorney's Offices), BIA, and AOUSC's Office of Defender Services have partnered to develop the Tribal Court Trial Advocacy Training Program, which will consist of a series of trainings for tribal court personnel, including defenders, prosecutors, and judges.[28] The first such training occurred in August 2011, and the second in March 2012. According to DOJ and BIA officials, an additional six trainings are planned through January 2013. A BIA official responsible for conducting the trainings stated that the trainings have resulted in court personnel coming together to create an improved tribal justice system.

Table 3. DOJ Grant Programs for which Allocating Funding for Indigent Defense is Allowed, but Not Required or a Priority

Name of grant program	Purpose	Type	Appropriated amounts,fiscal years 2005-2010
Juvenile Justice and Delinquency Prevention Title II	Supports state and local efforts in planning, establishing, operating, coordinating, and evaluating projects for the development of more effective education, training, research, prevention, diversion, treatment, and rehabilitation programs in the area of juvenile delinquency, as well as programs to improve the juvenile justice system.	Formula	2005:$84 million 2006:$80 million 2007:$79 million 2008:$74.3 million 2009: $75 million 2010: $75 million
Tribal Court Assistance Program	Helps develop and enhance the operation of tribal justice systems and provides funding for training and technical assistance to tribal court and justice system staff.	Discretionary	2005: $8 million 2006: $8 million 2007: $8 million 2008: $8.6 million 2009: $9 million 2010: $25 million
Justice and Mental Health Collaboration	Facilitates collaboration among criminal justice and mental health treatment systems to increase access to services.	Discretionary	2007: $5 million 2008: $6.5 million 2009: $10 million 2010: $12 million
Adult Drug Court Discretionary	Expands the drug court capacity at the state, local, and tribal levels.	Discretionary	2005: $40 million 2006: $ 10 million 2007: $10 million 2008: $15.2 million 2009: $40 million 2010: $45 million

Source: GAO analysis of DOJ grant documents and data.

Note: DOJ did not receive appropriations for the Justice and Mental Health Collaboration Grant Program in fiscal years 2005 and 2006.

UNLESS REQUIRED, FEW RECIPIENTS ALLOCATED OR PLANNED TO USE ANY FEDERAL FUNDING FOR INDIGENT DEFENSE, IN PART DUE TO COMPETING PRIORITIES

Recipients of the four grant programs requiring funds to be used in whole or in part for indigent defense from fiscal years 2005 through 2010 allocated or planned to use $13.3 million out of $21.2 million—or 63 percent—of available funds for state, local, and tribal indigent defense.[29]

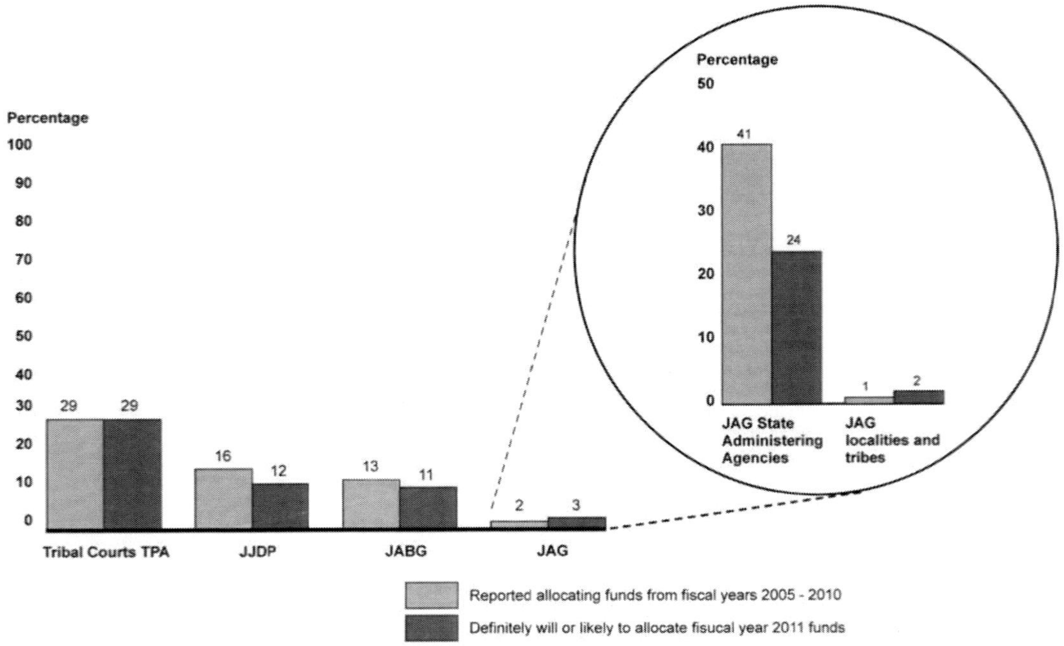

Source: GAO analysis of survey responses.

Note: We provide separate data on JAG State Administering Agencies—which directly receive 60 percent of the state's JAG allocation—and localities and tribes that receive JAG funding—which directly receive 40 percent of the state's JAG allocation. Survey response rates upon which these data were based were 68 percent for Tribal Courts TPA distribution recipients; 46 percent for JAG (89 percent for SAAs and 45 percent for localities and tribes); 89 percent for JJDP; 82 percent for JABG. Because of the relatively low response rates among recipients of BIA Tribal Courts TPA distributions and local and tribal JAG recipients, their results should not be generalized to the recipients of BIA Tribal Courts TPA distributions or local and tribal JAG recipient populations.

Figure 1. Percentage of Survey Respondents that Received DOJ Formula Grants or BIA Tribal Courts TPA Funds and Reported Allocating These Funds for Indigent Defense.

For instance, 19 of 33 grantees of the Capital Case Litigation Initiative used $3.3 million to provide training to indigent defense attorneys who handle death penalty cases.[30] See appendix II for additional information about the allocation and use of these grants for indigent defense.

However, two-thirds or more of the survey respondents who were recipients of the DOJ formula grants for which indigent defense was not a required use or Tribal Courts TPA distributions reported that they did not allocate funding for indigent defense, partly because of other competing priorities, such as law enforcement needs. As shown in figure 1, survey respondents for JAG State Administering Agencies (SAA)—the designated agencies in each state that establish funding priorities and coordinate JAG funds among state and local justice initiatives—and survey respondents for Tribal Courts TPA distributions more frequently reported allocating funds for indigent defense than JJDP, JABG, or local and tribal JAG survey respondents.[31] (See appendix III for additional information on the percentages of respondents who reported allocating nondiscretionary funding for indigent defense.) Similarly, as displayed in figure 2, our analysis of discretionary grants showed that no more than 25 percent was awarded for indigent defense from fiscal years 2005 through 2010. For example, the percentage of grants that was awarded fully or in part for indigent defense ranged from 1.3 percent for the Justice and Mental Health Collaboration program to 25 percent for the TCCLA grant.32 See appendix IV for additional information on the number of discretionary grants awarded for indigent defense.

In general, DOJ and BIA funding recipients who responded to our surveys most frequently reported that other criminal or juvenile justice areas were a higher priority and extremely or very important to their decisions not to allocate funding for indigent defense, while public defenders generally reported that they did not apply for discretionary grants because they were not aware they were eligible to do so. Figures 3 and 4, as well as the following sections, illustrate these responses in more detail.

Competing priorities: JAG respondents most frequently reported that funding for law enforcement, such as overtime for police officers; equipment, such as surveillance equipment or street lighting; and technology, such as cameras for police vehicles, were higher priorities than indigent defense. For instance, one JAG administrator with whom we spoke explained that his city was laying off over 30 police officers. Because there will now be fewer officers on the street to identify, report, and respond to crime as it happens, his jurisdiction gave priority to obtaining technology that would allow citizens to better report crimes as opposed to providing funding for indigent defense.

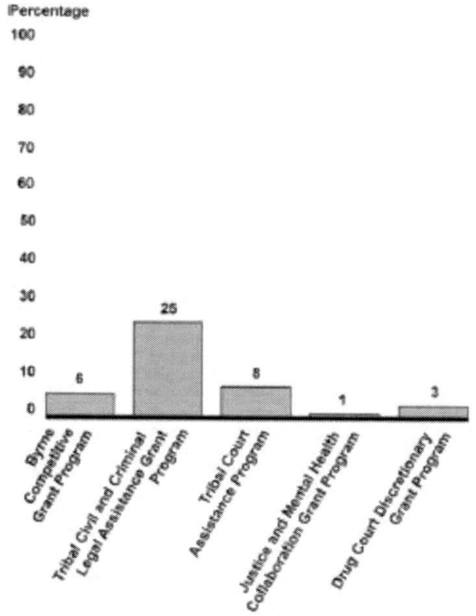

Source: GAO analysis of DOJ grant data.

Note: No grants were awarded for indigent defense in the Tribal Juvenile Accountability Discretionary Grant Program. For the years focused on in this review, DOJ awarded grants under the Byrne Competitive Grant Program in fiscal years 2007 through 2010, the Tribal Civil and Criminal Legal Assistance Grant Program in fiscal year 2010, the Tribal Court Assistance Program in fiscal years 2005 through 2010, the Justice and Mental Health Collaboration Grant Program in fiscal years 2007 through 2010, and the Drug Court Discretionary Grant Program in fiscal years 2005 through 2010.

Figure 2. Percentage of Discretionary Grants That Were Awarded Fully or in Part for Indigent Defense during Fiscal Years 2005 through 2010.

As figure 5 shows, respondents to our JAG survey reported allocating the largest proportion of funding to the law enforcement purpose area, followed by the planning, evaluation, and technology improvement purpose area, in which funds may be used for criminal justice information systems, such as automated fingerprint identification systems.

See figures 5 and 6 for the percentage of total JAG funding that respondents reported allocating to each of the seven JAG purpose areas, compared to indigent defense.

See appendix V for additional information about survey respondents' reported allocations across purpose areas and for indigent defense in each fiscal year.

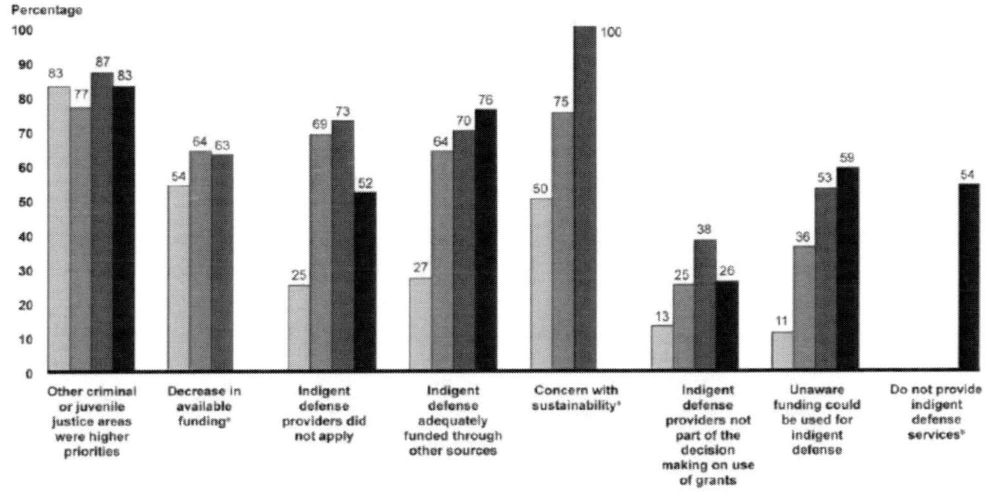

N=								
JAG	963	564	774	520	100	763	837	
JJDP	39	33	32	11	8	20	14	
JABG	30	27	26	10	6	16	15	
Tribal courts TPA	34		25	25		43	37	41

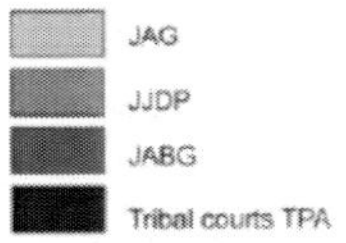

Source: GAO analysis of survey responses.

Note: The percentages are calculated out of only those respondents who indicated that the reasons were valid in their jurisdiction. Concerns with sustainability refer to grantee's concerns that indigent defense positions funded through the grant would not be sustainable after the funding ended.

[a] In order to compare responses across tribes, we did not ask Tribal Courts TPA or tribal JAG respondents about decreased funding or funding sustainability because BIA funding through the Tribal Courts TPA has been relatively constant from fiscal year 2005 through 2010.

[b] We did not ask the remaining JAG, JABG, or JJDP respondents about the importance of not providing indigent defense services because the respondents were generally representing state and local government offices, and states and local governments are required to afford defendants, including indigent defendants, the right to counsel.

Figure 3. Percentage of JAG, JJDP, JABG, and Tribal Courts TPA Survey Respondents Reporting Reasons That Were Extremely or Very Important to Their Decisions Not to Allocate Funding for Indigent Defense.

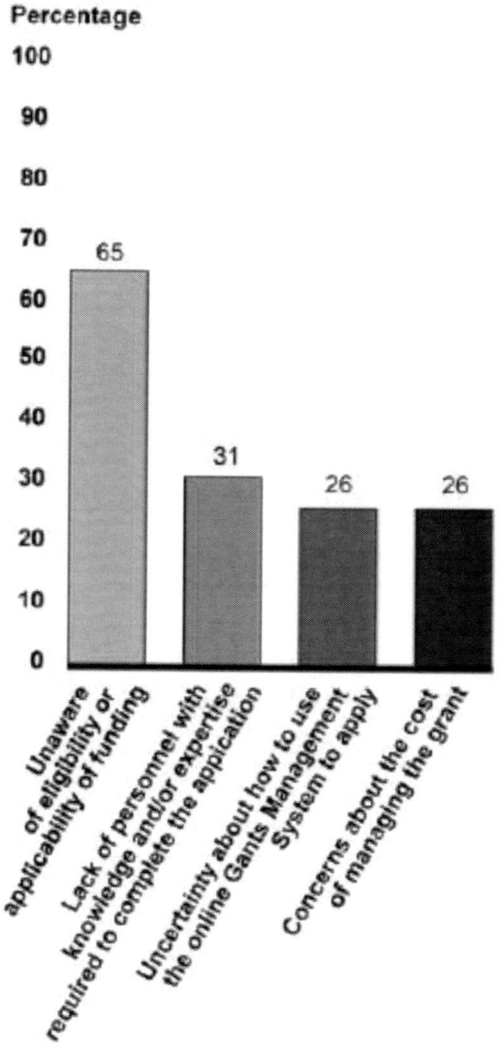

Source: GAO analysis of survey responses.

Figure 4. Percentage of Public Defender Survey Respondents Reporting Reasons That Were Extremely or Very Important for Why They Did Not Apply for Grant Funding (N=103).

The three JJDP and five JABG survey respondents who provided specific examples of other activities that were higher priorities than indigent defense most frequently cited alternatives to detention, such as services provided to a juvenile offender in the community as an alternative to incarceration, and programs to address the disproportionate number of juveniles of minority groups who come into contact with the juvenile justice system.[33]

Further, our review of the DOJ discretionary grants that can be, but are not required to be, used for indigent defense also showed that, generally, grantees that received these awards more frequently planned to use these awards for other criminal justice priorities. For example, Byrne Competitive grantees more frequently planned to use their awards to support law enforcement and other criminal justice areas than indigent defense. Figure 7 illustrates other criminal justice areas, such as law enforcement, that grantees commonly planned to fund with Byrne Competitive grants awarded from fiscal years 2007 through 2010.

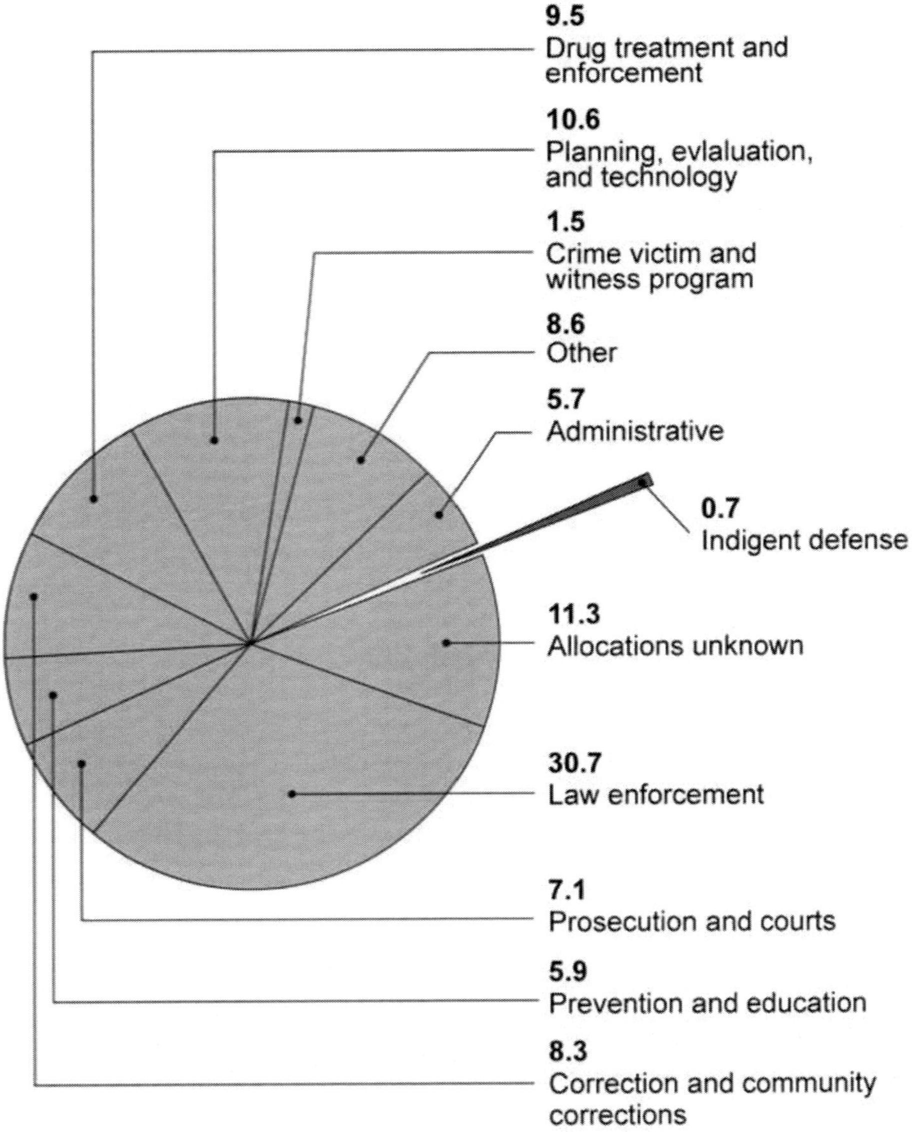

Source: GAO analysis of survey responses.

Note: Funding for indigent defense can be allocated in multiple purpose areas, as indigent defense is not its own purpose area. As a result, to obtain the percentages allocated for each purpose area, we subtracted the amount respondents reported allocating for indigent defense out of the specified purpose area. As discussed in appendix I, dollar amount data reported have limitations and should be considered estimates. In particular, in this figure, our data may overrepresent allocations to law enforcement because it was the first category listed in our survey and respondents that were unable to split their funding across purpose areas may have reported allocating all funding to law enforcement. Similarly, our data may overrepresent allocations for indigent defense because JAG recipients that allocated funding to indigent defense may have been more likely to respond to our survey than recipients that had never done so. Other includes funds not yet allocated. Percentages do not add up to 100 due to rounding.

Figure 5. Percentage of Funding That JAG SAA Respondents Reported Allocating to Each Purpose Area, Including Indigent Defense, during Fiscal Years 2005 through 2010.

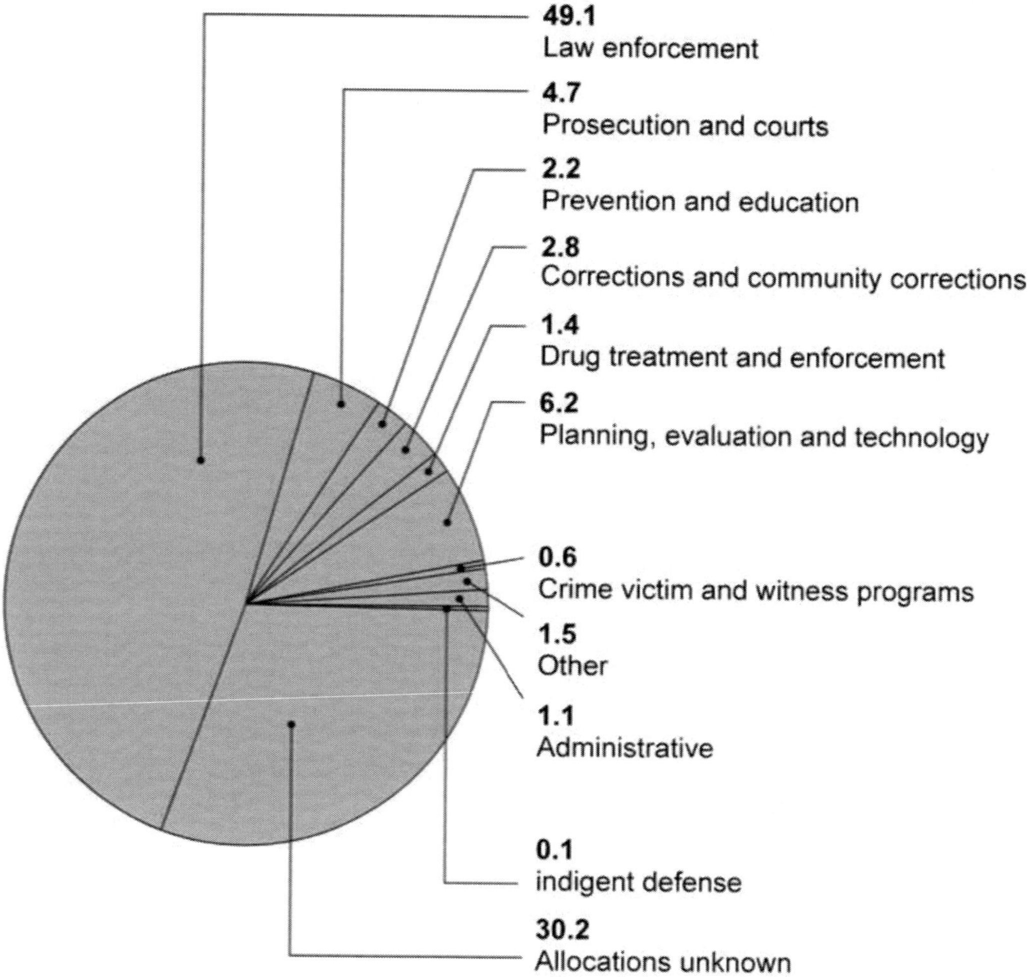

Source: GAO analysis of survey responses.

Note: Funding for indigent defense can be allocated in multiple purpose areas, as indigent defense is not its own purpose area. As a result, to obtain the percentages allocated for each purpose area, we subtracted the amount respondents reported allocating for indigent defense out of the specified purpose area. As discussed in appendix I, dollar amount data reported have limitations and should be considered estimates. In particular, in this figure, our data may overrepresent allocations to law enforcement because it was the first category listed in our survey and respondents that were unable to split their funding across purpose areas may have reported allocating all funding to law enforcement. Similarly, our data may overrepresent allocations for indigent defense because JAG recipients that allocated funding to indigent defense may have been more likely to respond to our survey than recipients that had never done so. Other includes funds not yet allocated. Percentages do not add up to 100 due to rounding.

Figure 6. Percentage of Funding That JAG Local and Tribal Respondents Reported Allocating to Each Purpose Area, As Well As Indigent Defense, during Fiscal Years 2005 through 2010.

Several factors may help to explain why grants were more frequently allocated or used for other criminal justice areas as opposed to indigent defense. For instance, a JAG administrator with whom we spoke indicated that JAG recipients often allocate funding to law enforcement because the JAG grant has historically been a law enforcement grant.[34]

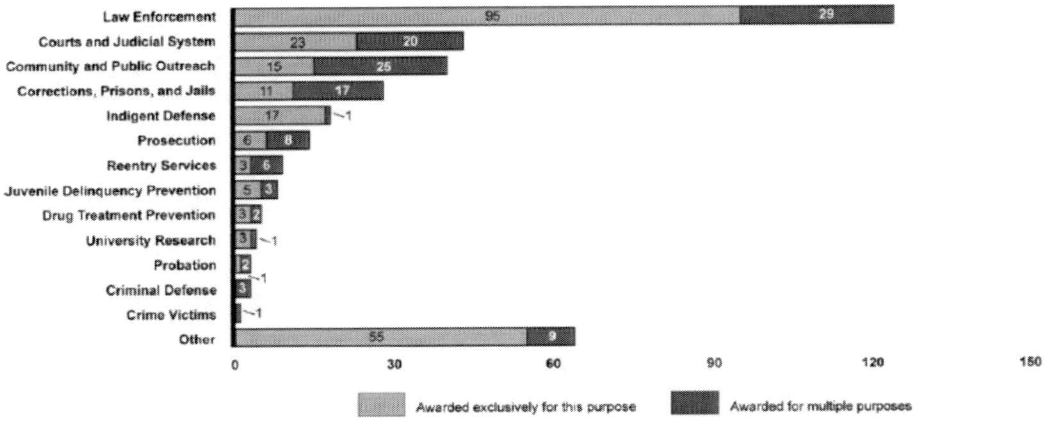

Source: GAO analysis of survey responses.

Note: Other may include crime prevention, funding to prevent or address domestic violence, pretrial justice, and county and state government criminal justice practitioners. For the years focused on in this review, DOJ awarded Byrne Competitive Grants in fiscal years 2007 through 2010.

Figure 7. Criminal Justice Areas Awarded Byrne Competitive Grants during Fiscal Years 2007 through 2010 (N=287).

In addition, 83 percent (1,484 of 1,779) of JAG survey respondents reported that their organization was a law enforcement entity—either a police department or sheriff's office—which may not naturally allocate funding for indigent defense.

Further, 64 percent (21 of 33) of JJDP, 63 percent (17 of 27) of JABG, and 54 percent (302 of 564) of JAG survey respondents reported that a decrease in the available grant funding was extremely or very important to their decision not to allocate funding for indigent defense.[35] Specifically, according to one JAG administrator, decreases in JAG funding make it even less likely that jurisdictions that have traditionally allocated funding for law enforcement will allocate funding for indigent defense because the law enforcement agencies need the money. Further, DOJ officials explained that OJP follows a "state and local assistance model" in administering the JAG program, whereby DOJ provides funding to states and localities but does not determine how the jurisdictions allocate the funding. Instead, the states and localities independently determine what issues within their respective jurisdictions need funding, and then allocate funds for those purposes. As a result, states and localities may choose not to allocate funding for indigent defense but instead allocate it to these higher-priority areas.

The Attorney General stated that DOJ is continuing to work to bring all criminal justice stakeholders, including indigent defense providers, together to plan comprehensive criminal justice strategies, which will help jurisdictions ensure that decisions are made with an eye toward strengthening the criminal justice system. For instance, DOJ issued new guidelines to JAG grantees in March 2012, within the fiscal year 2012 JAG solicitation, that encourage stakeholders to come together in a comprehensive criminal justice planning process. Specifically, these recommended guidelines specify that, at a minimum, the strategic planning process include law enforcement, courts, prosecutors, indigent defense providers, victim advocates, and corrections officials. Further, the JAG solicitation asks applicants to identify, among other things, the stakeholders currently participating in the strategic planning process. According to DOJ officials, these guidelines may benefit indigent defense providers in two ways. First, JAG funding is more likely to be shared with a broader range of stakeholders if they are included in the planning process, which our survey responses also suggest may be true. Specifically, among the 4 percent of JAG grantees who reported that representatives of the indigent defense community were involved in the decision making process, 22 percent reported allocating funding for indigent defense. In contrast, among the 52 percent who reported that representatives of the indigent defense community were not involved in the decision making process, 2 percent reported allocating funding for indigent defense.[36] Second, if indigent defense providers are included in the planning process, they can provide input to other stakeholders, such as law enforcement personnel, about the impact that their use of JAG funding may have on both the indigent defense provider and, correspondingly, the criminal justice system. For instance, an indigent defense expert explained that, when law enforcement or prosecutorial agencies receive additional funding, arrests and prosecutions may increase, which in turn increase indigent defense providers' caseloads. If the indigent defense provider does not receive additional funding to handle the caseload, cases may take longer to move through the judicial process.

Lack of awareness of eligibility for funding: Public defender offices or agencies responding to our survey most frequently reported (67 of 103) that their lack of awareness about their eligibility for funding was an extremely or very important reason they did not apply for DOJ discretionary grant funding from fiscal year 2005 through 2011.[37] For instance, 3 public defenders who submitted additional comments also reported that they would like to have a centralized source of information on available grants, training, and best practices that they could use for assistance. In addition, as shown in figure 8, no more than 54 percent of Tribal Courts TPA, JABG, JAG, and JJDP survey respondents reported that they were aware that funding could be allocated for indigent defense.

DOJ has undertaken efforts to make grantees aware of available funding. It has provided training and technical assistance on the grant process and a list of available grants on OJP's Web site. DOJ has also provided a list of grants that may be of interest to, among others, defender agencies, on ATJ's Web site. Further, ATJ officials reported that they collaborate with public defender membership organizations, such as the National Legal Aid and Defender Association and the National Association of Criminal Defense Lawyers, to make indigent defense providers aware of grants. In addition, they mention funding opportunities during speeches to the indigent defense community. Moreover, DOJ officials reported that all available grant opportunities are listed on grants.gov, the federal government's grant clearinghouse, and grantees can search the site using keywords that would help them identify grants of interest, such as those related to indigent defense. DOJ officials reported that they encourage potential applicants to sign up to receive information from grants.gov. In addition, BIA officials stated that during the contracting process tribes go through to obtain TPA funds, BIA may inform tribes that they could use funding available through their Tribal Courts TPA distribution for indigent defense—or any other component of tribal courts—but did not know of any explicit efforts to make tribes aware. Despite these efforts, no more than 54 percent of grantees or public defender offices or agencies that responded to our survey were aware of funding that could be used to support indigent defense. Moreover, 59 percent (22 of 37) of Tribal Courts TPA distribution, 53 percent (8 of 15) of JABG, and 36 percent (5 of 14) of JJDP survey respondents reported that such lack of awareness was an extremely or very important reason why they did not allocate funding for indigent defense.[38] While relatively few JAG recipients who responded to our surveys reported that lack of awareness was an extremely or very important reason why they did not allocate funding for indigent defense in the past, these states, localities, and tribes could make indigent defense a higher priority in the future. As a result, increasing awareness that federal funding can be used for this purpose could help DOJ and BIA to ensure that potential funding recipients are better positioned to respond to changing priorities.39 In addition, JAG (50 of 105), JABG (5 of 11), and JJDP (5 of 13) survey respondents most frequently suggested in open-ended responses that, to increase allocations for indigent defense, DOJ could take steps to increase awareness that funding could be allocated for indigent defense, such as by communicating this through e-mail, or during training sessions or conferences. Given that funding through these grant programs can be used, consistent with applicable authorizing statutes, to support indigent defense, and because the Attorney General has identified a crisis in criminal defense and has committed the department to focusing on indigent defense issues, increasing awareness among grantees and indigent defense providers about available funding could help DOJ better ensure that it meets its commitment to supporting indigent defense. DOJ grant administrators and ATJ officials acknowledged that opportunities exist to enhance grantees' awareness of funding that can be allocated or awarded for indigent defense. Further, in open-ended responses, 14 tribes stated that BIA should take actions to clarify that Tribal Courts TPA distributions may be used for indigent defense. Consistent with BIA's authority to provide financial assistance to tribes through contracts, compacts, or other means, to support the development, enhancement, and continuing operation of tribal justice systems, including for the employment and training of public defenders and appointed defense counsel, increasing tribes' awareness that funding may be used for indigent defense could better position BIA and tribes to support such systems. BIA officials responsible for providing assistance to tribal courts agreed that they could take additional actions to help increase tribes' awareness of funding available for indigent defense.

WHEN RECIPIENTS ALLOCATED FUNDING FOR INDIGENT DEFENSE, IN GENERAL, THE AMOUNT WAS SMALL RELATIVE TO THE TOTAL AWARD AND FUNDING WAS USED FOR PERSONNEL AND TRAINING

Those recipients who chose to allocate or use funding for indigent defense generally reported providing a small amount of funding for indigent defense relative to their total awards.[40] Specifically, the award amounts reported by JAG, JABG, JJDP, and Tribal Courts TPA recipients who allocated funding to indigent defense ranged from 2 percent of the total award (in the JJDP program) to 14 percent (in the JABG program). Similarly, in our review of discretionary grants, awards for indigent defense were generally small relative to total awards, ranging from at most 0.4 percent of the total award (in the Justice and Mental Health Collaboration and Drug Court Discretionary Grant programs) to at most 8.1 percent (in the Tribal Court Assistance Program).[41]Figure 9 shows indigent defense allocations as a percentage of these survey respondents' total awards, in current dollars unadjusted for inflation, while figure 10 shows discretionary awards for indigent defense as a percentage of total awards, in current dollars. See appendix IV for additional details about these allocations and awards by year.

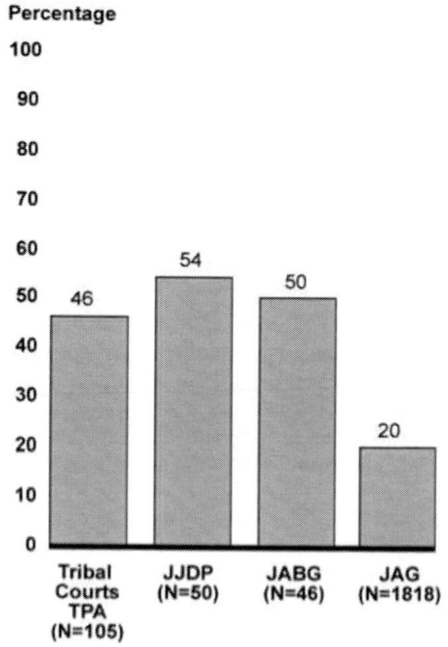

Source: GAO analysis of survey responses.

Figure 8. Survey respondents who reported they were aware that funding could be used for indigent defense.

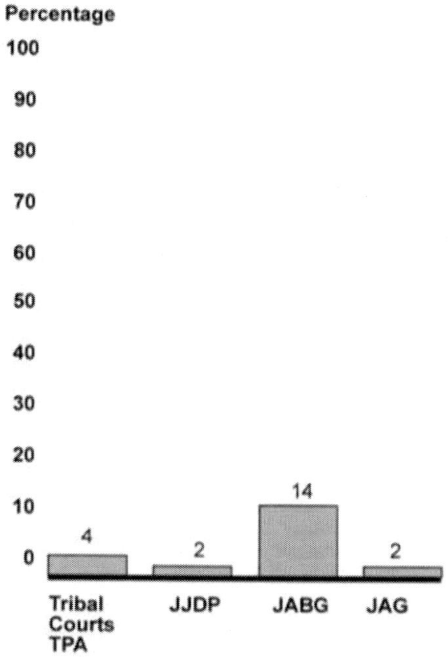

Source: GAO analysis of survey responses.

Note: As discussed in appendix I, there are limitations to these data, particularly for JAG respondents. As a result, these numbers should be considered estimates.

Figure 9. Allocations for Indigent Defense as a Percentage of Total Awards among Those Who Reported Allocating Funding for Indigent Defense, Fiscal Years 2005 through 2010.

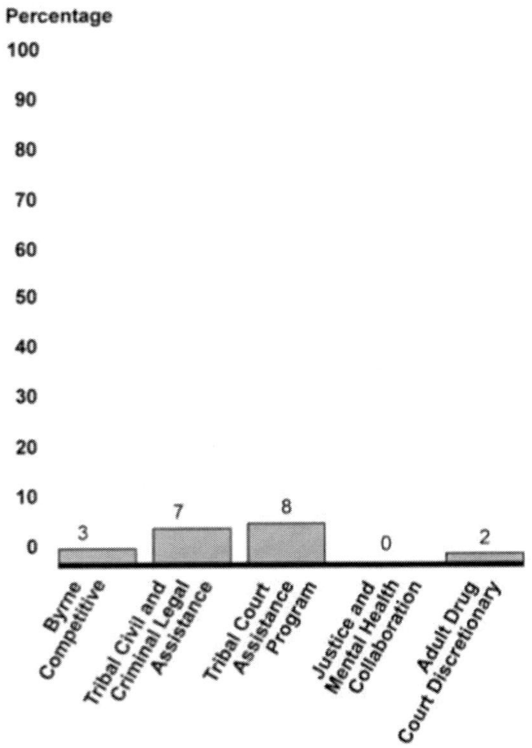

Source: GAO analysis of DOJ grant data.

Note: Includes grants that were used fully or in part for indigent defense. Thus, these percentages may represent the upper bound of the amounts awarded for indigent defense. Because the amount awarded for indigent defense as a percentage of total awards in the Justice and Mental Health Collaboration grants was so small, the percentage rounded to zero. No grants were awarded for indigent defense from the Tribal Juvenile Accountability Discretionary Grant Program.

Figure 10. Amounts Awarded Fully or In Part for Indigent Defense, as a Percentage of Total Amounts Awarded for Selected Discretionary Grants, during Fiscal Years 2005 through 2010.

Recipients most frequently reported using indigent defense funding for personnel and training, which may help to address challenges that public defenders face. More specifically, public defenders that responded to our survey most frequently reported that financial challenges very greatly or greatly impacted their ability to increase compensation for people working in the indigent defense system, hire additional attorneys, travel to or register for external training, and hire clerical support or investigators. Further, indigent defense providers we spoke with during a panel discussion at the National Legal Aid and Defender Association's annual conference confirmed this position, stating that critical funding needs for public defender programs included personnel—both attorneys and support staff—as well as training.

JABG and JJDP recipients who had allocated funding for indigent defense most commonly reported using this funding for training and personnel, and our review of discretionary grants found that indigent defense funding was generally used for these same purposes. Figures 11 and 12 illustrate the most frequently reported uses of the grants. Similarly, selected recipients of JAG and BIA Tribal Courts TPA distributions with whom we spoke most commonly reported using funding for personnel.

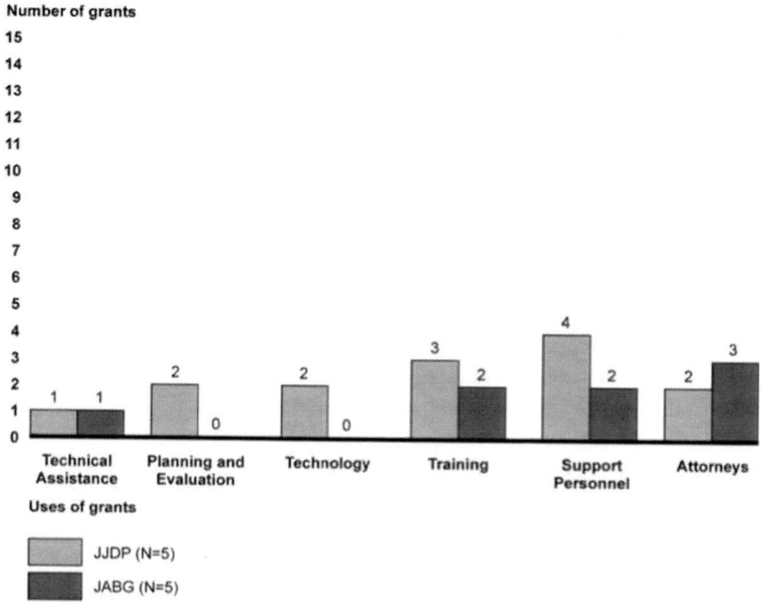

Source: GAO analysis of interview data.

Note: Grants may be used for multiple purposes; therefore, single grants may be counted more than once in the above graphic.

Figure 11. Reported Uses of JABG and JJDP Grants Allocated for Indigent Defense.

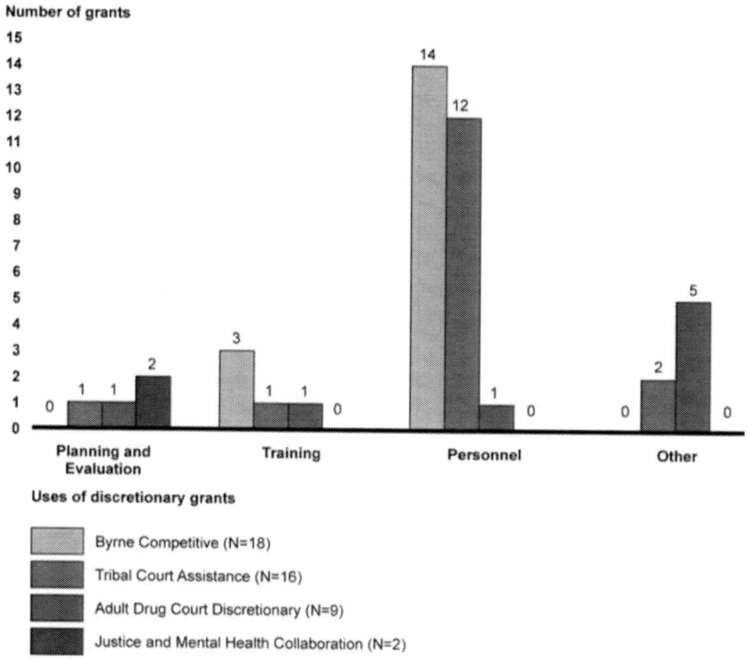

Source: GAO analysis of DOJ grant data.

Note: Grants may be used for multiple purposes; therefore, single grants may be counted more than once in the above graphic.

Figure 12. Uses of Discretionary Grants Awarded for Indigent Defense.

In terms of personnel, grantees funded both attorneys and support staff, including social workers, investigators, or substance abuse and treatment specialists. Support staff help to conduct investigations, process clients as they come in for assistance, or address needs clients have beyond their court case, such as challenges with substance abuse, mental health, employment, or housing. For instance, one JAG grantee reported that funds were used to hire an attorney in a county public defender office to represent veterans in the criminal court systems. The attorney represents the veterans at the county's veterans' court and also conducts significant outreach to treatment providers in the county to help ensure veterans can obtain any additional treatment they may need. In terms of training, grantees funded activities that included instruction on juvenile law and technology. Moreover, one grantee—The Bronx Defenders—received a Byrne Competitive grant to provide technical assistance to other public defender organizations on the public defense model they use, known as holistic defense (see sidebar).

The Bronx Defenders

In 2009, The Bronx Defenders, a public defender organization located in the South Bronx, New York, received a Byrne Competitive grant from DOJ. With this grant, it created The Center for Holistic Defense at The Bronx Defenders, which provides 6 months of technical assistance for selected public defender offices throughout the United States to implement a holistic model of defense, a model that targets both the causes and consequences of involvement in the criminal justice system. The Bronx Defenders operates using interdisciplinary teams of criminal, civil, and family defense lawyers, social workers, parent advocates, investigators, and community organizers to work with clients and their families to overcome the challenges they face. According to The Bronx Defenders, whether addressing the root causes of criminal justice system involvement such as addiction, mental illness, and joblessness or the collateral consequences of their criminal case, it works to provide quality legal representation and to make a long-term difference in clients' lives.

Source: GAO.

DOJ Could More Consistently Collect Data on the Amount of Funding Allocated for Indigent Defense When Programs Identify It as a Priority

For grant programs that require funding be used at least in part for indigent defense, DOJ collects data on whether recipients have allocated funding for indigent defense and the allocation amounts, which allows DOJ to determine if funding was used in accordance with grant requirements. For instance, in the John R. Justice Program, which funds student loan repayments for public defenders and prosecutors, DOJ collects data on the number and amount of loan repayments made to state and local public defenders. In addition, for the Capital Case Litigation Initiative, DOJ can determine the amounts allocated for indigent defense because the grant funds must be allocated equally between prosecution and defense.[42]

In addition, DOJ collected data on indigent defense funding for the Byrne Competitive and TCCLA grants when funding for indigent defense was a priority. Specifically, in 2009, when hiring public defenders was a national initiative for the Byrne Competitive grant, DOJ collected data on awards by national initiative and, thus, collected data on grant funding awarded for indigent defense under this initiative. Similarly, for the TCCLA grant, DOJ collects data on the grant category under which awards are made and, therefore, can identify funding awarded under the grant category related to indigent defense.

Further, DOJ has developed mechanisms to collect data on whether JAG recipients have allocated funding for indigent defense and the amount allocated. First, so that DOJ can determine the number of grantees that are using funds for a particular purpose, when applicants apply for JAG funding, DOJ allows them to identify which of the more than 150 "project identifiers" best describe the proposed activities for which they plan to use the funding.[43] According to BJA officials, DOJ created an indigent defense "project identifier" in fiscal year 2011 to better track indigent defense spending, given that indigent defense is listed as a priority in the fiscal years 2010 and 2011 JAG solicitations. Further, in its fiscal year 2011 solicitation, DOJ required that JAG applicants identify up to 5 project identifiers to catalogue their allocations. According to DOJ grant program officials, they established this requirement because they wanted to be able to track grantees' uses of the funds and respond to questions from Congress and others about these uses. DOJ officials stated that they limited the requirement to 5 project identifiers to help ensure that the identifiers selected were most representative of the projects being funded. BJA also noted that, during its application review, BJA staff have the option to select additional project identifiers that would assist in the description and tracking of projects being funded.

Second, as part of its efforts to revise JAG performance measures, which were made partly in response to our review, BJA has drafted a performance measure for the amount of funding spent on defense. Moreover, DOJ recently improved its efforts to collect data on the extent to which JAG grantees have allocated funds for indigent defense, but DOJ does not collect data on whether JABG or TJADG grantees have allocated funding for this purpose. According to an OJP official responsible for the grant system, all project identifiers are available to any priority. Specifically, in 2009, when hiring public defenders was a national initiative for the Byrne Competitive grant, DOJ collected data on awards by national initiative and, thus, collected data on grant funding awarded for indigent defense under this initiative. Similarly, for the TCCLA grant, DOJ collects data on the grant category under which awards are made and, therefore, can identify funding awarded under the grant category related to indigent defense.

Further, DOJ has developed mechanisms to collect data on whether JAG recipients have allocated funding for indigent defense and the amount allocated. First, so that DOJ can determine the number of grantees that are using funds for a particular purpose, when applicants apply for JAG funding, DOJ allows them to identify which of the more than 150 "project identifiers" best describe the proposed activities for which they plan to use the funding.[43] According to BJA officials, DOJ created an indigent defense "project identifier" in fiscal year 2011 to better track indigent defense spending, given that indigent defense is listed as a priority in the fiscal years 2010 and 2011 JAG solicitations. Further, in its fiscal year 2011 solicitation, DOJ required that JAG applicants identify up to 5 project identifiers to catalogue their allocations.

According to DOJ grant program officials, they established this requirement because they wanted to be able to track grantees' uses of the funds and respond to questions from Congress and others about these uses. DOJ officials stated that they limited the requirement to 5 project identifiers to help ensure that the identifiers selected were most representative of the projects being funded. BJA also noted that, during its application review, BJA staff have the option to select additional project identifiers that would assist in the description and tracking of projects being funded.

Second, as part of its efforts to revise JAG performance measures, which were made partly in response to our review, BJA has drafted a performance measure for the amount of funding spent on defense.

Moreover, DOJ recently improved its efforts to collect data on the extent to which JAG grantees have allocated funds for indigent defense, but DOJ does not collect data on whether JABG or TJADG grantees have allocated funding for this purpose. According to an OJP official responsible for the grant system, all project identifiers are available to any OJP grantees, including JAG as well as JABG and TJADG grantees. However, unlike the JAG program, JABG and TJADG grantees are not required to identify project identifiers to describe proposed project activities when applying for funding; therefore grantees may choose not to use them. Moreover, 3 of the 5 JABG survey respondents who reported allocating funding for indigent defense with whom we spoke reported that they were unaware of an indigent defense project identifier, and an additional respondent reported being aware, but unlikely to use it.[44]

DOJ officials responsible for the JABG program explained that they collect data on grantees' allocation of funds for the JABG purpose area that includes hiring court-appointed defenders, but the data are not detailed enough to identify allocations specifically for indigent defense.

Moreover, the officials noted that this purpose area is only 1out of 17 JABG purpose areas. Similarly, the purpose area that includes hiring court-appointed defenders is only 1 out of 17 TJADG purpose areas, and TJADG data we obtained from DOJ did not identify whether funding was awarded for indigent defense.

In addition, JABG and TJADG applicants have not been required to identify project identifiers because, according to an official from OJJDP, the office that administers the programs, OJJDP was not aware that the project identifiers available to JAG grantees could also be used by OJJDP staff and grantees.

We have previously reported that agencies should collect sufficiently complete, accurate, and consistent data to measure performance and support decision making at various organizational levels.[45]

Given that the Attorney General has identified a crisis in criminal defense and committed the department to focusing on indigent defense issues and developing and implementing solutions, collecting data on whether grantees have allocated or awarded funding for indigent defense could help DOJ better assess whether funding is supporting this commitment.

DOJ Assesses the Impact of Indigent Defense Grant Funding and Has Mechanisms to Help Indigent Defense Providers Evaluate Services

DOJ Has Measures to Assess the Impact of Indigent Defense-Related Grant Funding

According to the Office of Management and Budget (OMB), performance measurement indicates what a program is accomplishing and whether results are being achieved.[46]

For all DOJ grant programs that either require funding be used for indigent defense or identify it as a priority, DOJ has or is developing indigent defense-related performance measures and requires grantees to provide data to inform these measures. For example, for the Byrne Competitive, TCCLA, TJADG, and JABG programs—where DOJ has prioritized indigent defense-related funding—DOJ requires grantees to report indigent defense-related measures such as the number of public defenders hired.

In the JAG program, DOJ is developing a measure—the number of cases defended—in its revisions to its online performance measures.[47] For a list of performance measures DOJ uses to assess the impact of funding used for indigent defense-related activities, see appendix VI.

OMB guidance outlines four types of performance measures agencies may use to assess program impact: those that describe the level of activity that will be provided over a period of time (output measures), those that describe the intended result of carrying out the program (outcome measures), those that indicate how well a procedure, process, or operation is working (process measures), and those that describe the resources used to produce outputs and outcomes (input measures).[48] While each type of measure provides information that can help assess the impact of the program, OMB also states that appropriate performance goals should, among other things, focus on outcomes, but use outputs when necessary.[49] In addition, OMB strongly encourages the use of outcomes because they are more meaningful to the public than outputs.[50] As we have previously reported, developing output measures is a step toward developing outcome measures, and an important initial step in measuring progress.[51]

However, we have also previously reported that leading organizations promote accountability by establishing results-oriented, outcome goals and corresponding performance measures by which to gauge progress towards attaining these goals.[52]

We found that all nine of the DOJ grant programs that required or prioritized funding for indigent defense included output measures that described the level of grant activity. In addition, seven of the nine grant programs included outcome-oriented performance measures that described the intended results of the program. For example, for the Juvenile Indigent Defense National Clearinghouse Grant, DOJ developed the outcome measure "percentage of people exhibiting increased knowledge of the program area," which demonstrates a clear linkage to the program goals to improve juvenile indigent defense, to build the capacity of the juvenile indigent defense bar, and to promote the zealous and effective advocacy for juvenile indigent defendants. See appendix VI for our more detailed analysis of the measures used.

The John R. Justice and JAG programs do not include indigent defense-related outcome-oriented performance measures that gauge impacts or results. However, DOJ requires states that receive John R. Justice funding to submit, at the conclusion of the grant, an assessment of the program's impact on retention of prosecutors and defenders in the state, which would allow DOJ to assess whether the program is achieving intended results. DOJ officials explained that they required grantees to submit this assessment because the DOJ Inspector General is required in the statute establishing the John R. Justice program to report on the program's impact on the retention of prosecutors and public defenders.[53] As a result, DOJ decided to require these assessments from recipients in order to provide this information to the Inspector General, if requested.

In addition, according to DOJ officials, they have not developed indigent defense-related outcome-oriented performance measures for the JAG program because the ways in which JAG funds can be used vary significantly across and within the seven purpose areas, making the development of outcome-oriented measures that could capture the intended results of the program difficult. Even among grantees that allocated funding for indigent defense, the purposes varied significantly.

For instance, one JAG grantee with whom we spoke reported using indigent defense-related JAG funds to update the case management system at a public defender's office, for which an outcome measure could be the increase in the efficiency with which cases are handled, while another used the funds to pay for an attorney, for which an outcome measure could be the decrease in the number of cases each attorney handles.

Further, OMB has acknowledged that developing performance measures for programs that, like JAG, address multiple objectives and support a broad range of activities can be challenging. For programs that focus funds on specific purpose areas, as JAG does, OMB states that agencies can address the challenge by articulating national goals, and then working with state and local entities to identify specific objectives and measures linked to the national goals that the grantee will address.[54]

However, because indigent defense is not a JAG purpose area, such a solution would not result in indigent defense-related measures. In addition, DOJ officials stated that asking grantees to develop measures would place an additional reporting burden on the grantees. DOJ officials also stated that while they do not have indigent defense-related outcome-oriented measures in the JAG program, they do ask grantees to report on what they have accomplished with their grants. Like an outcome measure, this could allow DOJ to assess the results of the program.

Indigent Defense Providers Generally Reported That Evaluations of Their Services Have Not Been Conducted; DOJ Has Mechanisms to Support Such Evaluations

With its indigent defense-related performance measures, DOJ can assess the impact of a grantee's use of funds, such as whether the funding resulted in an increase in the number of defenders hired. However, its assessments are not intended to evaluate the effectiveness of a grantee's, or any indigent defense provider's, programs or services, such as whether the defender's ability, training, and experience match the complexity of the case, which is one of ABA's principles for public defense delivery systems. Instead, as we have previously reported, evaluations may be used to assess a program's effectiveness, identify how to improve performance, or guide resource allocation. Moreover, evaluation can play a key role in strategic planning and in program management, providing feedback on both program design and execution.[55] For example, respondents to our survey of public defender offices and agencies reported using evaluations for purposes such as enacting system improvements (8), supporting funding requests (8), and addressing caseload issues (4), among others. Of the 118 public defender offices or agencies that responded to our survey, 9 provided us with copies of evaluations that they had conducted of their office or agency or that another entity conducted, such as a consultant or oversight body.[56] For example, one evaluation—conducted by the oversight committee for a local jurisdiction's indigent defense services— collected data and used it to assess compliance with local indigent defense standards. The evaluation considered professional independence; attorney qualifications; training; supervision; workload; performance evaluation and discipline; support services; case management and quality control; and reporting. Appendix VII provides additional details on these evaluations.

Sixty-two percent (68 of 109) of public defender offices or agencies that responded to our survey reported that no evaluation had been conducted of their office or agency. Respondents who reported reasons for not conducting an evaluation most frequently cited lack of personnel (46 percent, 29 of 63) and lack of expertise and/or the need for technical assistance (43 percent, 27 of 63) as the reasons.[57] Moreover, respondents identified challenges to collecting data on factors that affect their ability to provide indigent defense services—information that could be used to conduct an evaluation. For example, 50 percent (59 of 118) reported that the amount of face-to-face time a public defender spends with a client—a potential indicator of effectiveness—is difficult or burdensome to collect, and data on client satisfaction are also costly to collect (18 percent, 21 of 118), difficult to measure (47 percent, 56 of 118), and imprecise (32 percent, 38 of 118). However, respondents also reported currently collecting data on factors that DOJ and indigent defense stakeholders report could affect the quality of indigent defense services. For example, according to BJA, managing defender workloads is important to ensuring that the administration of justice is fair and equitable, and quality of service may be impacted when public defenders are forced to manage too many clients with inadequate resources.[58] According to respondents, data currently being collected includes both average caseload per public defender (86 percent, 96 of 111), and the number of active cases per public defender (84 percent, 94 of 112). Respondents also reported collecting data on average salary or hourly rate of public defenders (76 percent, 83 of 109)—a factor that indigent defense stakeholders have identified as relevant to the ability to attract and retain qualified attorneys.59 Appendix VIII provides additional information on the extent to which public defender offices or agencies reported collecting data that could be used to conduct an evaluation and the associated challenges or limitations of the data.

DOJ has mechanisms that could help to address some of the evaluation challenges that indigent defense offices and agencies reported, including a lack of expertise or the need for technical assistance. For instance, BJA provides technical assistance with evaluation through its Center for Program Evaluation and Performance Measurement website, and makes technical assistance available to SAAs and BJA applicants, among others.

Further, DOJ reported that it has funded more narrowly scoped, nongeneralizable, case studies intended to help inform a broader study of indigent defense and provide insights, as well as available resources, for criminal justice stakeholders.

For instance, from fiscal years 2005 through 2010, the period of our review, the National Institute of Justice (NIJ) funded one study that described how outcomes differed when murder defendants were represented by public defenders versus court-appointed private attorneys in one city.[60] The study found that, in the city evaluated, there were significant differences between the two groups on several dimensions. Specifically, defendants represented by the public defender office had shorter average sentences, were less likely to receive a life sentence, had less expected time served, and were more likely to plead guilty.

In addition, in 2010, OJP held a National Symposium on Indigent Defense, which about 500 participants attended, including public defenders and state and local criminal and juvenile justice policymakers and practitioners. The symposium included presentations by experts on topics related to indigent defense, such as managing limited indigent defense resources in difficult economic times, among other things. 61 Further, in 2011, NIJ collaborated with ATJ to hold a workshop to identify domestic and international best practices for indigent defense and to develop an agenda on criminal indigent defense research. In addition to providing suggestions for future research, the workshop produced a report containing 40 recommendations to ATJ and NIJ.[62] Among the major themes highlighted in the report was participant support for evidence-based research on indigent defense, including evaluation of successful domestic and international practices.[63]

DOJ officials stated that this report was completed consistent with NIJ's practice of documenting conference proceedings and gathering information from stakeholders.

Further, DOJ has taken steps to identify characteristics of model programs, including awarding grant funding to the National Criminal Justice Association to identify innovative use of JAG funds to support indigent defense, among other criminal justice areas. [64]

Moreover, in addition to the studies it has conducted or funded in the past, in February 2012, NIJ issued a solicitation—Social Science Research on Indigent Defense—that seeks applications for research on the fundamental issues surrounding access to legal services and the need for quality representation at the state and local level.[65]

Proposed topics include three areas: juvenile and adult defendants' waiver of their right to counsel, the importance of defense team members in indigent defense cases—issues indigent defense stakeholders identify as impediments to effective representation—as well as other research focused on important issues surrounding indigent defense.[66]

This solicitation—which will provide up to $1 million for research projects—will fund a rigorous, scientific study that will identify barriers defendants commonly face in securing effective representation. DOJ officials stated that they developed this solicitation after conducting a review of existing indigent defense research, which they used to identify the areas of research they believed to be most important. Given that public defenders in our survey reported the need for assistance in conducting evaluations, NIJ's study could help provide these defenders with the information, framework, and tools to conduct such evaluations, and identify factors that may affect the provision of indigent defense services.

CONCLUSIONS

Identifying a crisis in the nation's criminal defense system, DOJ has stated its commitment to focusing on indigent defense issues and developing and implementing solutions.

Moreover, both DOJ and BIA have undertaken efforts to assist state, local, and tribal indigent defense providers in overcoming barriers to providing effective indigent defense services. However, consistent with OJP's commitment to identify and address the most pressing challenges confronting the justice system and BIA's authority to support the development, enhancement, and continuing operation of tribal justice systems, they could do more to meet the needs of indigent defense providers. Specifically, by increasing awareness among JAG, JABG, and JJDP grantees, as well as indigent defense providers, that funding is available for indigent defense, DOJ could be in a better position to ensure that eligible grantees are aware that they can access federal funding to help address their needs. In addition, by increasing awareness among recipients of Tribal Courts TPA distributions that funding can be used for indigent defense, BIA could better help tribes enhance all aspects of their criminal justice system.

DOJ collected data on the amount of funding allocated for indigent defense for the Byrne Competitive and TCCLA grants when funding for indigent defense was a priority, and has developed mechanisms to do so in the JAG program, but does not consistently do so in the JABG and TJADG programs, where indigent defense is also a priority. Since DOJ seeks to focus on indigent defense issues and develop solutions, taking steps to collect data on allocations for indigent defense would position DOJ to better assess if it is meeting its commitment to indigent defense and help inform future funding priorities.

Recommendations for Executive Action

To ensure that OJP is best positioned to identify and address critical needs in the indigent defense community, determine whether it has met its commitment to indigent defense, and improve accountability in grants administration, we recommend that the Assistant Attorney General of OJP take the following three actions:

- take steps to increase JAG, JABG, and JJDP grantees' awareness that funding can be allocated for indigent defense;
- inform indigent defense providers about grants for which they are eligible to apply; and
- take steps to collect data on allocations and spending for indigent defense in the JABG and TJADG programs.

To ensure that the Office of Justice Services is best positioned to support the development, enhancement, and continuing operation of tribal justice systems, we recommend that the Director of the Bureau of Indian Affairs take actions to increase awareness among recipients of Tribal Court TPA distributions that funding can be allocated for indigent defense.

Agency and Third Party Comments and Our Evaluation

We provided a draft of this report for review and comment to DOJ and DOI. In addition, we provided relevant sections of the report to The Bronx Defenders and the Administrative Office of the U.S. Courts (AOUSC). DOI did not provide official written comments to include in our report. However, in an email received April 23, 2012, the DOI liaison stated that DOI concurred with our recommendation. In its written comments, DOJ concurred with the recommendations in this report. DOJ, The Bronx Defenders, and AOUSC also provided technical comments which we incorporated throughout the report as appropriate.

DOJ identified several actions that OJP will take to implement the recommendations related to increasing JAG, JABG, and JJDP grantees' awareness that funding can be allocated for indigent defense and informing indigent defense providers about grants for which they are eligible to apply. These actions include updating its "Frequently Asked Questions" document for grantees; communicating this information to grantees through email, technical assistance websites, and during national meetings; and working with national organizations, such as ABA and NLADA, to disseminate information on available funding to indigent defense providers through conferences, meetings, emails, newsletters, and publications. Increasing grantee awareness that funding can be allocated for indigent defense could help DOJ better ensure that it meets its commitment to supporting indigent defense. OJP's proposed steps, if implemented across eligible grant programs, should address the intent of our recommendations. With regard to the recommendation that OJP take steps to collect data on allocations and spending for indigent defense in the JABG and TJADG programs, we originally included language in the recommendation that described examples of actions OJP could take to collect such data. Specifically, we stated that such actions could include increasing JABG and TJADG applicants' awareness of the indigent defense project identifier, to ensure more consistent use of the identifiers and allow DOJ to collect data on allocations of the grants to indigent defense, and requiring JABG and TJADG grantees to select project identifiers. After sending the draft report to DOJ for comment, officials from OJP and ATJ stated that they plan to work together to determine internally the best way to collect data on allocations and spending for indigent defense in the JABG and TJADG programs, which could include the actions we identified in the original recommendation or other measures. Thus, they requested that we remove the language that described examples of how OJP could collect this data. We agreed that DOJ was best positioned to determine how to implement the recommendation and modified the recommendation by removing the language that described such examples to address the recommendation. OJP stated that, by September 30, 2012, OJJDP will determine the mechanism by which data on allocations and spending for indigent defense in the JABG and TJADG programs can best be collected. Collecting such data would position DOJ to better assess if it is meeting its commitment to indigent defense.

Eileen R. Larence
Director, Homeland Security and Justice Issues

APPENDIX I: OBJECTIVES, SCOPE, AND METHODOLOGY

We addressed the following questions as a part of our review:

1. What type of support, if any, have the Department of Justice (DOJ) and Bureau of Indian Affairs (BIA) provided for state, local, and tribal indigent defense?
2. For fiscals years 2005 through 2010, to what extent was eligible DOJ and BIA funding allocated and awarded for indigent defense, what factors affected decisions

to allocate and award funding for this purpose, and what actions have DOJ and BIA taken, if any, to address these factors?

3. When fiscal year 2005 through 2010 federal funding was allocated or awarded for indigent defense, how did it compare to the total allocations or awards made, and how did recipients use the funding?
4. To what extent does DOJ collect data on indigent defense funding when the grant program specifies that funds be allocated or awarded for this purpose or highlights it as a priority?
5. When a grant program specifies that funds be spent for indigent defense or highlights it as a priority, to what extent can DOJ assess the impacts of this grant funding, and to what extent have there been evaluations of indigent defense programs and has DOJ supported these evaluation efforts ?

To determine what DOJ grant programs and BIA funding could be used to support state, local, and tribal indigent defense from fiscal years 2005 through 2010, we reviewed the Catalog of Federal Domestic Assistance, DOJ's website, and BIA's annual budget justifications.[1] In addition, we spoke with public defenders and state and local government offices in selected states to determine whether there were additional grants they had applied for or received related to indigent defense that we had not already identified. We selected these states based on geographical location, the extent to which state and local government offices had received federal funding, and the structure of the state's indigent defense system. We also met with agency officials in DOJ's Office of Justice Programs (OJP), who are responsible for administering the programs, and BIA's Office of Justice Services, who provide support to tribal courts, to discuss the federal funding programs in more detail. Once our determinations were made, we sent OJP officials a list of funding programs to be included in our review, and asked for confirmation of this list. The DOJ grants included in our review were the Edward Byrne Memorial Justice Assistance Grant (JAG) Program; the Juvenile Accountability Block Grant (JABG); the Juvenile Justice and Delinquency Prevention Title II (JJDP); John R. Justice Program; Byrne Competitive Program; Capital Case Litigation Initiative; Wrongful Conviction Review Program; Tribal Civil and Criminal Legal Assistance Program; Tribal Courts Assistance Program; Juvenile Indigent Defense Clearinghouse Grant; Tribal Juvenile Accountability Discretionary Grant; Juvenile Justice and Mental Health Collaboration Grant; and Adult Drug Court Discretionary Grant. The BIA funding included in our review was the Tribal Courts tribal priority allocation (TPA) distributions. We obtained records of all recipients of these grants from DOJ and by reviewing BIA's budget documentation. Further, we interviewed knowledgeable agency officials about the source of the grant data and the controls in place to maintain the integrity of the data and determined that the data were sufficiently reliable for our purposes. In addition, to determine what other assistance DOJ and BIA made available to support indigent defense, we interviewed DOJ and BIA officials responsible for training and technical assistance to identify assistance other than funding that the agencies provide to support indigent defense.

To determine the extent to which state, local, and tribal governments allocated federal funding for indigent defense, the factors that influenced their decisions, and the amounts allocated, we conducted separate Web-based surveys of all recipients of fiscal year 2005 through 2010 DOJ formula grants that could be allocated for indigent defense—the JAG, JJDP, and JABG grants—and tribal governments that received BIA Tribal Courts TPA distributions from fiscal years 2005 through 2010.[2] To develop the survey questionnaires, we reviewed existing literature about the provision of indigent defense, and interviewed state JAG, JABG, and JJDP recipients, local JAG recipients, and tribes. We designed draft questionnaires in close collaboration with a GAO social science survey specialist. We conducted pretests with five state and local JAG recipients, three JABG recipients, three JJDP recipients, two tribal JAG recipients, and two recipients of BIA Tribal Court TPA distributions to help further refine our questions, develop new questions, and clarify any ambiguous portions of the survey.

We developed and administered the web-based questionnaires accessible through a secure server. We emailed each recipient a unique identification number and password, and a link to the questionnaire for their population. See table 4 for further details about the population, response rates, and generalizabilty of these surveys.

Because all recipients of JABG and JJDP funding were included in our survey, and our results are therefore not subject to sampling error, and we received response rates of 82 and 89 percent, we consider our results generalizable to the populations of JABG and JJDP recipients. While we also included all eligible members of the target populations in our state and local JAG, tribal JAG, and Tribal Courts TPA surveys, because of their relatively low response rates and the possibility of other errors all questionnaire surveys face, our results represent only respondents participating in these surveys and should not be generalized to the populations. Specifically, certain members of these populations may have been more or less likely to respond to our survey and this may affect our data. For instance, our data may overrepresent allocations for indigent defense because recipients that allocated funding for indigent defense may have been more likely to respond to our survey than recipients that had never done so. In addition, on the JAG survey, recipients of larger amounts of money and recipients of multiple years of funding were more likely to respond, but recipients of funding awarded solely pursuant to amounts appropriated through the American Recovery and Reinvestment Act were less likely to respond. However, the responses provide insights into the extent to which JAG and BIA Tribal Courts TPA funding has been allocated for indigent defense.

The practical difficulties of conducting any survey may introduce errors in estimates. For example, difficulties in interpreting a particular question, sources of information available to respondents, or entering data into a database or analyzing them can introduce unwanted variability into the survey results. We took steps in developing the questionnaire, collecting the data, and analyzing them to minimize these errors. In addition, as indicated above, social science survey specialists designed the questionnaire in collaboration with GAO staff that had subject matter expertise. We then conducted pretests to check that (1) the questions were clear and unambiguous, (2) terminology was used correctly, (3) the questionnaire did not place an undue burden on respondents, (4) the information could feasibly be obtained, and (5) the survey was comprehensive and unbiased. We made multiple contact attempts with nonrespondents during the survey by e-mail, and some nonrespondents were also contacted by telephone. When we analyzed the data, an independent analyst checked all computer programs. Since this was a web-based survey, respondents entered their answers directly into the electronic questionnaire, eliminating the need to key data into a database, minimizing error.

Table 4. Survey Distribution, Populations, Respondents and Rates, and Generalizability

Grant program	Date survey distributed	Eligible population	Number of respondents	Response rate, in percent	Considered generalizable?
Juvenile Justice and Delinquency	September 22, 2011	56	50	89	Yes
Prevention Title II					
Juvenile Accountability Block Grant	September 22, 2011	56	46	82	Yes
Justice Assistance Grant (overall state	October 17, 2011				
and local)		3,934[a]	1,807	46	No
States		56	50	89	Yes
Localities		3878	1757	45	No
Justice Assistance Grant (tribes)[b]	December 22, 2011	29	11	38	No
Tribal Courts TPA	December 21, 2011	154	105	68	No

Source: GAO analysis of survey data.

[a]For the state and local JAG survey, we provisionally identified, and on October 17, 2011, attempted to contact 3,970 recipients. We later determined that 36 were ineligible or duplicates. Therefore, our final eligible population was 3,934.

[b]For the purposes of this report, we have combined all the tribal JAG responses with the responses of state and local JAG recipients.

We assessed the reliability of funding allocation data that was provided by including a series of questions pertaining to the accuracy of reported data in our survey and reviewing the data for obvious errors. Dollar amounts reported through our surveys, particularly by JAG respondents, have limitations and should be treated as estimates. For instance, respondents may have had difficulty identifying the precise amount of funding allocated for indigent defense in the earlier years of our time frame (fiscal years 2005 through 2010), may have been unable to determine the exact amount of funding that was allocated for indigent defense if grant funds were used for multiple purposes, or may not have had sufficient information to provide total amounts allocated to indigent defense because they had not yet fully allocated their grant funds. In addition, our JAG data may overrepresent allocations to law enforcement because it was the first category listed in our survey and respondents that were unable to split their funding across purpose areas may have reported allocating all funding to law enforcement.

To determine the extent to which DOJ awarded discretionary grants for indigent defense, we obtained project descriptions for all discretionary grants that could have been awarded for indigent defense in fiscal years 2005 through 2010 from DOJ. We then reviewed these descriptions to determine the recipients of the grant services. In addition to indigent defense providers, this included the following categories: civil defenders, criminal defenders, prosecutors, law enforcement providers, court offices, correctional agencies, crime victims, reentry service providers, juvenile delinquency prevention organizations, appellate defenders, drug treatment providers, community and public outreach providers, non-attorney staff, innocence projects, and universities. Many grants had multiple recipients of grant services. In these instances, we classified the grants to reflect all recipients; as a result, grants may be counted in more than one category. For each grant program we determined the number of grants used exclusively for indigent defense, the number of grants used for indigent defense with another grant recipient category, and the number and amount of grants that were not used for indigent defense. Two analysts made these classifications in order to verify each other's work.

Table 5. Public Defender Offices by Stratum and Population, Cases Selected, and Sample Size

Stratum	Stratum name	Population	Number of cases	Effective sample	Response rate
	Certainty strata				
1	State offices	22	22	22	100%
2	Territories	6	6	4.8	100%
3	Tribes	17	17	13.6	59%
4	Public defender offices—major metro areas	53	52	42.4	50%
5	Secondary offices not in major metro areas	71	71	56.8	41%
	Subtotal certainties	169	169	139.6	
	Random sample				
6	Primary offices[a]	672	85	68.8	29%
	Total sample	841	253	208.4	

Source: GAO analysis of survey population.

[a]By primary office, we mean the office or agency which has been designated by a local jurisdiction as its chief provider of indigent defense services. In general, the primary office will handle the bulk of indigent defense services in its respective jurisdiction, with other services being provided by another office, agency or individual in accordance with predetermined contractual agreement, capacity limitations (where applicable), or compliance with ethical and professional standards relating to conflicts of interest.

To determine what factors influenced public defenders' decisions to apply for funding, we conducted a web-based survey of public defenders. To develop the survey questionnaire, we reviewed existing literature about the provision of indigent defense, and interviewed stakeholder groups knowledgeable about the provision of these services. We designed draft questionnaires in close collaboration with a GAO social science survey specialist. We conducted pretests with four public defenders to help further refine our questions, develop new questions, and clarify any ambiguous portions of the survey.

We drew our survey sample from 841 public defender offices identified nationwide. To identify the population of public defender offices nationwide, we started with the Census of Public Defender Offices, which was conducted in 2007 by the Bureau of Justice Statistics (BJS).[3] This Census collected data from all state and county funded public defender offices across the country. We further worked in partnership with the National Legal Aid and Defender Association (NLADA) to update existing contact information and identify additional offices that should be included.

We drew a stratified sample of 253 of the 841 public defenders nationwide. From this population of 841 public defenders, we sampled 100 percent of: 22 state-level offices, 6 territories, 17 tribes, 52 public defender offices in major metropolitan areas, and 71 secondary offices not in major metropolitan areas. The remaining 85 public defenders were drawn within strata defined by region. The six strata are shown in table 5.

We developed and administered the web-based questionnaire accessible through a secure server, and emailed unique identification numbers and passwords to the 253 public defenders beginning December 6, 2011. We sent follow-up e-mail messages beginning December 13, 2011, to those who had not yet responded. Then we contacted all remaining nonrespondents by telephone, starting January 5, 2012. The questionnaire was available online until February 29, 2012.

We received 118 responses from the sample of 253, for an unweighted response rate of 47 percent. Because of this relatively low response rate, our results represent only respondents participating in our survey and should not be generalized to the population of public defenders; thus we report results based only on the respondents and do not present population estimates. However, the responses provide insights into the factors that influence public defenders' decisions to apply for federal funding. We took steps similar to those in our grant recipient surveys when developing the questionnaire, collecting the data, and analyzing them to minimize errors.

To determine what efforts, if any, DOJ has taken to address factors influencing recipients' decisions to allocate funding for indigent defense, we interviewed DOJ and BIA officials responsible for each type of funding. We also reviewed DOJ's guidance to recipients to determine the extent to which DOJ communicated that funding could be used for indigent defense programs. We compared this guidance against the grant and BIA statutes, and DOJ's stated commitment to support indigent defense.

To determine the allocation amounts and uses of formula grants and Tribal Courts TPA distributions that were allocated for indigent defense, we asked a question pertaining to funding amounts in our state and local JAG, JABG, JJDP, tribal JAG, and Tribal Courts TPA surveys described above and also performed follow-up interviews with select grant recipients to determine the purposes for which funds were used. We contacted all 6 JABG and 7 JJDP recipients that reported allocating any fiscal year 2005 through 2010 funding for indigent defense, all 16 state and local JAG recipients that reported allocating fiscal year 2010 funding for indigent defense, and 7 recipients of BIA Tribal Courts TPA distributions that reported allocating any fiscal year 2005 through 2010 funding for indigent defense and asked them to describe how they used grants funds that were allocated for indigent defense. We conducted interviews with 5 of 6 JABG, 5 of 7 JJDP, 9 of 16 state and local JAG, and 7 of 20 recipients of BIA Tribal Courts TPA distributions that reported allocating to indigent defense. To determine the allocation amounts and uses of discretionary grants which were awarded for indigent defense, during our review of all project descriptions of DOJ discretionary grants that could have been awarded for indigent defense from fiscal years 2005 through 2010, in addition to determining the recipient of the grant services, we also determined the use for each grant. We identified the following possible uses: training, technical assistance, personnel, planning and evaluation, technology initiatives, equipment, case management, conflict counsel, outreach and public education, facilities, codes and legal rules, and representation from an outside source. For each grant, two analysts came to agreement on the categorization. As with the recipients of grant services, many grants had multiple uses. In these instances, we classified the grants to reflect all their uses; as a result, grants may be counted more than one time in our overall analysis. With this information we were able to provide the amount and use for all discretionary grants that were used all or in part for indigent defense.

To determine the extent to which DOJ collects data on whether recipients allocate funds for indigent defense when such funding is required or highlighted as a priority, we reviewed all grant solicitations to determine whether DOJ required that funding be allocated or awarded for indigent defense or identified indigent defense as a purpose area or priority. For grants in which we found that it was, we spoke with DOJ officials about why they chose to do so. In addition, through document requests and interviews with DOJ officials, we asked the agency to provide information that describes the extent to which they track how grantees have allocated funding, including for indigent defense, and how they do or could do so. We analyzed this information to ascertain the status of their efforts and the mechanisms available to conduct such tracking.

As part of this analysis, we requested data from DOJ on its fiscal year 2011 JAG grantees because—beginning in fiscal year 2011—JAG grantees were required to select up to five project identifiers to indicate how their 2011 JAG funds would be used, and DOJ developed a project identifier for indigent defense. We compared this data with our survey results from JAG grantees to determine the extent to which grantees that indicated in our survey that they are likely to allocate funding for indigent defense also selected indigent defense as a project identifier in their fiscal year 2011 grant application in order to assess the accuracy of the project identifier data. We compared DOJ's data collection efforts against our prior work on implementing the Government Performance and Results Act, which states that agencies should collect sufficiently complete, accurate, and consistent data to measure performance and support decision making at various organizational levels.[4]

To determine the extent to which DOJ can assess the impact of grant programs that specify that funds must be spent for indigent defense or highlight it as a priority, we reviewed performance measures outlined in DOJ grant solicitations. We compared DOJ's measures against criteria in Office of Management and Budget (OMB) guidance[5] and our prior work on performance measures, which states that leading organizations promote accountability by establishing results-oriented, outcome goals and corresponding performance measures by which to gauge progress towards attaining these goals.[6] Two analysts also independently reviewed performance measures DOJ established or is establishing for all grant programs in which indigent defense funding is required or a priority to assess whether the measures focused on the intended result of the program (were outcome-oriented). The analysts then met to discuss and resolve any differences in the results of their analysis. In addition, we spoke with DOJ officials about the feasibility of collecting performance measures for grant programs.

To determine the extent to which evaluations have been conducted of indigent defense programs, and the extent to which DOJ has supported these evaluation efforts, we asked public defender offices and agencies in our survey whether an evaluation had been conducted of their office and the challenges associated with conducting such an evaluation. We reviewed the evaluations of the 9 respondents who reported they were willing to share them, but did not assess the quality of the evaluations or their results. In addition, we conducted a literature search of peer-reviewed journals using databases such as ProQuest, PolicyFile, and LexisNexis. In December 2011, we also held a listening session at a National Legal Aid and Defender Association conference where public defenders described challenges to conducting evaluations, among other topics. Finally, to identify actions DOJ has taken to evaluate indigent defense systems, we reviewed studies funded or conducted by DOJ and interviewed DOJ officials about its efforts to evaluate indigent defense systems.

We conducted this performance audit from February 2011 to May 2012 in accordance with generally accepted government auditing standards. Those standards require that we plan and perform the audit to obtain sufficient, appropriate evidence to provide a reasonable basis for our analysis based on our audit objectives. We believe that the evidence obtained provides a reasonable basis for our analysis based on our audit objectives.

APPENDIX II: ALLOCATIONS AND USES OF DOJ GRANTS THAT REQUIRED INDIGENT DEFENSE FUNDING

As table 6 demonstrates, grantees of the four programs that we determined require funding for indigent defense—the John R. Justice Program, Capital Case Litigation Program, Wrongful Conviction Review Program, and Juvenile Indigent Defense National Clearinghouse—have allocated or used these grants in accordance with grant requirements for indigent defense.

Table 6. Number and Amount of Awards for Indigent Defense for DOJ Grant Programs That Required Funding for Indigent Defense

	Fiscal years in which the grant was active from fiscal year 2005-2010	Number of grants awarded in all active fiscal years	Total amount awarded for indigent defense	Awards to indigent defense as percentage of total funding
John R. Justice[a]	2010	51	$5.1 million	50%
Capital Case Litigation Initiative[b]	2007-2010	33	$3.3 million	63%
Wrongful Conviction Review[c]	2009-2010	24	$4.6 million	89%
Juvenile Indigent Defense National Clearinghouse	2010	1	$500,000	100%

Source: GAO analysis of DOJ data.

[a] John R. Justice data include $244,834 (2 percent of total funding) for federal public defenders; the remaining amounts were awarded to state and local public defenders. One state obtained a waiver from the requirement to allocate funding equally to prosecutors and defenders as it had few eligible defenders and no defenders with any outstanding student loans to qualify for the repayment in the state, and thus awarded all of its funding to prosecutors.

[b] Capital Case Litigation data are greater than the 50 percent required for indigent defense because they include 18 grants for $3.2 million that were awarded to indigent defense in combination with another purpose, but we were unable to determine the exact amount of funding awarded for indigent defense alone.

[c] Wrongful Conviction data do not reflect that all grants and funding were awarded for indigent defense because, due to our methodology for categorizing grantees, two grantees were categorized as state appellate defender offices, which we classified as a separate group from indigent defense providers that handle defendants' initial cases, and one as a nonprofit organization. However, these grantees' project descriptions indicated that they would utilize the grant to provide representation in post-conviction claims of innocence, in accordance with grant requirements.

APPENDIX III: PERCENTAGE OF SURVEY RESPONDENTS THAT ALLOCATED FUNDING FOR INDIGENT DEFENSE AND ALLOCATION AMOUNTS

Figures 13, 14, and 15 show the percentages of Edward Byrne Memorial Justice Assistance Grant (JAG); Juvenile Accountability Block Grant (JABG); Juvenile Justice and Delinquency Prevention Title II (JJDP); and Bureau of Indian Affairs (BIA) Tribal Courts Tribal Priority Allocation (TPA) Distribution survey respondents who reported allocating funding for indigent defense from fiscal year 2005 through 2010.[1] As the figures demonstrate, the percentage was highest among JAG State Administering Agencies (SAA)—the state agencies that administer JAG funds—in receipt of grants awarded pursuant to amounts appropriated through the American Recovery and Reinvestment Act (ARRA). In addition, the percentage of JJDP and JABG recipients that reported allocating funding for indigent defense increased and decreased, respectively, in fiscal year 2009. Further, the percentage of BIA tribal courts survey respondents that reported allocating funding for indigent defense has increased over time.

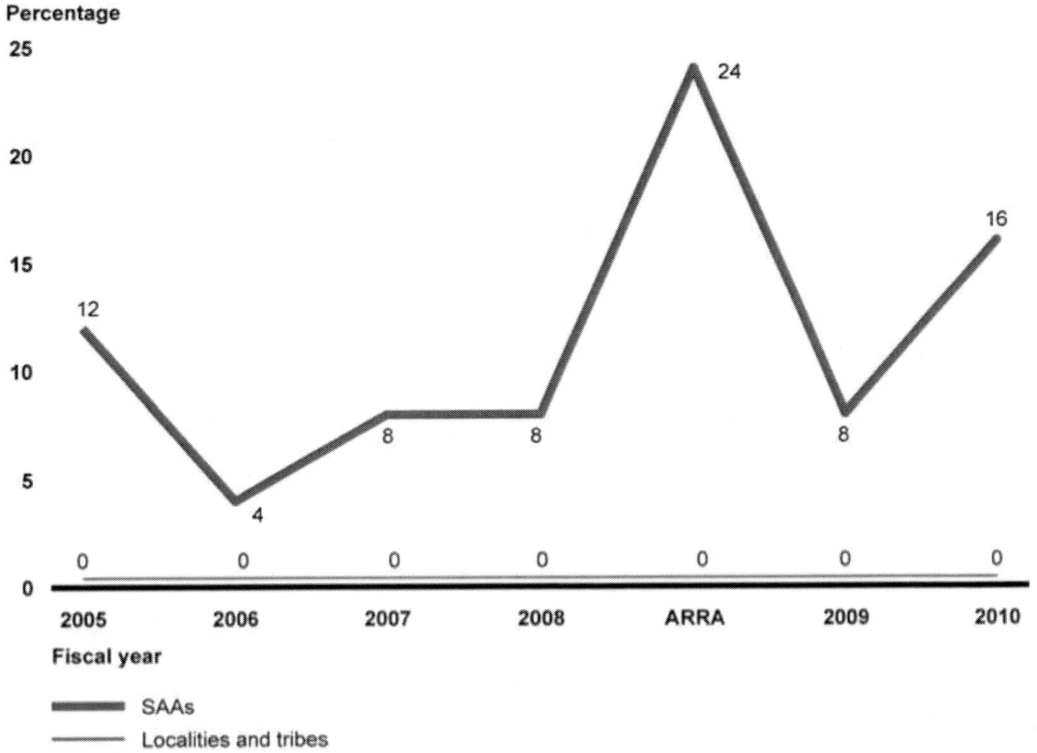

Source: GAO analysis of survey data.

Note: Because so few localities and tribes reported allocating funding for indigent defense, the numbers rounded to zero.

Figure 13. Percentage of JAG State, Local, and Tribal Survey Respondents That Reported Allocating Funding for Indigent Defense, by Fiscal Year.

As figures 16, 17, and 18 illustrate, among survey respondents who reported allocating funding for indigent defense, allocations for indigent defense as a percentage of total awards reported by survey respondents were generally small, but varied slightly across time.

For instance, in the JAG program, reported allocations as a percentage of total awards were highest among localities and tribes in fiscal years 2009 and 2010.

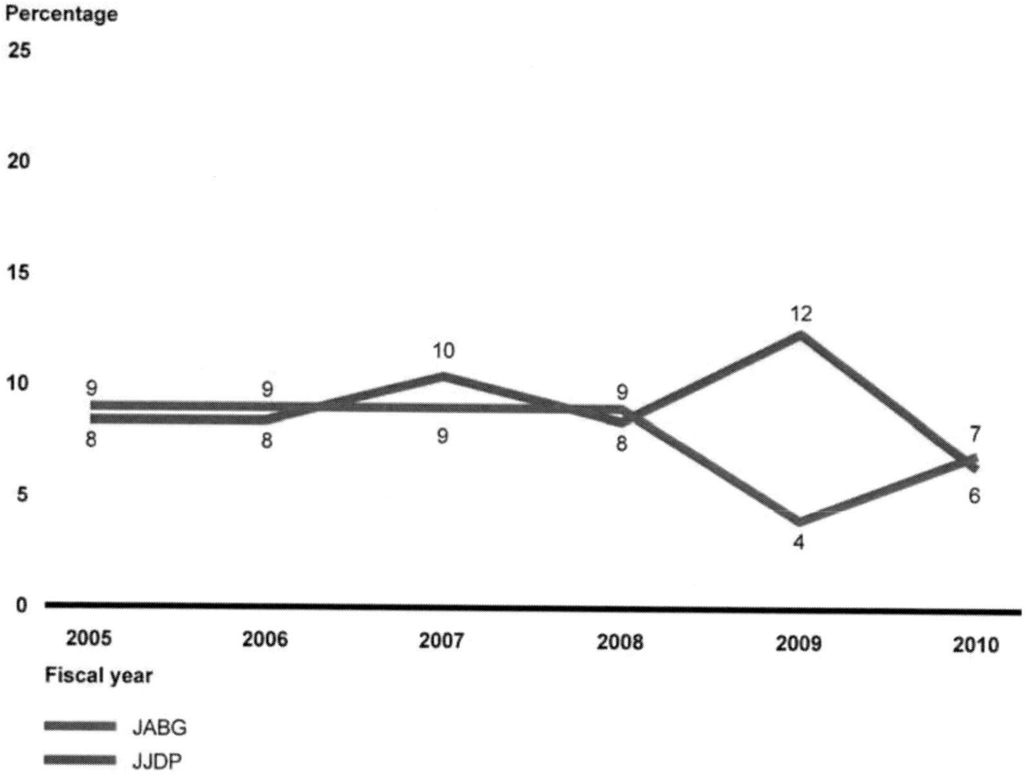

Source: GAO analysis of survey data.

Figure 14. Percentage of JJDP and JABG Survey Respondents That Reported Allocating Funding for Indigent Defense, by Fiscal Year.

In addition, reported allocations as a percentage of total awards are highest in the JABG program, but have been decreasing over time. Further, reported allocations as a percentage of total awards among BIA Tribal Courts TPA recipients have been increasing over time.

However, these data, particularly the allocation amounts, have limitations and should be treated as estimates.

For instance, respondents may have had difficulty identifying the precise amount of funding allocated for indigent defense in the earlier years of our time frame (fiscal years 2005 through 2010), been unable to determine the exact amount of funding that was allocated for indigent defense if grant funds were used for multiple purposes, or not have had sufficient information to provide total amounts allocated to indigent defense because they had not yet fully allocated their grant funds. In addition, our JAG data may overrepresent allocations to law enforcement because it was the first category listed in our survey and respondents that were unable to split their funding across purpose areas may have reported allocating all funding to law enforcement.

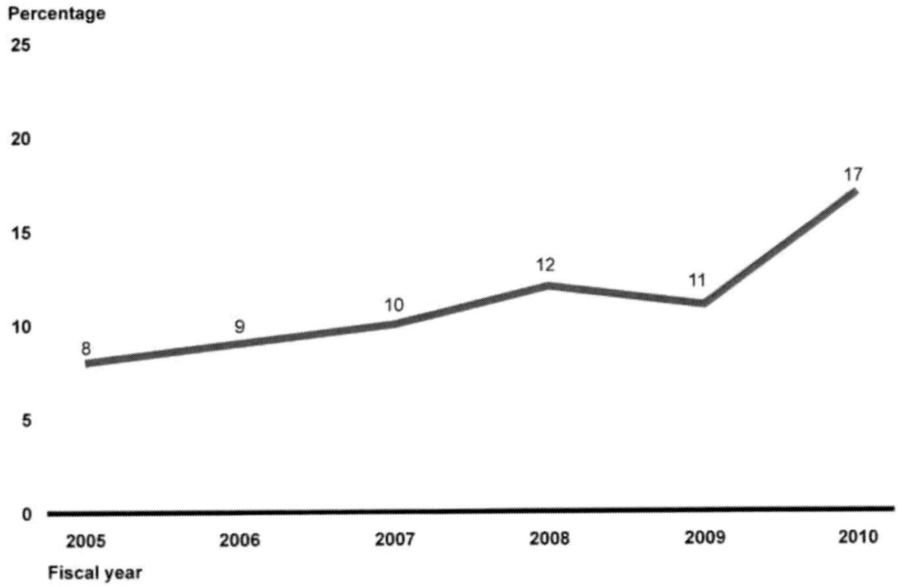

Source: GAO analysis of survey data.

Figure 15. Percentage of BIA Tribal Courts TPA Funding Survey Respondents That Reported Allocating Funding for Indigent Defense, by Fiscal Year.

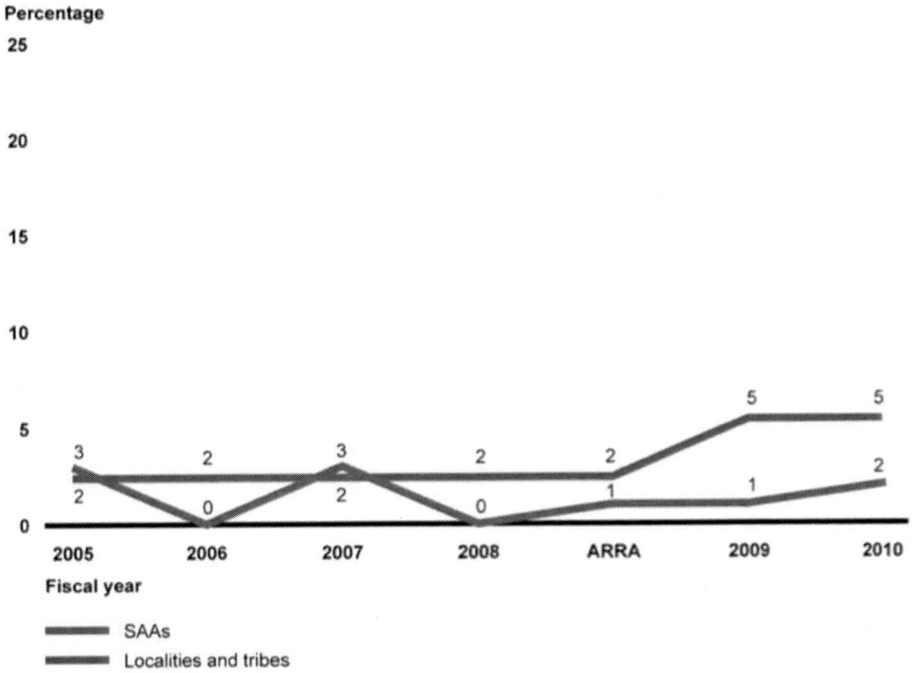

Source: GAO analysis of survey data.

Figure 16. Reported Allocations as a Percentage of Total Award, by Fiscal Year, among JAG Respondents Who Reported Allocating Funding for Indigent Defense.

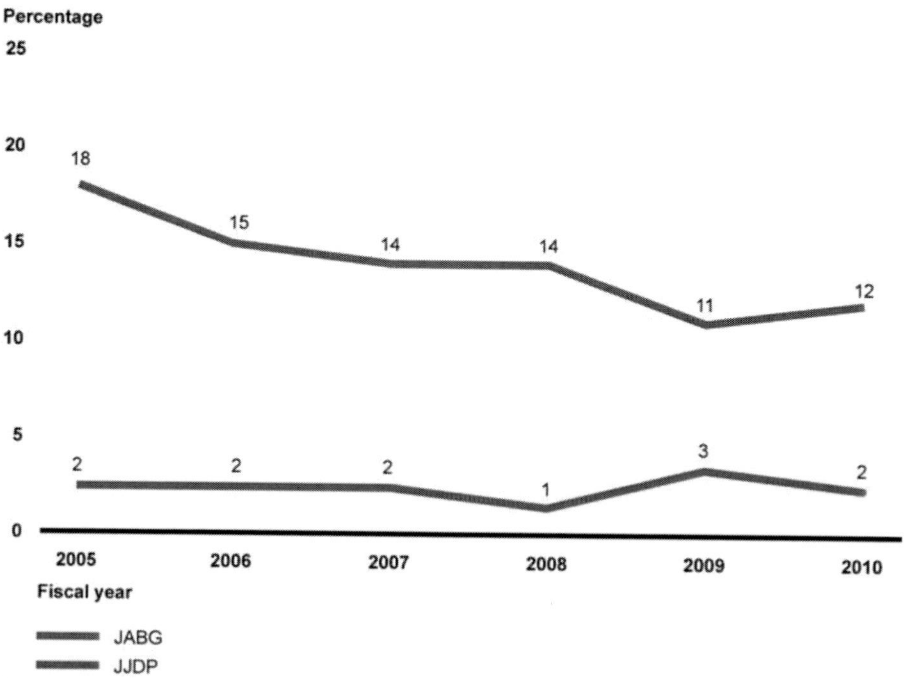

Source: GAO analysis of survey data.

Figure 17. Reported Allocations as a Percentage of Total Award, by Fiscal Year, among JABG and JJDP Respondents Who Reported Allocating Funding for Indigent Defense.

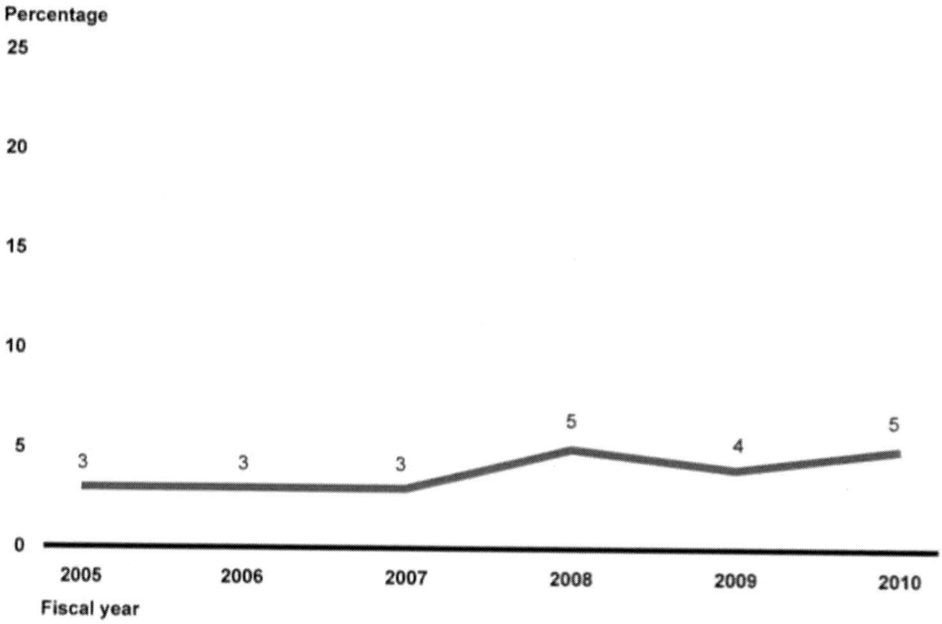

Source: GAO analysis of survey data.

Figure 18. Reported Allocations as a Percentage of Total Award, by Fiscal Year, among BIA Tribal Courts TPA Respondents Who Reported Allocating Funding for Indigent Defense.

APPENDIX IV: ADDITIONAL DETAILS ON NUMBER OF INDIGENT DEFENSE DISCRETIONARY AWARDS AND AWARD AMOUNTS

Table 7 shows, by DOJ discretionary grant, the number of grants awarded in whole or in part for indigent defense, this number as a percentage of total awards, total allocations for indigent defense, and these allocations as a percentage of total awards. These data, particularly the award amounts, have limitations. For instance, we reviewed project descriptions that were based on grantees' applications; however, the descriptions did not identify the amount of funding specifically planned for indigent defense.

Therefore, the amounts reported represent the maximum possible awards for indigent defense.

Table 7. Awards and Allocations in Whole or in Part for Indigent Defense, by Discretionary Grant that Did Not Require Spending for this Purpose

	Number of grants awarded, fiscal years 2005 through 2010	Percentage of total grants awarded that were for indigent defense	Maximum possible total allocation to indigent defense	Maximum possible allocation to indigent defense, as percentage of total funding
Byrne Competitive	18	6.3%	$4,058,585	2.7%
Adult Drug Court Discretionary Grant Program	9	2.8%	$2,088,137	2.5%
Justice and Mental Health Collaboration Grant Program	2	1.3%	$99,955	0.4%
Tribal Courts Assistance Program	16	7.9%	$3,863,679	8.0%
Tribal Civil and Criminal Legal Assistance	2	25.0%	$281,400	7.1%
Tribal Juvenile Accountability Discretionary Grant	0	0%	$0	0%

Figures 19 and 20 show the percentage of grants awarded in whole or in part for indigent defense as well as maximum possible awards for indigent defense as a percentage of total grant awards from 2005 through 2010.

As figure 19 demonstrates, the percentage of grants awarded for indigent defense was highest for fiscal year 2010 TCCLA grants, and in the fiscal year 2009 Byrne Competitive grant program, when indigent defense was part of a national initiative.

In addition, as figure 20 illustrates, awards to indigent defense as a percentage of total awards were highest in the Tribal Court Assistance Program, although they were decreasing over time.

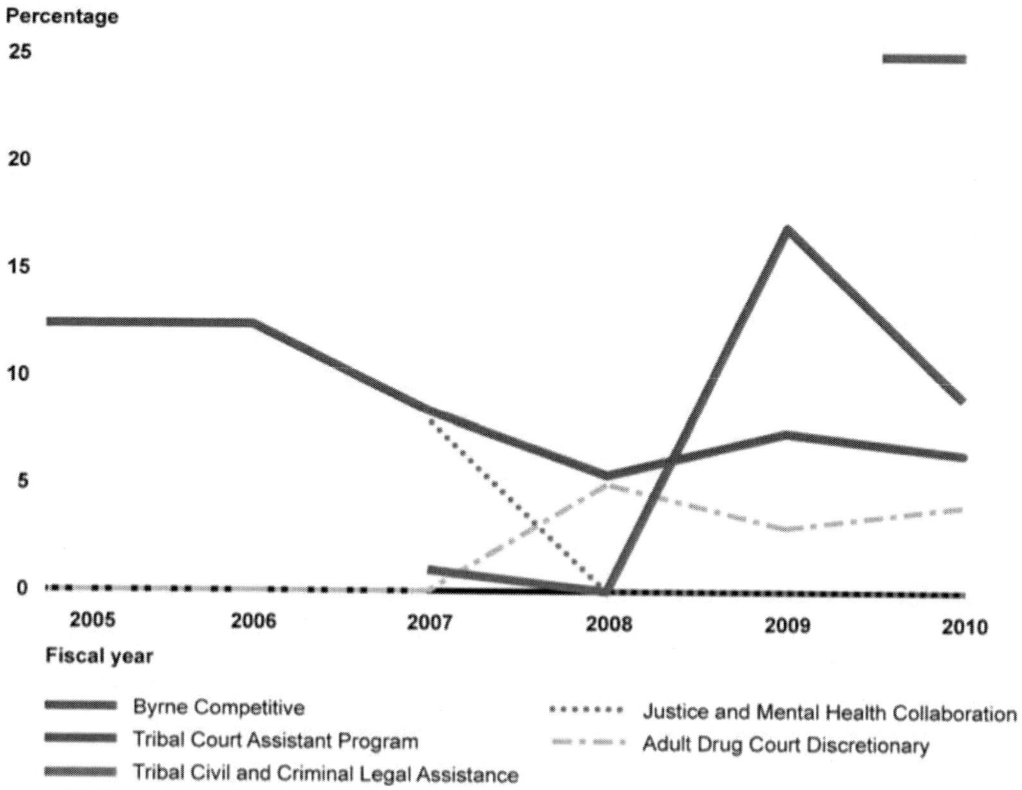

Source: GAO analysis of DOJ data.

Note: DOJ determined that 35 percent of TCCLA funding was awarded for indigent defense in fiscal year 2010, and 51 percent was awarded for indigent defense in fiscal year 2011. The fiscal year 2010 percentage differs from our analysis due to the differences in the methodologies used to determine the percentage of grants awarded for indigent defense. Specifically, DOJ calculated its percentage by dividing the grants awarded under Category 2—the purpose of which is to provide criminal legal assistance services—by the total awards under the grant. In contrast, we reviewed each of the project descriptions submitted by TCCLA grantees to determine whether the descriptions indicated that the grantee planned to use the funds for indigent defense. Because the project descriptions may not have included all the planned activities of the grantee, our methodology may not have captured all grants that were awarded for indigent defense.

Figure 19. Percentage of Grants Awarded in Whole or in Part for Indigent Defense; Fiscal Years 2005 through 2010.

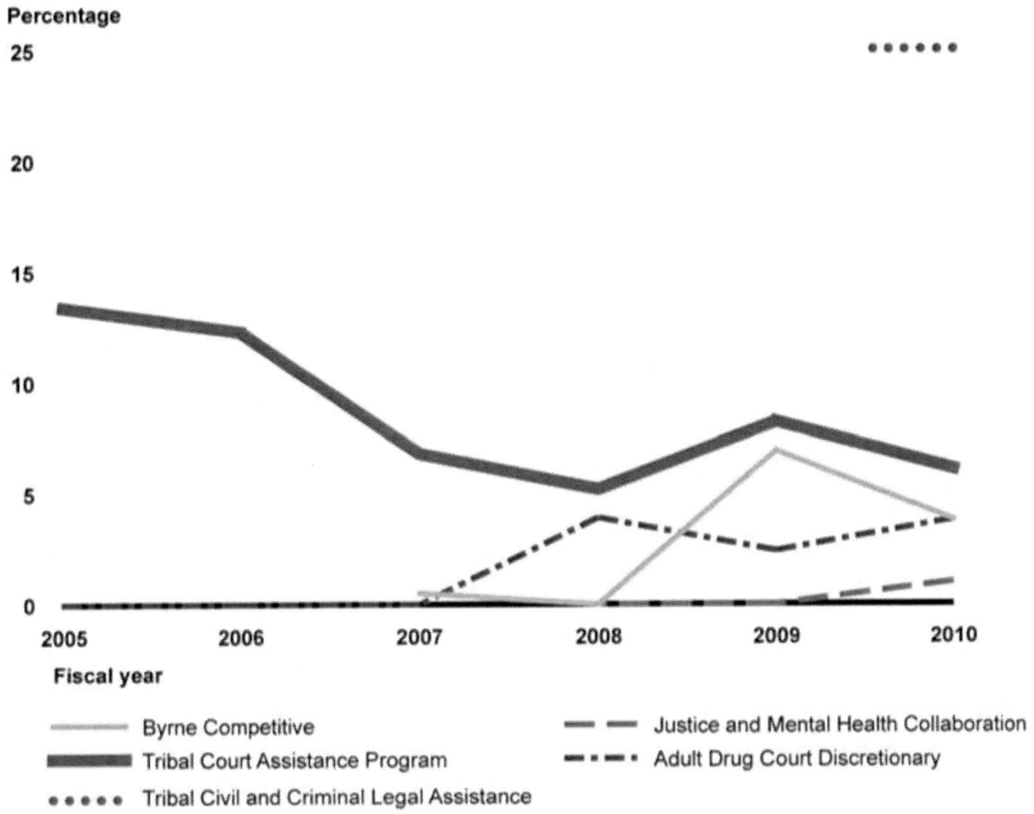

Source: GAO analysis of DOJ data.

Note: The figure includes grants that were used fully or in part for indigent defense. The Tribal Juvenile Accountability Discretionary Grant Program had no grants awarded for indigent defense and, thus, is not included in the figure.

Figure 20. Indigent Defense Awards, as a Maximum Possible Percentage of Total Awards; Fiscal Years 2005 through 2010.

APPENDIX V: JAG SURVEY RESPONDENTS' ALLOCATIONS ACROSS PURPOSE AREAS AND FOR INDIGENT DEFENSE, BY FISCAL YEAR

Figures 21 through 34 display the percentages of their total awards that Edward Byrne Memorial Justice Assistance Grant (JAG) State Administering Agencies (SAA)—state agencies that administer JAG funds—and local and tribal JAG recipients that responded to our survey reported allocating for all seven JAG purpose areas by fiscal year.[1] The figures also include the percentage of their total awards that these respondents reported allocating for indigent defense.[2]

However, our data have limitations and should be treated as estimates. Specifically, respondents may have had difficulty identifying the precise amount of funding allocated for indigent defense in the earlier years of our timeframe (fiscal years 2005 through 2010, including funding awarded pursuant to amounts appropriated through the American Recovery and Reinvestment Act (ARRA)), been unable to determine the exact amount of funding that was allocated for each purpose area if grant funds were used for multiple purposes, or not have had sufficient information to provide total amounts allocated to each purpose area because they had not yet fully allocated their grant funds.

In addition, the data may overrepresent allocations to law enforcement because it was the first category listed in our survey and respondents that were unable to split their funding across purpose areas may have reported allocating all funding to law enforcement.

Finally, our data may overrepresent allocations for indigent defense because JAG recipients that allocated funding to indigent defense may have been more likely to respond to our survey than recipients that had never done so.

As figures 21 through 27 illustrate, SAAs who responded to our survey reported allocating the largest proportion of funding to the law enforcement purpose area.

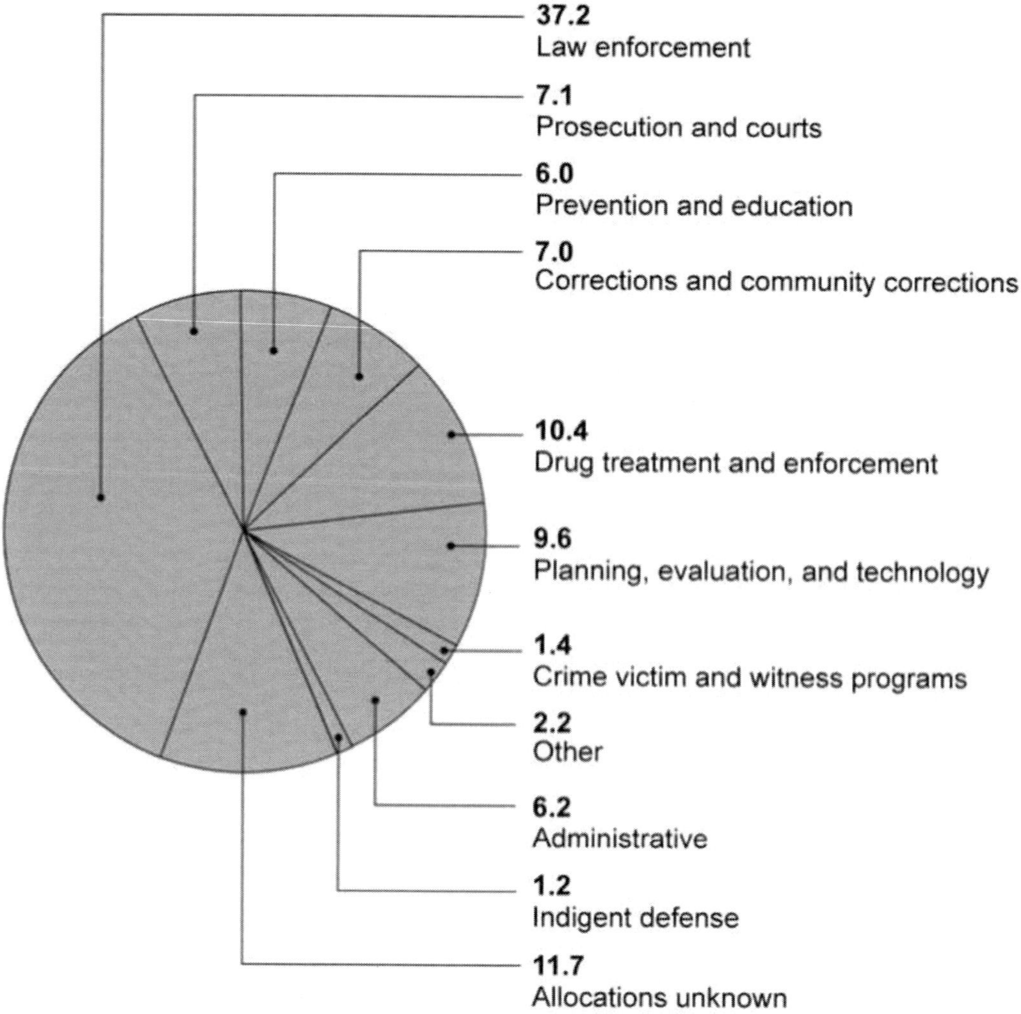

Source: GAO analysis of survey data.

Note: Other includes funds not yet allocated.

Figure 21. SAAs' Reported Allocations across JAG Purpose Areas and for Indigent Defense as a Percentage of Total Awards, Fiscal Year 2005.

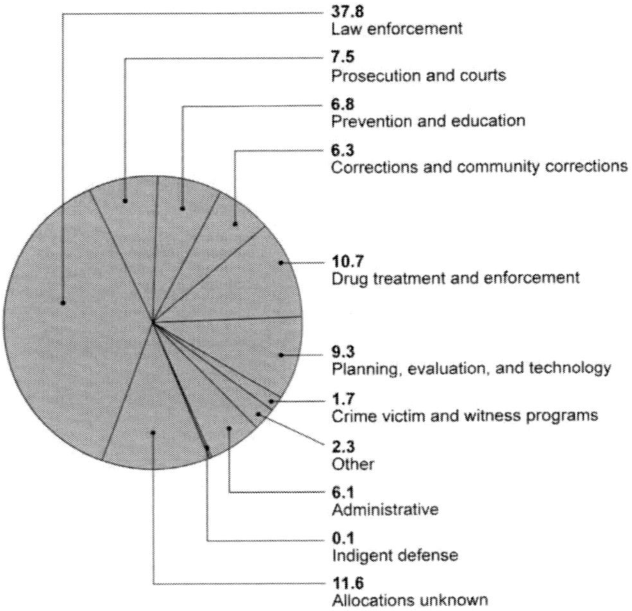

Source: GAO analysis of survey data.

Note: Other includes funds not yet allocated. Percentages do not add up to 100 due to rounding.

Figure 22. SAAs' Reported Allocations across JAG Purpose Areas and for Indigent Defense as a Percentage of Total Awards, Fiscal Year 2006.

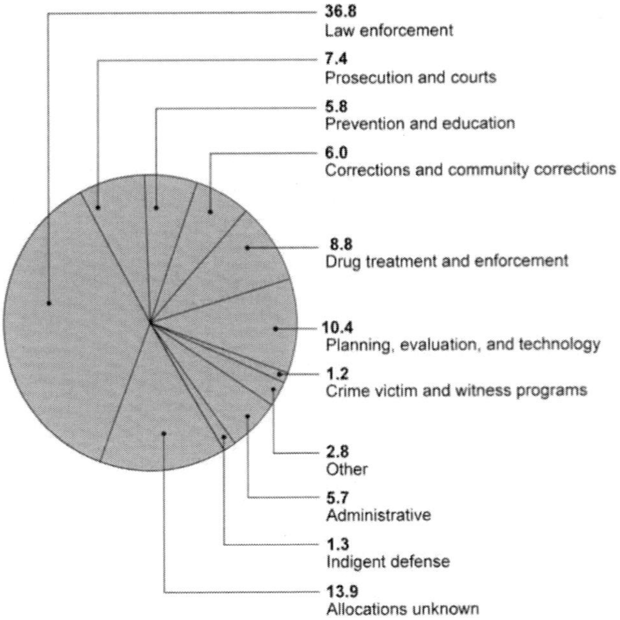

Source: GAO analysis of survey data.

Note: Other includes funds not yet allocated. Percentages do not add up to 100 due to rounding.

Figure 23. SAAs' Reported Allocations across JAG Purpose Areas and for Indigent Defense as a Percentage of Total Awards, Fiscal Year 2007.

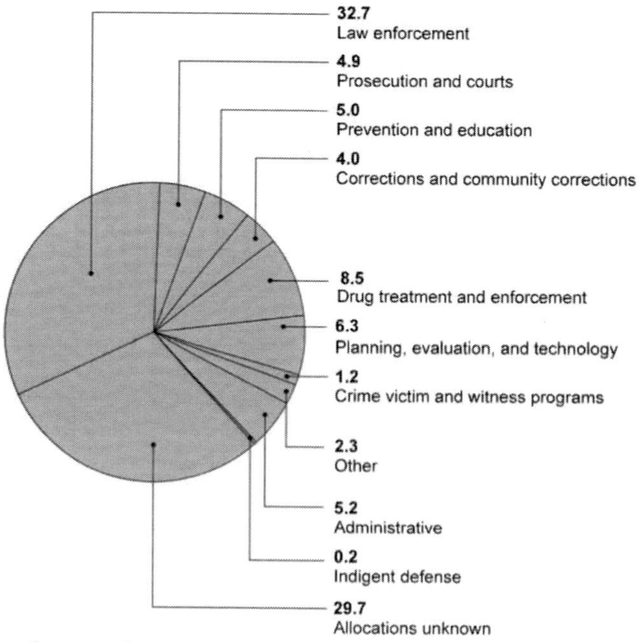

Source: GAO analysis of survey data.

Note: Other includes funds not yet allocated.

Figure 24. SAAs' Reported Allocations across JAG Purpose Areas and for Indigent Defense as a Percentage of Total Awards, Fiscal Year 2008.

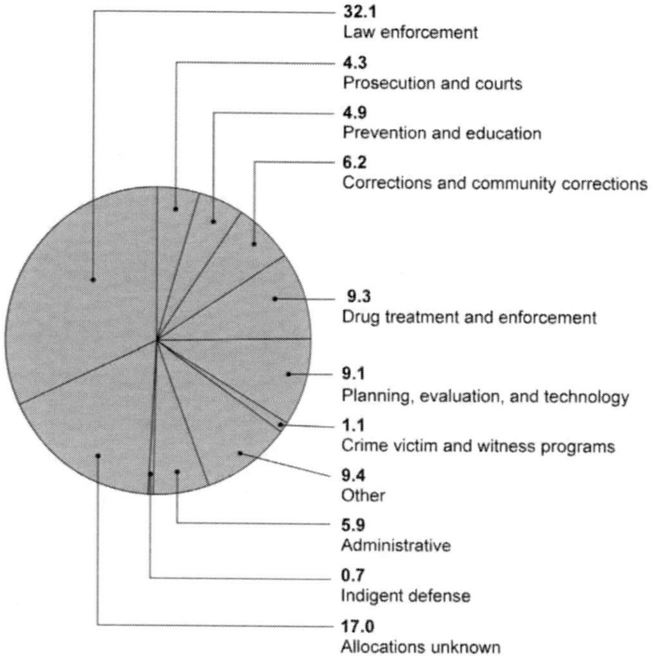

Source: GAO analysis of survey data.

Note: Other includes funds not yet allocated.

Figure 25. SAAs' Reported Allocations across JAG Purpose Areas and for Indigent Defense as a Percentage of Total Awards, Fiscal Year 2009.

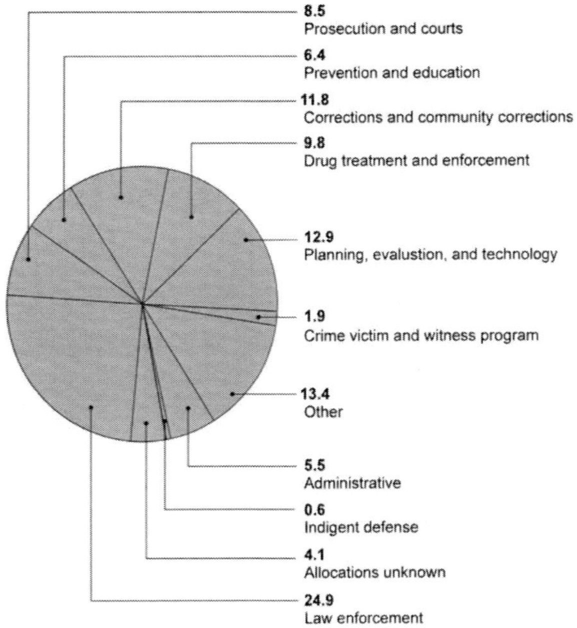

Source: GAO analysis of survey data.

Note: Other includes funds not yet allocated. Percentages do not add up to 100 due to rounding.

Figure 26. SAAs' Reported Allocations across JAG Purpose Areas and for Indigent Defense as a Percentage of Total Awards, ARRA.

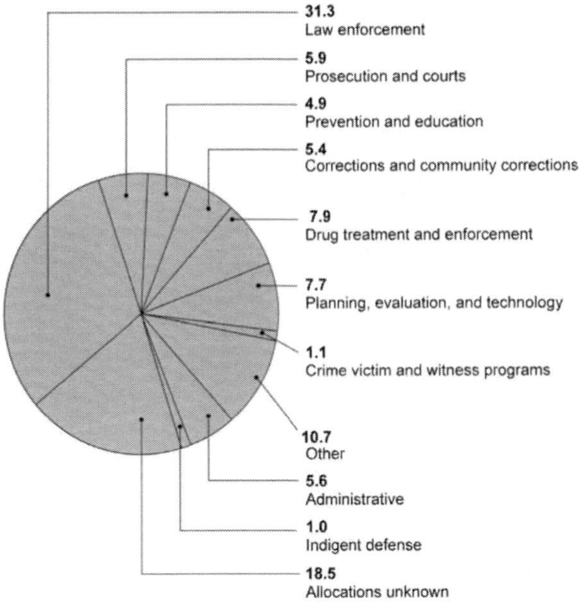

Source: GAO analysis of survey data.

Note: Other includes funds not yet allocated.

Figure 27. SAAs' Reported Allocations across JAG Purpose Areas and for Indigent Defense as a Percentage of Total Awards, Fiscal Year 2010.

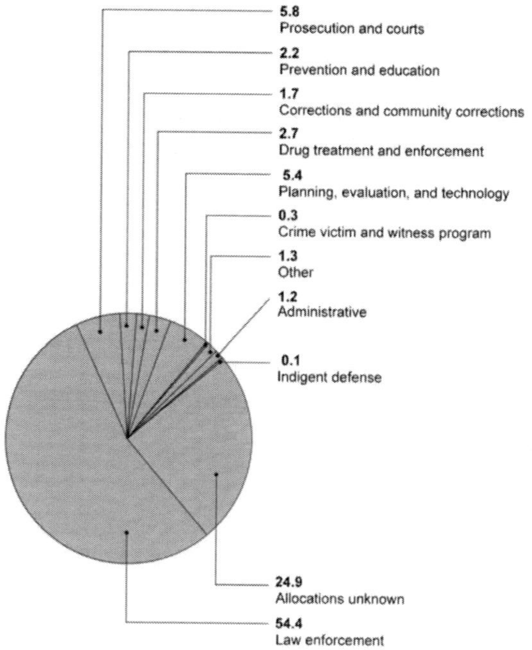

Source: GAO analysis of survey data.

Figure 28. Local and Tribal JAG Recipients' Reported Allocations across JAG Purpose Areas and for Indigent Defense as a Percentage of Total Awards, Fiscal Year 2005'

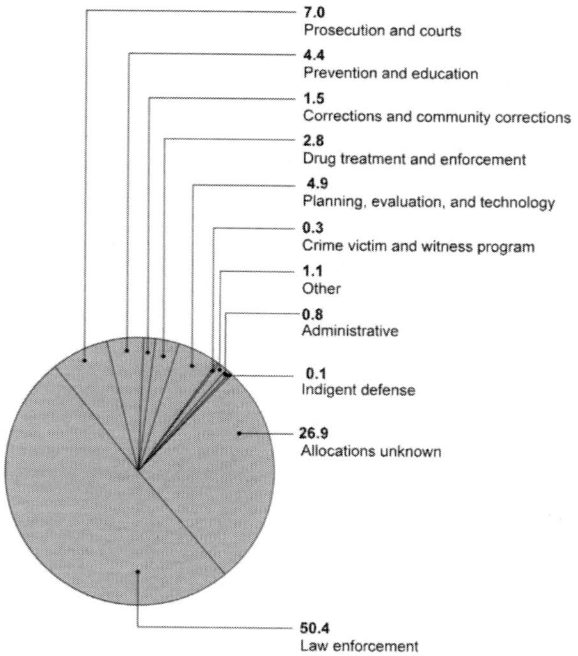

Source: GAO analysis of survey data.

Note: Percentages do not add up to 100 due to rounding.

Figure 29. Local and Tribal JAG Recipients' Reported Allocations across JAG Purpose Areas and for Indigent Defense as a Percentage of Total Awards, Fiscal Year 2006.

As figure 28 through 34 demonstrate, localities and tribes that received JAG funding and responded to our survey reported allocating the largest proportion of their funding to the law enforcement purpose area.

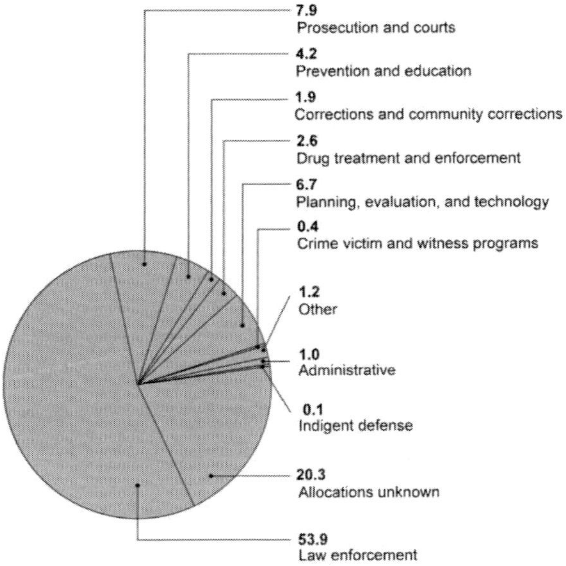

Source: GAO analysis of survey data.
Note: Percentages do not add up to 100 due to rounding.

Figure 30. Local and Tribal JAG Recipients' Reported Allocations across JAG Purpose Areas and for Indigent Defense as a Percentage of Total Awards, Fiscal Year 2007.

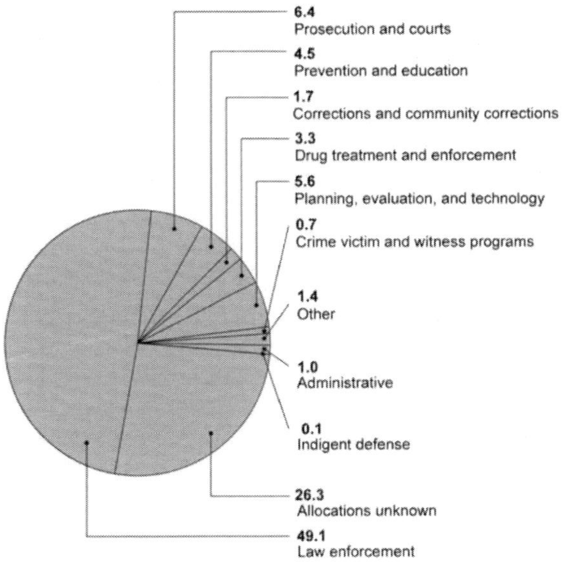

Source: GAO analysis of survey data.
Note: Percentages do not add up to 100 due to rounding.

Figure 31. Local and Tribal JAG Recipients' Reported Allocations across JAG Purpose Areas and for Indigent Defense as a Percentage of Total Awards, Fiscal Year 2008.

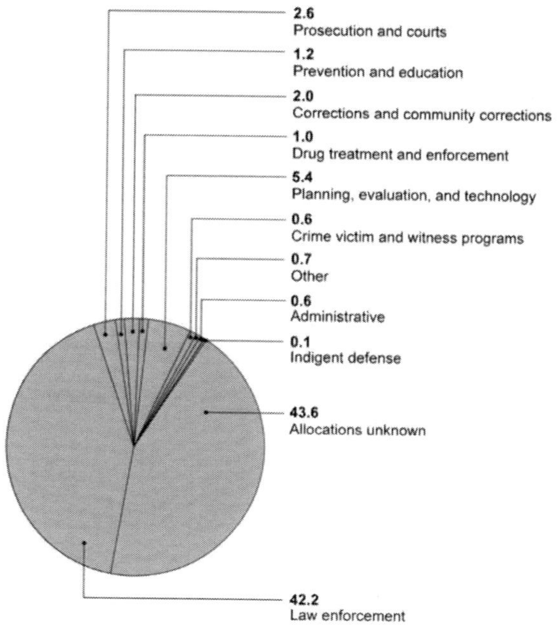

Source: GAO analysis of survey data.

Note: Other includes funds not yet allocated.

Figure 32. Local and Tribal JAG Recipients' Reported Allocations across JAG Purpose Areas and for Indigent Defense as a Percentage of Total Awards, Fiscal Year 2009.

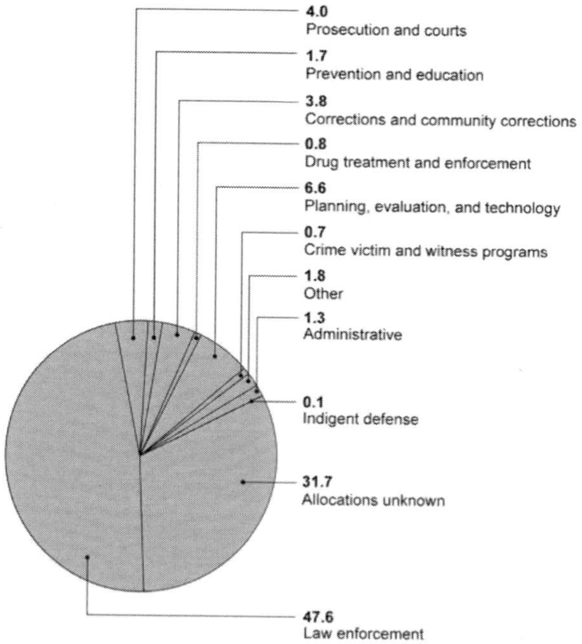

Source: GAO analysis of survey data.

Note: Other includes funds not yet allocated. Percentages do not add up to 100 due to rounding.

Figure 33. Local and Tribal JAG Recipients' Reported Allocations across JAG Purpose Areas and for Indigent Defense as a Percentage of Total Awards, ARRA.

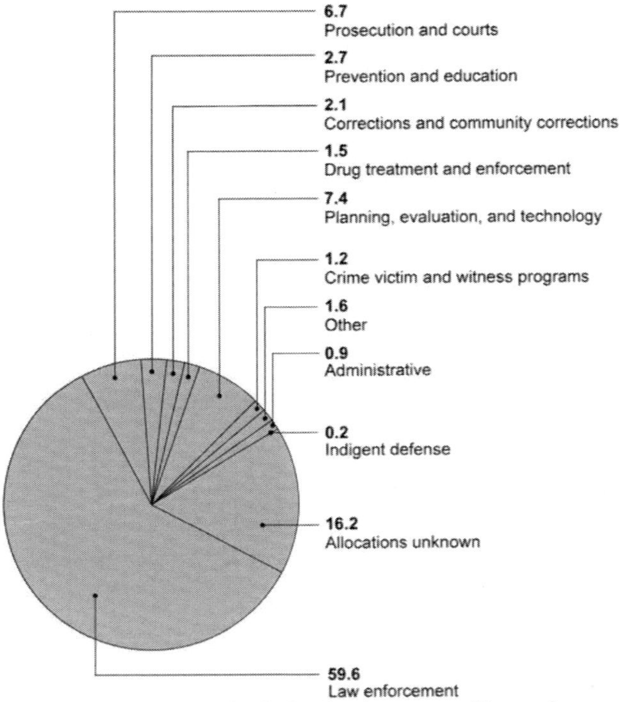

Source: GAO analysis of survey data. Other includes funds not yet allocated.
Note: Percentages do not add up to 100 due to rounding.

Figure 34. Local and Tribal JAG Recipients' Reported Allocations across JAG Purpose Areas and for Indigent Defense as a Percentage of Total Awards, Fiscal Year 2010.

Appendix VI: Analysis of Indigent Defense Related Performance Measures for Department of Justice Grant Programs

For all grant programs in which funding for indigent defense is required or prioritized—the John R. Justice Grant Program; the Capital Case Litigation Initiative; the Wrongful Conviction Review Program; the Juvenile Indigent Defense National Clearinghouse; the Edward Byrne Memorial Justice Assistance Grant (JAG); the Juvenile Accountability Block Grant (JABG); the Byrne Competitive Grant Program; the Tribal Juvenile Accountability Discretionary Grant Program; and the Tribal Civil and Criminal Legal Assistance Grant Program (TCCLA)—the Department of Justice (DOJ) has developed or is developing indigent defense-related performance measures.

Table 8 identifies these measures and whether the measures are output measures, or those that describe the level of activity that will be provided over a period of time; outcome measures, or those that describe the intended result of carrying out the program; input measures, or those that describe the resources used to produce outputs and outcomes; or process measures, or those that indicate how well a procedure, process, or operation is working.

Table 8. Indigent Defense-Related Performance Measures and Type of Measure for DOJ Grant Programs

Grant	Objectives	Performance measure	Output	Outcome	Input	Process
Byrne Competitive Grant Program– National Initiative: Adjudicationa	Increase the number of trained public defenders.	Percentage of trainees who successfully completed the program	X			
	Increase the knowledge of criminal justice practitioners through in-person training.	Percentage of trainees who completed the training whose post test indicated an improved score over their pre-test		X		
	Increase the knowledge of criminal justice practitioners through web-based learning.	Percent increase in trained public defenders	X			
	Increase the knowledge of criminal justice practitioners through distance learning using CD/DVDs.	Percentage of trainees who completed the training who rated the training as satisfactory or better				X
	Increase a criminal justice agency's ability to solve problems and/or modify policies or practices.	Percentage of organizations that completed the survey who expressed satisfaction that the CD/DVD met their training needs				X
	Increase the knowledge of criminal justice practitioners through the development and/or revision of training curricula.	Percentage of requesting agencies who rated services as satisfactory or better in terms of timeliness and quality following completion of an onsite visit				X
	Increase information provided to the criminal justice community	Percentage of requesting agencies that were planning to implement at least some of the report recommendations six months after the onsite visit		X		
		Percentage of requesting agencies of other onsite services who rated the services provided as satisfactory or better				X
		Percentage of advisory/focus groups evaluated as satisfactory or better				X
		Percentage of curricula that were pilot tested			X	
		Percentage of curricula that were revised after pilot testing			X	
Byrne Memorial Justice Assistance Grant Program	JAG funds may be used for state and local initiatives, technical assistance, training, personnel, equipment, supplies, contractual support, and criminal justice information	Number of cases defended				

Grant	Objectives	Performance measure	Output	Outcome	Input	Process
	systems that will improve or enhance such areas as:					
	• Law enforcement programs					
	• Prosecution and court programs					
	• Prevention and education programs		X			
	• Corrections and community corrections programs					
	• Drug treatment and enforcement programs					
	• Planning, evaluation, and technology improvement programs					
	• Crime victim and witness programs (other than compensation)					
Capital Case Litigation Initiative	Provide training on death penalty issues to attorneys who litigate death penalty cases. Increase the knowledge of criminal justice practitioners through in-person training.	Percent increase in the number of capital litigation attorneys trained in capital case procedures and strategies	X			
		Percentage of in-person trainees who successfully completed the program	X			
		Percentage of in-person trainees who completed the training whose post-test indicated an improved score over their pre-test		X		
		Number of attorneys trained	X			
		Percentage of in-person trainees who completed the training who rated the training as satisfactory or better				X
John R. Justice Grant Program	To encourage qualified individuals to enter and continue employment as prosecutors and public defenders.	Number and amount of loan repayments awarded	X			
		Percent increase in outreach to eligible beneficiaries	X			

Table 8. (Continued)

Grant	Objectives	Performance measure	Output	Outcome	Input	Process
		Average number of days between application for repayment benefits and the loan repayment occurring	X			
Juvenile Accountability Block Grant Program[b]	The goal of the JABG program is to reduce juvenile offending through accountability-based programs focused on the offender and juvenile justice system.	Percent of people exhibiting an increased knowledge of the program area during the reporting period		X		
	The objective is to ensure that states address 1 or more of 17 purpose areas and receive information on best practices from OJJDP. *[Note: indigent defense is included within the purpose area "Hiring Court Staff/Pretrial Services."]*	Number of program policies changed, improved, or rescinded during the reporting period		X		
		Percent of organizations reporting improvements in operations based on training and technical assistance (TTA)		X		
		Number of hours per week and percent of staff time (including defenders) spent directly serving clients	X			
		Amount of funds awarded for system improvement			X	
		Number and percent of defenders hired	X			
		Number of cases per staff member	X			
		Number and percent of vacant positions for defenders			X	
		Number of training requests received			X	
		Number of technical assistance requests received			X	
		Number of program materials developed during the reporting period	X			
		Number of planning or training events held during the reporting period	X			
		Number of people trained during the reporting period	X			
		Percent of those served by TTA who reported implementing an evidence based program and/or practice during or after the TTA		X		

Grant	Objectives	Performance measure	Output	Outcome	Input	Process
Juvenile Indigent Defense National Clearinghouse Program	To improve juvenile indigent defense; objectives include to increase:	Percentage of people exhibiting increased knowledge of the program area		X		
	• training opportunities for juvenile indigent defense	Percentage of organizations reporting improvements in operations based on training and technical assistance		X		
	• technical support efforts for juvenile indigent defense	Number of program policies changed, improved, or rescinded		X		
	• publications and resources for juvenile indigent defense	Percentage of those served by TTA who reported implementing an evidence-based program/practice during/after TTA		X		
	• policy development and leadership opportunities	Number of training requests received			X	
		Number of technical assistance requests received			X	
		Number of program materials developed	X			
		Number of planning or training events held	X			
		Number of people trained	X			
Tribal Civil and Criminal Legal Assistance Program[c]	(Category 2) Provide criminal legal assistance services for Indian tribes, members of Indian tribes, and tribal justice systems, pursuant to the federal poverty guidelines. Criminal legal assistance services may include adult criminal actions, juvenile delinquency actions, guardian ad litem appointments arising out of criminal or delinquency acts[d]	Percent increase in number of defendants served Percent of defendants who rated the services of their grant-funded attorney as satisfactory or better				X
Tribal Juvenile Accountability Discretionary Grant Program[e]	To provide funds to federally recognized American Indian and Alaska Native (AI/AN) communities to develop and implement programs that hold AI/AN youth accountable for their delinquent behavior and strengthen tribal juvenile justice systems.	Percentage of eligible youth served using graduated sanctions approaches[f]	X			

Table 8. (Continued)

Grant	Objectives	Performance measure	Output	Outcome	Input	Process
	Among the 17 purpose areas is the following: "hiring juvenile court judges, probation officers,. and court-appointed defenders and special advocates, and funding pretrial services (including mental health screening and assessment) for juvenile offenders, to promote the effective and expeditious administration of the juvenile justice system	Percentage of funds awarded for system improvement			X	
		Percentage of program youth completing program requirements	X			
		Percentage of programs employing evidence-based practices, i.e., a practice shown through rigorous evaluation and replication to be effective in preventing or reducing delinquency or related risk factors	X			
		Percentage of youth with whom an evidence-based practice was used	X			
		Percentage of program youth who reoffend (rearrested or seen at juvenile court for a new offense)		X		
		Number and percent of defenders hired	X			
		Number of cases per staff member	X			
		Number and percent of vacant positions for defenders			X	
		Number of hours per week and percent of staff time spent directly serving clients	X			
Wrongful Conviction Review Program[g]	Provide representation to defendants in post-conviction claims of innocence cases.	Number of cases in which actual perpetrators are identified though re-examination of evidence		X		
		Percent of cases in which actual perpetrators are identified through re-examination of evidence in post-conviction innocence claims		X		
		Percent increase in number of cases evaluated for potential wrongful convictions	X			
		Number of people/experts	X			

Grant	Objectives	Performance measure	Output	Outcome	Input	Process
		consulted.				
		Number of hours of forensic re-analysis services provided	X			
		Number of hours of screening, evaluation, and litigation services provided	X			

Source: GAO analysis of DOJ grant documents.

a The measures for the Byrne Competitive Grant Program were only for the year and category for which indigent defense funding was a priority.

[b] Measures displayed for the Juvenile Accountability Block Grant Program include those which are related to indigent defense; measures unrelated to indigent defense are not displayed.

[c] The measures for the Tribal Civil and Criminal Legal Assistance Program were for fiscal year 2010 and only for the category for which indigent defense funding was a priority.

[d] A guardian ad litem is an individual, usually a lawyer, appointed by the court to represent the interests of a minor or incompetent person in a legal action.

[e] Measures displayed for the Tribal Juvenile Accountability Discretionary Grant Program include those which are related to indigent defense; measures unrelated to indigent defense are not displayed.

[f] For example, the term "graduated sanctions" has been defined as an accountability-based, graduated series of sanctions (including incentives, treatment, and services) applicable to juveniles within the juvenile justice system to hold such juveniles accountable for their actions and to protect communities from the effects of juvenile delinquency by providing appropriate sanctions for every act for which a juvenile is adjudicated delinquent, by inducing their law-abiding behavior, and by preventing their subsequent involvement with the juvenile justice system. See 42 U.S.C. § 5603(24).

[g] The Wrongful Conviction Review Program limits eligibility for funding to non-profit organizations as well as public defender offices that represent convicted defendants (who, according to DOJ, are indigent), in claims of innocence. As a result, we consider the grant to be related to indigent defense.

APPENDIX VII: SELECT MEASURES, FINDINGS, AND RECOMMENDATIONS FROM PUBLIC DEFENDER OFFICE AND AGENCY EVALUATIONS AND REPORTS

Of the 118 respondents to our survey of public defender offices or agencies, 9 provided us with, or directed us to, copies of evaluations of or reports on their office or agency. Table 9 shows select measures used in these evaluations or reports, and their findings and recommendations.

Table 9. Summary of Select Measures, Findings, and Recommendations from Public Defender Evaluations and Reports

Office or Agency (Random Identifier)	Measures	Findings	Recommen-dations	Reporting period	Evaluator
1	• Caseload (for each attorney; weighted by case type) • Training (number of staff that attended each offering)	N/A	N/A	Year	Internal

Table 9. (Continued)

Office or Agency (Random Identifier)	Measures	Findings	Recommen-dations	Reporting period	Evaluator
1	• Cases opened and closed (sum totals) • Length of cases (average number of days open) Active and inactive cases (sum totals)				
2	• Attorney staffing levels • Caseloads (office total by case type; quarterly caseload by attorney for select case types as percentage of office total) • Training (attorney attendance at continuing legal education programs offered during reporting period) • Representation at clients' first appearances • Timeliness of jail visits • Client complaints • Investigator staffing and use of investigators (rate) • Use of experts • Supervision • Motions Practice • Trials (number and type) • Use of interpreters • Overall quality of representation • Conflicts	Attorney turnover rate is high. Jail visits and use of investigators are inconsistent across attorneys. Expert witness requests are not always handled properly. Supervision of attorneys does not provide quality control.	Increase use of investigators, as appropriate; consider providing training on this topic. Provide defenders with training opportunities each quarter. Supervisor should be more proactive in monitoring staff. Address continued problems related to sealing motions.	Quarter	External (appoint-ted monitor)
3	• Number of cases assigned to ad hoc counsel over ten yearsa • Debentures received for ad hoc casesb • Cost per disposed ad hoc case	The ad hoc program is the most fiscally unpredictable and costly method of providing public defense services, with little or no check on the quality of representation provided.	Continue to expand the assigned counsel contract program. Maintain the Serious Felony Units. Impose firm caps consistent with administrative order. Enforce strict standards for identifying conflicts. Refuse payment of assignments for frivolous post conviction relief matters.	Year	Internal
4	• Independence • Attorney qualifications • Training • Supervision	Agency is a model provider of indigent defense services, meeting	Consider evaluating the need to reduce supervisory	Snapshot of current conditions	External (consultant)

Office or Agency (Random Identifier)	Measures	Findings	Recommen-dations	Reporting period	Evaluator
	• Workload • Attorney-client relationships • Parity between prosecution and defense • Involvement of private bar	or exceeding all recognized national standards for the delivery of indigent defense services.	caseload. Consider formalizing rotations to reduce turnover. Consider creating a full-		
		Agency is independent; controls caseloads; and has sufficient funding to represent every client competently.	time training director. Consider creating the position of a full-time assigned counsel administrator. Draft bylaws.		
5	• Professional independence • Attorney qualifications • Training • Supervision • Workload • Evaluation, performance and discipline • Support services • Case management and quality control • Reporting	Provider exceeded the contractual requirement. Moreover, the percentage of felonies and misdemeanors was sufficiently high as to cause that caseload to exceed the maximum standard in each year of the reporting period. Provider has failed to institute a sufficiently formalized system of supervision and review.	Monitor case intake to prevent workload from exceeding caseload standard. Meet level of basic compliance standard regarding attorney evaluation and discipline. Increase the number of formal checks of management and quality controls.	2 years	External (oversight body)
6	• Office space • Technology • Organizational Leadership and Structure • Attorney recruitment, retention & staff needs • Education and development programs	Provider has the leadership capacity and present ability to successfully fulfill its obligations to its clients, to the courts and justice systems, to its community, and to the county.	Plan ahead for replacement and/or upgrading of hardware and software, and work together to sustain the current high level of technology competence. Implement management reorganization that establishes a clear, integrated line of supervision and authority that would, among other things, preserve a chief	Multi-year	External (consultant)

Table 9. (Continued)

Office or Agency (Random Identifier)	Measures	Findings	Recommen-dations	Reporting period	Evaluator
			defender responsible and accountable for all aspects of the operation, but also include supervisors authorized to direct and manage particular administrative and representational responsibilities. Consider adding staff to meet current and anticipated case and workload challenges.		
7	• Uniformity of the public defender system across the state • Performance assessment and accountability • Reliance on part-time public defenders • Strategic planning and budgeting • Management of resource reductions • Size and nature of public defender workloads • Impact of public defender workloads on how they do their		The Board of Public Defense (BPD) should ensure that district chief public defenders' presentations to the board focus more on district performance and challenges rather than	Multi-year	External (government auditor)
	work • Case outcomes • Court efficiency • Statutory framework for determining eligibility for	Public defender workloads are too high, resulting in public defenders spending limited time with clients, difficulties preparing cases, and scheduling problems that hinder the efficient operation of criminal courts. Staff reductions are the most immediate cause of high workloads, but case complexity and other factors add	descriptive characteristics of the district. The state public defender should establish stricter criteria for the structure and content of district chiefs' work plans. BPD and the state public defender should establish standards for and measures of quality representation of clients.		

Office or Agency (Random Identifier)	Measures	Findings	Recommen-dations	Reporting period	Evaluator
		to the time required per case. Heavy reliance on part-time public defenders presents risks that need to be addressed, but the public defender's office has few staff resources	BPD and the state public defender should improve		
	appointment of a public defender • Application of statutory eligibility criteria by judges and court staff • Procedures for determining eligibility • Accuracy of eligibility determinations • Ordering, collection, and distribution of reimbursements	available for planning, research, and policy development activities. Oversight body has strengthened accountability in the public defender system but could do more to measure and supervise the quality of services. Standards for determining eligibility for a public defender are not clearly defined in law, and judges reported wide differences in how they weigh eligibility factors. Judges reported having little confidence in the accuracy of information they use to assess defendants' financial circumstances, but it appears that the vast majority of applicants cannot afford a private attorney. Law requires defendants with some financial means to reimburse a portion of their public defender costs, but	management practices that ensure active supervision of full- and part-time assistant public defenders to monitor their performance representing clients and litigating in court. BPD and the state public defender should complete long-range planning efforts to: estimate future staffing needs in light of anticipated retirements among long time public defenders; evaluate the proper balance of full-time and part-time public defenders needed in the future; study the costs associated with establishing additional public defender satellite offices; and consider other options to recruit and retain public defenders. BPD should seek the resources necessary to fund a planning and		

Table 9. (Continued)

Office or Agency (Random Identifier)	Measures	Findings	Recommen-dations	Reporting period	Evaluator
		reimbursements are inconsistently ordered and collected.	analysis position in the administrative services office.		
			When funding becomes available, BPD should conduct a caseload study that includes methods sufficient to develop separate caseload standards for metropolitan area, suburban, and rural public defender districts. The state public defender should ensure that the office collects and records staff counts by position at regular intervals during the fiscal year.		
8	• Case processing • Structure and number of public defense contractors • Quality of representation	In juvenile cases, the average period from first appearance to jurisdiction is more than 90 days. Attorneys need training on how to conform to performance standards. There is a need for additional attorneys in the county.	Consider structure of current public defense systems and the need for additional attorneys in developing a service delivery plan. Consider offering longer contracts to indigent defense providers who are willing to relocate or live in remote areas. Consider supplementing insufficient trial-level caseloads with appellate	Snapshot of current conditions	External (oversight[b]ob ody)

Office or Agency (Random Identifier)	Measures	Findings	Recommen-dations	Reporting period	Evaluator
			work. Consider law school recruitment and specialized apprenticeship training for new lawyers interested in relocating. Consider assisting providers with office space and initial capital needs.		
9	• Caseloads • Indigency standards and eligibility requirements • Attorney turnover rates • Staffing and personnel issues • Compensation • Organizational practices (overhead, office location, technology, resources, etc.)	There has been no increase in staff in prior 6 years while caseload has increased by 12,000 cases. Attorney turnover rate is high. Attorney supervisors carry full caseloads, resulting in inadequate training, mentoring, and supervision. Office space is inadequate.	Research and consider specifying circumstances that would trigger the right to be represented by a public defender in probation violation cases. Take efforts to return the caseloads to the caseload standard. Contract out certain cases involving misdemeanors, traffic violations, and probation violations to private attorneys when economically feasible in order to reduce the numbers of cases for which	Snapshot of current conditions	External (oversightbod y)
			each public defender is responsible. Promulgate a rule requiring prosecuting attorneys to file all charges against the same defendant arising out of the same		

Table 9. (Continued)

Office or Agency (Random Identifier)	Measures	Findings	Recommen-dations	Reporting period	Evaluator
			transaction or occurrence in a single document. Eliminate certain unconstitutional court costs and replace them with a lesser court cost to help fund the public defender system and provide revenue to pay contract attorneys, fund an increase in support staff and fund an increase in base salary for public defenders. Research the feasibility of creating a student loan forgiveness program. Make technology available to the counties of the state to allow attorneys to meet with their clients via videoconference or teleconference.		

Source: GAO analysis of evaluations and reports from select public defender offices or agencies who responded to GAO survey and provided GAO with copies or directed GAO to publicly available copies.

Note: The evaluations summarized above were conducted by or on behalf of survey respondents; GAO has not assessed the quality of the evaluations or their results.

[a] Consistent with Office 3 documentation, ad hoc cases are those cases in which representation is provided by assigned attorneys who are not staff employees of the public defender office or agency to avoid a conflict of interest.

[b] In this context, a debenture is a submission by assigned counsel to the public defender office or agency to request compensation for time and funding expended in providing representation in ad hoc cases.

APPENDIX VIII: POSSIBLE DATA ELEMENTS FOR EVALUATING PUBLIC DEFENDER OFFICES, EXTENT TO WHICH RESPONDENTS COLLECT RELATED DATA, AND DATA CHALLENGES AND LIMITATIONS

Respondents to our public defender office survey reported collecting data that could be used to conduct an evaluation, but also reported challenges to collecting this data. Table 10 shows the percentage of survey respondents collecting each data element, and the associated challenges.

Table 10. Survey Respondents Collecting Data Elements and Associated Challenges

Data element	Percentage collecting data[a]	Challenges and limitations associated withdata (based on 118 possible respondents)
Average caseload per defender	87% (97 of 112)	Costly to collect: 6% (7) Difficult/burdensome to collect:10% (11) Difficult to measure: 7% (8) Imprecise: 7% (8)
Number of active cases per defender	84% (95 of 113)	Costly to collect: 6% (7) Difficult/burdensome to collect: 10% (12) Difficult to measure: 3% (4) Imprecise:11% (13)
Average salary or hourly rate of defenders, as applicable	76% (83 of 109)	Costly to collect: 3% (4) Difficult/burdensome to collect: 6% (7) Difficult to measure: 3% (3) Imprecise: 5% (6)
Whether or not defenders are in compliance with professional and ethical standards	67% (74 of 111)	Costly to collect:6% (7) Difficult/burdensome to collect:11% (13) Difficult to measure:14% (16) Imprecise: 13% (15)
Whether or not salary is accompanied by additional benefits (e.g., loan repayment, health insurance)	66% (72 of 109)	Costly to collect:4% (5) Difficult/burdensome to collect: 6% (7) Difficult to measure: 3% (4) Imprecise: 3% (4)
Ratio of attorneys to non-attorney support staff (e.g., clerical, paralegal, etc.)	65% (72 of 110)	Costly to collect: 3% (4) Difficult/burdensome to collect: 7% (8) Difficult to measure: 7% (8) Imprecise: 2% (2)
Whether or not cases are handled using a case management system	62% (68 of 111)	Costly to collect: 12% (14) Difficult/burdensome to collect: 8% (9) Difficult to measure: 3% (4) Imprecise: 7% (8)
Whether or not the same defender represents a client in all stages of proceedings once he or she is assigned the case (vertical representation)	61% (69 of 113)	Costly to collect: 9% (10) Difficult/burdensome to collect:13% (15) Difficult to measure: 5% (6) Imprecise: 6% (7)
Average number of defenders' continuing legal education (CLE) and/or training hours completed per year	59% (66 of 112)	Costly to collect: 3% (4) Difficult/burdensome to collect: 6% (7) Difficult to measure: 3% (3) Imprecise: 3% (3)

Table 10. (Continued)

Data element	Percentage collecting data[a]	Challenges and limitations associated withdata (based on 118 possible respondents)
Average caseload per defender, relative to any established caseload standard (e.g. some percent or number higher or lower than whatever standard is used, as applicable)	57% (64 of 112)	Costly to collect: 5% (6) Difficult/burdensome to collect: 10% (12) Difficult to measure: 15% (17) Imprecise: 15% (17)
Ratio of attorneys to investigators	56% (61 of 108)	Costly to collect: 4% (5) Difficult/burdensome to collect: 5% (6) Difficult to measure: 5% (6) Imprecise: 3% (4)
Type(s) of cases a defender has ever handled (e.g. capital, felony, misdemeanor, juvenile, etc.)	54% (60 of 112)	Costly to collect: 11% (13) Difficult/burdensome to collect: 27% (3) Difficult to measure: 10% (12) Imprecise: 10% (12)
Number of requests for funding for expert witnesses	48% (51 of 107)	Costly to collect: 8% (9) Difficult/burdensome to collect: 18% (2) Difficult to measure: 8% (9) Imprecise: 7% (8)
Number of times expert witnesses are used	42% (46 of 110)	Costly to collect: 10% (12) Difficult/burdensome to collect: 22% (26) Difficult to measure: 5% (6) Imprecise: 9% (10)
Individual defender performance ratings, as determined by a methodology in place at your office or agency	40% (44 of 110)	Costly to collect: 7% (8) Difficult/burdensome to collect: 19% (22) Difficult to measure: 31% (36) Imprecise: 18% (21)
Number of cases a defender has ever handled	41% (45 of 111)	Costly to collect: 11% (13) Difficult/burdensome to collect: 34% (40) Difficult to measure: 18% (21) Imprecise: 15% (17)
Whether or not a defender is present for the client's first appearance	38% (43 of 113)	Costly to collect: 12% (14) Difficult/burdensome to collect: 24% (28) Difficult to measure: 13% (15) Imprecise: 10% (12)
Meetings held between defender and client (per case)	38% (42 of 111)	Costly to collect: 12% (14) Difficult/burdensome to collect: 39% (46) Difficult to measure: 11% (13) Imprecise: 12% (14)
Amount of time defender spends per case	33% (37 of 113)	Costly to collect: 12% (14) Difficult/burdensome to collect: 45% (53) Difficult to measure: 23% (27) Imprecise: 19% (22)
Complexity of cases a defender has ever handled (e.g. number and/or severity of charges)	32% (36 of 112)	Costly to collect: 14% (16) Difficult/burdensome to collect: 36% (42) Difficult to measure: 26% (30) Imprecise: 27% (32)
Amount of face-to-face time defender spends with client	23% (25 of 111)	Costly to collect: 16% (19) Difficult/burdensome to collect: 50% (59) Difficult to measure: 15% (18) Imprecise: 15% (17)
Elapsed time between arrest and appointment of counsel	20% (23 of 113)	Costly to collect: 15% (18) Difficult/burdensome to collect: 34% (40) Difficult to measure: 15% (18)

Data element	Percentage collecting data[a]	Challenges and limitations associated withdata (based on 118 possible respondents)
		Imprecise: 11% (1)
Satisfaction of other criminal justice partners	14% (15 of 109)	Costly to collect: 13% (15) Difficult/burdensome to collect: 27% (31) Difficult to measure: 36% (42) Imprecise: 30% (35)
Satisfaction of clients	8% (9 of 106)	Costly to collect: 18% (21) Difficult/burdensome to collect: 38% (44) Difficult to measure: 48% (56) Imprecise: 32% (37)

Source: GAO analysis of survey data.

[a] The number responding to each question varied.

End Notes

[1] See Gideon v. Wainwright, 372 U.S. 335 (1963) (holding that the Sixth Amendment's effective assistance of counsel provision is a fundamental and essential right made obligatory upon states by virtue of the Fourteenth Amendment's due process of law clause). Pursuant to the Sixth Amendment's right to effective assistance of counsel provision, a penalty of imprisonment may not be imposed upon any defendant, indigent or otherwise, absent representation by counsel or a knowing and intelligent waiver of counsel.

[2] Throughout this report, we use "indigent defense" to refer to direct and indirect activities that help ensure indigent defendants are afforded counsel in criminal cases. These activities may include hiring additional public defenders, investigators, or other support staff; providing training for public defenders; making technological improvements in public defenders' offices or systems; or providing loan repayments to help retain public defenders.

[3] See Santa Clara Pueblo v. Martinez, 436 U.S. 49, 55-56 (1978) (recognizing that although Indian tribes no longer possess the full attributes of sovereignty, they remain a separate people, with the power of regulating their internal and social relations, and that as separate sovereigns, tribes have historically been regarded as unconstrained by those constitutional provisions framed specifically as limitations on federal or state authority) (internal citations and quotations omitted). See also 25 U.S.C. § 1302(2) (defining an Indian tribe's power of self-government).

[4] We selected fiscal years 2005 through 2010 because you requested that we identify federal funding that was used for indigent defense during this time frame. The Catalog of Federal Domestic Assistance is a government-wide compendium of federal programs, projects, services, and activities that provide assistance or benefits to the American public. It contains financial and nonfinancial assistance programs administered by departments and establishments of the federal government.

[5] Amounts appropriated through the American Recovery and Reinvestment Act of 2009 (ARRA) are also included in our review. See Pub. L. No. 111-5, 123 Stat. 115, 130 (2009).

[6] An electronic supplement to this report—GAO-12-661SP (available June 2012)— provides survey results. Formula grants are funding programs for which the primary grantees do not compete, although they must submit an application and meet other specified requirements. These grants are usually administered and managed by State Administering Agencies (SAA), and the amount of the grant awards are calculated by a formula most often governed or established by statute, which may consider factors such as population or crime data. We provide further descriptions of these grants later in this report. In addition, we identified BIA funding to Courts of Indian Offenses (referred to as "CFR courts") that could be used for indigent defense. We did not include CFR courts in our survey of tribal courts because CFR courts constitute direct services administered by BIA officials. However, according to BIA officials, every CFR court has a law-trained public defender. Also, based on discussions with BIA officials, we did not include tribal courts in BIA's Alaska region.

[7] We surveyed tribal JAG recipients separately from state and local JAG recipients. However, we combined all JAG responses for the purposes of this report. See appendix I for additional details.

[8] Because we included all recipients in our survey, our results are not subject to sampling error.

[9] See appendix I for additional details on the number of number of respondents we followed up with and how they were selected.

[10] Discretionary grants are awarded directly to eligible recipients, most often on a competitive basis.

[11] OMB, Performance Measurement Challenges and Strategies (Washington, D.C.: June 2003).

[12] GAO, Executive Guide: Effectively Implementing the Government Performance and Results Act, GAO/GGD-96-118, (Washington, D.C.: June 1996).

[13] The 17 public defender office or agency leaders who attended the listening session also discussed characteristics of model public defender programs; factors that affect the ability of public defenders to provide effective representation; and critical funding needs facing public defender programs. We observed their discussion, recorded the information shared, and reviewed the information to identify common themes.

[14] State-based public defender offices functioned entirely under the direction of a central office that funded and administered all public defender offices in the state. BJS, State Public Defender Programs, 2007 (Washington, D.C.: September 2010). Similarly, the District of Columbia, Puerto Rico, American Samoa, Guam, the Northern Mariana Islands, and the US Virgin Islands have also established centralized indigent defense agencies. Maine funds 100 percent of indigent defense services, which are provided by assigned counsel, but does not have city, county or state public defender offices.

[15] See Santa Clara Pueblo v. Martinez, 436 U.S. 49, 55-56 (1978) (recognizing that although Indian tribes no longer possess the full attributes of sovereignty, they remain a separate people, with the power of regulating their internal and social relations, and that as separate sovereigns, tribes have historically been regarded as unconstrained by those constitutional provisions framed specifically as limitations on federal or state authority) (internal citations and quotations omitted). See also 25 U.S.C. § 1301(2) (defining an Indian tribe's power of self-government).

[16] See Pub. L. No. 90-284, tit. II, 82 Stat. 73, 77 (1968) (codified as amended 25 U.S.C. §§ 1301-41).

[17] See 25 U.S.C. § 1302(a)(1), (8).

[18] See 25 U.S.C. § 1302(a)(6), (c)(1)-(2). The Tribal Law and Order Act of 2010 (TLOA), Pub. L. No. 111-211, tit. II, 124 Stat. 2258, 2261, amended ICRA by authorizing tribal courts to imprison convicted offenders for up to 3 years if the defendant has been previously convicted of the same or a comparable offense by any jurisdiction in the United States (federal, state, or tribal) or if the defendant is being prosecuted for an offense comparable to an offense that, in any U.S. or state jurisdiction, would be punishable by more than 1 year of imprisonment if prosecuted in state or federal court. See § 1302(b). In addition, the maximum term of imprisonment that may be imposed in a criminal proceeding (i.e., where a defendant is charged with multiple offenses) is 9 years. See § 1302(a)(7)(D). A tribe may not, however, impose a term of imprisonment in excess of one year unless it affords the defendant certain rights enumerated in the statute, including the right to have counsel provided at the tribe's expense. See § 1302(c).

[19] Other types of funding include congressionally directed awards (also referred to as earmarks), cooperative agreements, and payment programs.

[20] Through the Indian Self-Determination and Education Assistance Act of 1975, Pub. L. No. 93-638, 88 Stat. 2203, as amended, the federal government established a policy of Indian self-determination whereby tribes, with the support and assistance of the federal government, would be afforded an "effective and meaningful" role in planning, conducting, and administering programs and services previously administered by federal entities. See 25 U.S.C. § 450a. Tribes generally obtain funding to assume these functions pursuant to self-determination contracts or self-governance compacts negotiated and entered into with BIA. See §§ 450h, 458cc. Self-governance compacts differ from self-determination contracts in that such compacts afford tribes more flexibility in how the agreed upon funding may be utilized.

[21] Our survey of public defender offices or agencies included a sample of 253 of the 841 offices. Because of the relatively low response rate, responses should not be generalized to all public defender offices or agencies. See appendix I for additional details on the survey. The total respondents differ by question because not all respondents provided answers to all questions.

[22] Hiring court-appointed defenders is an authorized use encompassed by one of the JABG program's and TJADG program's purpose areas, which are established in statute, not by DOJ.

[23] In addition, BIA provides direct services to tribes that do not operate certain programs themselves, such as tribes that rely upon CFR courts.

[24] American Bar Association, ABA Ten Principles of a Public Defense Delivery System. (Chicago, Ill.: February 2002).

[25] The AOUSC serves the federal judiciary in carrying out its constitutional mission to provide equal justice under law through a wide range of administrative, legal, financial, management, program, and information technology services to the federal courts. According to AOUSC officials, funding for indigent defense providers is limited to federal defender organizations, attorneys appointed to represent defendants financially unable to retain counsel in federal criminal proceedings (see 18 U.S.C. § 3006A), and expert service providers.

Similarly, all training and technical assistance is directed to persons providing representation in federal criminal and related matters.

[26] NTTAC offers training and technical assistance services in the following criminal justice areas: adjudication (includes indigent defense), corrections, counter-terrorism, crime prevention, information sharing, law enforcement, mental health, and substance abuse.

[27] The focus group, entitled National Indigent Defense Reform: The Solution is Multifaceted, produced a preliminary report suggesting DOJ endorse the following five core principles to demonstrably improve indigent defense reform: reclassify criminal offenses to reduce pressure on public defenders; support programs that ensure counsel is present for a criminal defendant's first appearance; protect the sixth Amendment right to "effective" assistance of counsel by taking actions to support the right to counsel at the state and local level; ensure the defense bar is consulted prior to adoption of new law enforcement strategies, which could impact defender caseloads; and better utilize the resources of the private bar.

[28] The U.S. Attorneys are the chief federal law enforcement officers in their districts, responsible for federal criminal prosecutions and civil cases involving the United States Government.

[29] The dollar figures are in current dollars not adjusted for inflation. Adjusting for inflation does not affect the percentages.

[30] DOJ did not receive appropriations for the Capital Case Litigation Initiative in fiscal years 2005 and 2006. Eighteen of the 19 grantees who used funding to provide training to defenders also provided training to nondefenders, such as prosecutors.

[31] 60 percent of JAG funding awarded to states is awarded directly to a SAA in each state, and each SAA must in turn allocate a formula-based share of these funds to local entities, for which SAAs may require that local entities apply. BJA awards the remaining 40 percent of the state's allocation directly to eligible units of local government, as determined by a statutorily prescribed formula, within the state.

[32] DOJ determined that 35 percent of TCCLA funding was awarded for indigent defense in fiscal year 2010, and 51 percent was awarded for indigent defense in fiscal year 2011. The fiscal year 2010 percentage differs from our analysis due to the differences in the methodologies used to determine the percentage of grants awarded for indigent defense. Specifically, DOJ calculated its percentage by dividing the grants awarded under Category 2—the purpose of which is to provide criminal legal assistance services—by the total awards under the grant. In contrast, we reviewed each of the project descriptions submitted by TCCLA grantees to determine whether the descriptions indicated that the grantee planned to use the funds for indigent defense. Because the project descriptions may not have included all the planned activities of the grantee, our methodology may not have captured all grants that were awarded for indigent defense.

[34] The JAG program was formed from two existing grants, one of which was a law enforcement-focused grant. Specifically, the JAG program was created following enactment of the Violence Against Women and Department of Justice Reauthorization Act of 2005, which merged the discretionary Edward Byrne Memorial Grant program with the formula-based Local Law Enforcement Block Grant Program. See 42 U.S.C. § 3750.

[35] Total population numbers of JAG, JABG, and JJDP that responded to this question do not match the overall total survey population because some respondents did not answer the question.

[36] These percentages do not total 100 percent because 45 percent of respondents reported that they did not know if an indigent defense provider was involved in the determination of how JAG funding would be used.

[37] We asked public defender offices or agencies about their awareness of discretionary grants because they could apply for these grants. We did not ask about their awareness of formula grants or other funding sources because they do not have the opportunity to apply directly to DOJ or BIA for these funds.

[38] These percentages are calculated only out of those respondents that indicated that they were not aware that funding could be used for indigent defense in any year from fiscal year 2005 through 2010.

[39] 11 percent (90 of 837) of JAG survey respondents reported that lack of awareness was an extremely or very important reason why they did not allocate funding for indigent defense.

[40] As previously discussed, recipients of grants that required that funding be allocated for indigent defense—JRJ, CCLI, WCR, and JIDNC—allocated or planned to use such funds for indigent defense in accordance with grant requirements. See appendix II for additional details on these allocations and uses.

[41] Because the discretionary awards include funding used in part for indigent defense, these calculations are an upper bound of allocations to indigent defense as a percentage of total award.

[42] Data collection on indigent defense funding for the Wrongful Conviction Review Program and Juvenile Indigent Defense National Clearinghouse is inherent because, according to DOJ, all funding for these programs must be awarded for indigent defense.

[43] GAO, Law Enforcement Body Armor: DOJ Could Enhance Grant Management Controls and Better Ensure Consistency in Grant Program Requirements, GAO-12-353 (Washington, D.C.: Feb. 15, 2012).

[44] These 5 respondents included all JABG recipients who reported allocating funding for indigent defense from fiscal years 2005 through 2010 with whom we were able to conduct an interview. We did not discuss the project identifiers with the remaining respondent. One additional JABG respondent who reported allocating funding did not respond to our requests for an interview.

[45] GAO/GGD-96-118.

[46] OMB, Performance Measurement Challenges and Strategies (Washington, D.C.: June 2003).

[47] BJA launched the online Performance Measurement Tool in 2007 to improve upon its previous grants management system and allow online performance data submission. However, we previously reported that DOJ acknowledged that weaknesses exist in the current JAG performance measures and were working to update the measures with input from JAG SAAs. See GAO-11-87. After developing draft revisions to the Performance Measurement Tool, DOJ posted the revised measures on its website and received stakeholder comments.

[48] OMB, Performance Measurement Challenges and Strategies (Washington, D.C.: June 2003); OMB, Circular No. A-11, Part 6: Preparation and Submission of Strategic Plans, Annual Performance Plans, and Annual Performance Reports (Washington, D.C.: August 2011).

[49] OMB, Performance Measurement Challenges and Strategies (Washington, D.C.: June 2003).

[50] OMB, Performance Measurement Challenges and Strategies (Washington, D.C.: June 2003).

[51] GAO, Warfighter Support: DOD Needs Strategic Outcome-Related Goals and Visibility over Its Counter-IED Efforts, GAO-12-280 (Washington, D.C.: February 22, 2012).

[52] GAO, Executive Guide: Effectively Implementing the Government Performance and Results Act, GAO/GGD-96-118 (Washington, D.C.: June 1996).

[53] See 42 U.S.C. § 3797cc–21(h) (requiring the Inspector of the Department of Justice to submit a report to Congress, not later than 3 years after the date of enactment of this section (enacted August 14, 2008), on the costs of the program and the impact of the program on the hiring and retention of prosecutors and public defenders).

[54] OMB, Performance Measurement Challenges and Strategies (Washington, D.C.: June 2003).

[55] GAO, Designing Evaluations, GAO-12-208G. Washington, D.C. January, 2012.

[56] An additional 23 public defender offices or agencies reported that an evaluation had been conducted, but did not provide us with or direct us to a copy.

[57] Respondents were permitted to select more than one factor influencing their decision not to conduct an evaluation.

[58] BJA, Keeping Defender Workloads Manageable (Washington, D.C.: January 2001).

[59] National Right to Counsel Committee, Justice Denied: America's Continuing Neglect of our Constitutional Right to Counsel (Washington, D.C.: April 2009).

[60] Preliminary findings on RAND's NIJ grant are available at Henderson, JM & P. Heaton, How Much Difference Does the Lawyer Make? The Effect of Defense Counsel on Murder Case Outcomes (Dec. 2011). According to NIJ officials, NIJ has been conducting and supporting research on issues related to indigent defense since the 1980s.

[61] See http://nij.gov/nij/topics/courts/indigent-defense/2010-symposium/ wel come.htm for information about the symposium. The 2010 symposium was an update to a 1999 National Symposium on Indigent Defense, after which a report was released. See http://www.sado.org/fees/icjs.pdf for this report.

[62] DOJ, Expert Working Group Report: International Perspectives on Indigent Defense, NCJ236022 (September 2011).

[63] According to OJP, practices are evidence-based when their effectiveness has been demonstrated by causal evidence, generally obtained through outcome evaluations, which documents a relationship between an intervention and its intended outcome, while ruling out, to the extent possible, alternative explanations for the outcome.

[64] In its 2011 report, Cornerstone for Justice: Byrne JAG and its Impact on the Criminal Justice System, the National Criminal Justice Association highlighted the state of Minnesota for using JAG funds to support public defenders.

[65] According to DOJ, the recommendations documented in the report produced by the workshop on domestic and international best practices for indigent defense informed this solicitation.

[66] Indigent defense stakeholders cite invalid waivers—which, according to stakeholders, occur when defendants are not properly informed of their right to counsel—and lack of experts, investigators and interpreters as impediments to competent and effective defense services. National Right to Counsel Committee, Justice Denied: America's Continuing Neglect of our Constitutional Right to Counsel (Washington, D.C.: April 2009).

End Notes for Appendix I

[1] We selected fiscal years 2005 through 2010 because you requested that we identify federal funding that was used for indigent defense during this time frame. The Catalog for Federal Domestic Assistance is a government-wide compendium of federal programs, projects, services, and activities that provide assistance or benefits to the American public. It contains financial and nonfinancial assistance programs administered by departments and establishments of the federal government.

[2] An electronic supplement to this report—GAO-12-661SP (available June 2012)— provides survey results. Amounts appropriated through the American Recovery and Reinvestment Act of 2009 (ARRA) are also included in our review. See Pub. L. No. 111-5, 123 Stat. 115, 130 (2009). Formula grants are funding programs for which the primary grantees do not compete, although they must submit an application and meet other specified requirements. These grants are usually administered and managed by State Administering Agencies (SAA), and the amount of the grant awards are calculated by a formula most often governed or established by statute, which may consider factors such as population or crime data. In addition, we identified BIA funding to Courts of Indian Offenses (referred to as "CFR courts") that could be used for indigent defense. We did not include CFR courts in our survey of tribal courts because CFR courts constitute direct services administered by BIA officials. However, according to BIA officials, every CFR court has a law-trained public defender. Also, based on discussions with BIA officials, we did not include tribal courts in BIA's Alaska region.

[3] BJS, County-based and Local Public Defender Offices, 2007 (Washington, D.C.: September 2010); BJS, State Public Defender Programs, 2007 (Washington, D.C.: September 2010).

[4] GAO, Executive Guide: Effectively Implementing the Government Performance and Results Act, GAO/GGD-96-118, (Washington, D.C.: June 1996).

[5] OMB, Performance Measurement Challenges and Strategies (Washington, D.C.: June 2003).

[6] GAO-10-95.

[7] The 17 public defender office or agency leaders who attended the listening session also discussed characteristics of model public defender programs; factors that affect the ability of public defenders to provide effective representation; and critical funding needs facing public defender programs. We observed their discussion, recorded the information shared, and reviewed the information to identify common themes.

End Note for Appendix III

[1] Forty-six percent of JAG recipients (1,818 of 3,963, including 89 percent of SAAs and 45 percent of localities and tribes) completed the JAG survey; 82 percent of JABG recipients (46 of 56) completed the JABG survey; 89 percent of JJDP recipients (50 of 56) completed the JJDP survey; and 63 percent (106 of 169) of recipients completed the Tribal Courts survey. Because all recipients of JABG and JJDP funding were included in our population and we received response rates of 82 and 89 percent, we consider our results generalizable to the population of JABG and JJDP recipients. While all eligible members of our target population of JAG and recipients of BIA Tribal Courts TPA distributions were included in our survey, due to the relatively low response rates and the possibility of other errors all questionnaire surveys face, our results represent only respondents participating in our survey and should not be generalized to the population of JAG recipients or recipients of BIA Tribal Courts TPA distributions.

End Notes for Appendix V

[1] Forty-six percent of JAG recipients (1,818 of 3,963, including 89 percent of SAAs and 45 percent of localities and tribes) completed the JAG survey. While all eligible members of our target population of JAG and recipients were included in our survey, due to the relatively low response rate and the possibility of other errors all questionnaire surveys face, our results represent only respondents participating in our survey and should not be generalized to the population of JAG recipients.

[2] Funding for indigent defense can be allocated in multiple purpose areas, as indigent defense is not its own purpose area. As a result, to obtain the percentages allocated for each purpose area, we subtracted the amount respondents reported allocating for indigent defense out of the specified purpose area.

In: Indigent Defense
Editors: Betty Nichols and Jeff Weaver
ISBN: 978-1-62257-441-4

Chapter 2

LEGAL SERVICES CORPORATION: BACKGROUND AND FUNDING*

Carmen Solomon-Fears

SUMMARY

The Legal Services Corporation (LSC) is a private, nonprofit, federally funded corporation that helps provide legal assistance to low-income people in civil (i.e., noncriminal) matters. The primary responsibility of the LSC is to manage and oversee the congressionally appropriated federal funds that it distributes in the form of grants to local legal services providers, which in turn give legal assistance to low-income clients in all 50 states, the District of Columbia, the US territories of Guam and the Virgin Islands, the Commonwealth of Puerto Rico, and Micronesia (including the Commonwealth of the Northern Mariana Islands, the Republic of the Marshall Islands, and Palau).

Although the authorization of appropriations for the LSC expired at the end of FY1980, the LSC has operated for the past 31 years under annual appropriations laws. On November 17, 2011, the House and the Senate passed the conference report on H.R. 2112 (H.Rept. 112-284). President Obama signed H.R. 2112 into law (P.L. 112-55) on November 18, 2011. P.L. 112-55 (the Consolidated and Further Continuing Appropriations Act, 2012) funded the LSC at $348 million for FY2012. The FY2012 appropriation for the LSC, $348 million, is 13.9% less than the FY2011 LSC appropriation of $404.2 million, 22.7% less than the Administration's budget request, 16% more than the House committee's recommendation, and 12.1% less than the amount passed by the Senate. In addition, since FY1996, all of the LSC appropriations laws have included language that restricts the activities of LSC grantees. The LSC appropriation for FY2012 included existing restrictions on LSC activities.

For FY2013, the Obama Administration requested $402.0 million for the LSC. This amount is $54.0 million (15.5%) above the FY2012 appropriation of $348.0 million for the LSC. The Senate Committee on Appropriations recommended $402 million for the LSC for FY2013. The House-passed appropriations bill (H.R. 5326) for Commerce, Justice, Science, and Related Agencies (CJS) recommended $328 million for the LSC for FY2013. The LSC statute requires that poverty population data from the most recent

---

* This is an edited, reformatted and augmented version of a Congressional Research Service publication RL34016, dated May 23, 2012.

decennial census be used to distribute LSC funds. Due to changes in the data sets obtained by the 2010 decennial census, information needed by the LSC is no longer available.

On September 19, 2011, the LSC Board recommended several changes to resolve the issue and improve distribution of LSC funds.

Under the LSC's competitive process, legal services providers in every jurisdiction bid to become the LSC grantee for a designated service area in a state. During 2010, the LSC funded 136 local programs/grantees in 919 offices employing 4,350 attorneys. Local programs establish their own eligibility criteria, in which clients served may not have income that exceeds 125% of the federal poverty guidelines. In 2010, 71% of LSC clients were females and 29% were males.

The majority of LSC clients (85%) were between the ages of 18 and 59, 13% were age 60 or older, and 2% were under the age of 18. Almost 47% of LSC clients were non-Hispanic white, 26% were non-Hispanic black, almost 9% were of other races, and about 19% were Hispanic. In 2010, LSC grantees closed 932,406 cases involving issues primarily related to families (divorce, child support, etc.), housing, consumer finance, income maintenance, and health.

Although the LSC is the largest single source of funding for the civil legal services system in the United States, it is not the only source of funding. Local legal services programs supplement their LSC grants with funds from a variety of governmental and private sources. LSC funding accounts for 44% of all funding for civil legal services for the poor in the United States.

INTRODUCTION

The Legal Services Corporation (LSC) is a private, nonprofit, federally funded corporation that helps provide legal assistance to low-income people in noncriminal (i.e., civil) matters. The LSC is governed by an 11-member board appointed by the President and confirmed by the Senate, of whom no more than 6 members may be of the same political party.

The primary responsibility of the LSC is to manage and oversee the congressionally appropriated federal funds that it distributes in the form of grants to local legal services providers, which in turn give legal assistance to *low-income* clients in all 50 states, the District of Columbia, the US territories of Guam and the Virgin Islands, the Commonwealth of Puerto Rico, and Micronesia (including the Commonwealth of the Northern Mariana Islands, the Republic of the Marshall Islands, and Palau).

The federal government has administered a program of legal services for the poor since 1966. Originally, the program was administered through the Office of Economic Opportunity, a now-defunct agency that had led the War on Poverty in the mid-1960s. In 1971, President Nixon proposed establishment of a separate corporation to deliver legal services to insulate the program from political pressure.[1]

Authorizing legislation was enacted in 1974 (P.L. 93-355), and the LSC came into existence the following year. In 1977, the LSC was extended through FY1980 (P.L. 95-222). Although Congress has not reauthorized the LSC statute since FY1980, it has continued to fund LSC every year, and has included legislative language affecting LSC activities in the annual appropriations laws.

PROGRAM MECHANICS

The LSC does not provide legal services directly. Rather, it funds local legal services providers, referred to by the LSC as "grantees." Grantees may include nonprofit organizations that have as a purpose the provision of legal assistance to eligible clients, private attorneys, groups of private attorneys or law firms, state or local governments, and certain sub-state regional planning and coordination agencies.

During 2009, the LSC funded 136 local programs in 918 offices employing about 4,200 attorneys.

These numbers are reduced from 1994, when 320 local programs employed about 4,500 attorneys. Each local program is governed by its own board of directors, of which a majority are attorneys and one-third are eligible clients. Local programs establish their own eligibility criteria, under which a client's household income may not exceed 125% of the federal poverty guidelines.[2]

Each local program must spend an amount equal to at least 12.5% of its basic grant to encourage private attorneys to provide pro bono legal aid to the poor.

LSC Laws and Appropriations
P.L. 93-355 (July 25, 1974)
P.L. 95-222 (Dec. 28, 1977)
P.L. 105-12 (Apr. 30, 1997)
P.L. 106-185 (Apr. 25, 2000)
P.L. 104-134 (Apr. 26, 1996)
P.L. 104-208 (Sept. 30, 1996)
P.L. 105-119 (Nov. 26, 1997)
P.L. 105-277 (Oct. 21, 1998)
P.L. 106-113 (Nov. 29, 1999)
P.L. 106-553 (Dec. 21, 2000)
P.L. 107-77 (Nov. 28, 2001)
P.L. 108-7 (Feb. 20, 2003)
P.L. 108-199 (Jan. 23, 2004)
P.L. 108-447 (Dec. 8, 2004)
P.L. 109-108 (Nov. 22, 2005)
P.L. 110-5 (Feb. 15, 2007)
P.L. 110-161 (Dec. 26, 2007)
P.L. 110-329 (Sept. 30, 2008)
P.L. 111-8 (Mar. 11, 2009)
P.L. 111-117 (Dec. 16, 2009)
P.L. 111-322 (Dec. 22, 2010)
P.L. 112-10 (April 15, 2011)
P.L. 112-55 (Nov. 18, 2011)

Since April 1996 (P.L. 104-134), LSC grantees (i.e., legal services agencies/ providers/programs) have been selected on a competitive basis.[3] Under the LSC's competitive process, legal services providers in every jurisdiction bid to become the LSC grantee for a designated service area in a state. Pursuant to its 1998 State Planning Initiative, the LSC has sought to streamline its delivery system. During the competition process, the LSC evaluates applications according to established quality standards and awards grants to those providers judged best qualified to provide high-quality legal services in accordance with applicable legal requirements. Federal regulations (Title 45 C.F.R. Part 1634) stipulate the procedures to be followed in awarding LSC grants. Grants are made for one to three years. Multi-year awardees must submit reports and grant renewal forms as part of the annual grant renewal process.

Before the implementation of the 1998 State Planning Initiative, LSC grantees often were unaware of other LSC grantees in the state. Work and training collaborations and other cooperative endeavors were rare among LSC grantees in the same state, and practically nonexistent among LSC grantees in other states. Further, most legal services programs only had superficial relationships and minimal contact with law firms and local judges. In anticipation of reduced federal funding, the LSC first encouraged and later directed grantees to form partnerships with the judiciary, private bar associations, and with each other. The 1998 State Planning Initiative was the means by which the LSC sought to ensure that LSC funds were efficiently and effectively used to provide legal services to poor persons in all areas of the states and jurisdictions. Pursuant to the 1998 Initiative, the LSC made participation in statewide civil legal services delivery systems a condition of receipt of LSC funding.[4] It is generally agreed that poor persons in need of legal assistance have benefitted from the LSC's statewide delivery system approach. The LSC has done this by requiring federally funded legal services providers to coordinate their work with other persons and organizations within a state, including groups historically considered funding "competitors" (other nonprofit organizations and non-LSC legal services programs) or "unlikely partners" (judges, legislators, bar leaders).[5]

Restrictions on Activities

Since its inception, the legal services program has been controversial, and Congress has imposed restrictions on activities of local attorneys. The authorizing statute contains restrictions against lobbying; political activities; class actions except under certain conditions; and cases involving abortion, school desegregation, and draft registration or desertion from the military. Additional restrictions have been included in appropriations laws each year. Under the current appropriations law, LSC grantees may not

- engage in partisan litigation related to redistricting;
- attempt to influence regulatory, legislative, or adjudicative action at the federal, state, or local level;
- attempt to influence oversight proceedings of the LSC;
- initiate or participate in any class action suit;

- represent certain categories of aliens, except that both LSC and non-LSC funds may be used to represent aliens who have been victims of domestic violence or child abuse;
- conduct advocacy training on a public policy issue or encourage political activities, strikes, or demonstrations;
- engage in litigation related to abortion;
- represent clients in eviction proceedings if the eviction was based on drug-related activities;
- represent federal, state, or local prisoners;
- participate in efforts to reform a federal or state welfare system;
- engage in activities related to assisted suicide, euthanasia, or mercy killing; or
- solicit clients.

LSC grantees must establish priorities, and staff must agree in writing not to engage in activities outside these priorities.

Moreover, federal law prohibits the LSC from receiving nonfederal funds, and grantees are prohibited from receiving non-LSC funds, unless the source of funds is told in writing that these funds may not be used for any activities prohibited by the LSC Act or the appropriations law.[6]

CLIENTS AND CASES

Legal services provided through LSC funds are available only in civil matters to individuals with household incomes of less than 125% of the federal poverty guidelines. The LSC places primary emphasis on the provision of routine legal services. Legal services cases deal with a variety of issues, including family-related issues (divorce, separation, child custody, support, adoption, spousal abuse, child abuse or neglect); housing issues (landlord/tenant matters, foreclosures); welfare or other income maintenance program issues (Supplemental Security Income, Supplemental Nutrition Assistance Program, unemployment compensation benefit claims); consumer and finance issues (debt collection, bankruptcy); and other issues such as health coverage and employment matters.

During 2010, legal services attorneys closed 932,406 cases. Family issues such as divorce and separation, custody and visitation, child support, and domestic abuse were the substance of 34.5% of cases handled by field offices; housing issues, including eviction cases, comprised 25.2% of cases; consumer finance comprised 12.2% of cases; and income maintenance issues represented another 12.7% of cases.

Issues related to health coverage (3.2%), employment (3.1%), juveniles (1.6%), individual rights (1.7%), education (0.7%), and other miscellaneous categories (5.1%) comprised 15.4% of cases.

Most of the cases handled by LSC are resolved through advice and referral. In 2010, only about 13% of cases were resolved in court, primarily because they involved family law issues (e.g., protective orders, child support, etc.) in which court action was required by state law.[7]

LSC Cases Closed

FY2002: 978,834

FY2003: 935,793

FY2004: 901,067

FY2005: 906,338

FY2006: 895,488

FY2007: 906,507

FY2008: 889,155

FY2009: 920,447

FY2010: 932,406

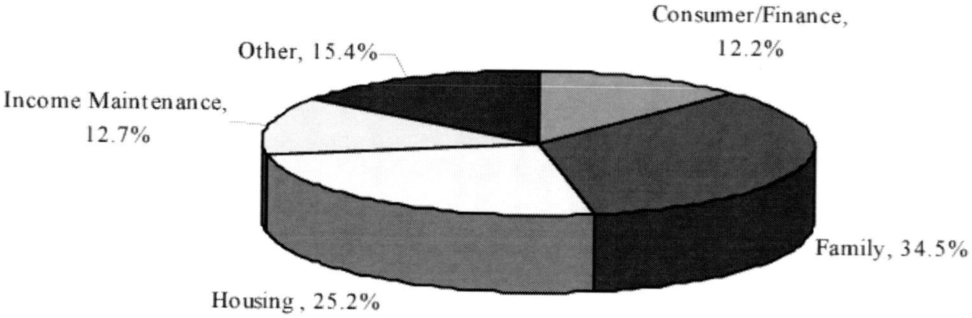

Source: Figure prepared by the Congressional Research Service, based on data from the Legal Services.

Figure 1. LSC Cases Closed in 2010, by Legal Problem.

LSC grantees have closed about 1 million cases annually for the last several years. In addition, they have handled another 4 million legal service "matters" such as helping self-represented (i.e., pro se) litigants obtain the information they need to pursue their lawsuits, disseminating legal services materials in communities, referring clients to appropriate services, and providing mediation assistance.[8]

According to the LSC Fact Book for 2010, LSC clients were of all races and ethnic groups. LSC clients include the working poor, veterans, family farmers, people with disabilities, battered women, women seeking divorces or child support, and victims of natural disasters. In 2010, 71% of LSC clients were females and 29% were males. Approximately 85% of LSC clients were between the ages of 18 and 59, 13% were age 60 or older, and about 2% were under age 18.

In 2005, LSC staff were directed by the LSC to document the extent to which the civil legal needs of low-income persons were not being met. In September 2009, the report was updated. The new report confirms the findings of the earlier report.

Race and Ethnicity of LSC Clients, 2010	
White, not Hispanic	46.6%
Black, not Hispanic	26.3%
Hispanic	18.7%
Native American	2.5%
Asian or Pacific Islander	2.1%
Other	3.9%

The LSC found that (1) 50% of potential clients requesting legal assistance were denied assistance because the LSC did not have the resources to help them; (2) at least 80% of persons who were eligible for LSC services do not get access to either a legal services attorney or a private attorney (pro bono or paid) when they need such assistance; and (3) there is one legal services attorney for every 6,415 low-income persons—the comparable number for the general population is one attorney for every 429 persons, a difference of 15 to 1.[9]

FUNDING HISTORY

When the LSC was first established, its initial goal was to provide all low-income people with at least "minimum access" to legal services, defined as the equivalent of one legal services attorney for every 5,000 poor persons. This goal was briefly achieved in FY1980, but not maintained due to inflation and subsequent budget cuts.

For example, in FY2004, the LSC estimated an appropriation of $683 million would have been needed for minimum access; however, the LSC received $335 million in appropriations that year. According to a 2009 LSC study (cited above), there is one legal services attorney for every 6,415 poor persons. Funds for the LSC are included in the annual appropriation for Commerce, Justice, Science, and Related Agencies (CJS). *Table 1* shows LSC appropriations for selected years from FY1976 (the first full year of LSC operations) to FY2011. Current funding ($404.2 million) is 3.8% below the FY2010 LSC funding level ($420 million) but surpasses the LSC's previous highest funding level of $400 million in both FY1994 and FY1995.

LSC funding accounts for less than half (42%) of all funding for civil legal services for the poor in the United States (discussed in more detail later in this report).

FY1996

From its inception through FY1995, LSC appropriations gradually increased. However, for FY1996, Congress funded the LSC at $278 million, for a reduction of almost 31% from the previous year. In its FY1996 budget resolution, the House assumed a three-year phase-out of the LSC, recommending appropriations of $278 million in FY1996, $141 million in

FY1997, and elimination by FY1998. The House Budget Committee stated in its report (H.Rept. 104-120):

> Too often, ... lawyers funded through federal LSC grants have focused on political causes and class action lawsuits rather than helping poor Americans solve their legal problems.... A phase out of federal funding for the LSC will not eliminate free legal aid to the poor. State and local governments, bar associations, and other organizations already provide substantial legal aid to the poor.

The FY1996 appropriation for the LSC entirely eliminated funding for supplemental legal assistance programs, including Native American and migrant farm worker support, national and state support centers, regional training centers, and other national activities.

Table 1. LSC Appropriations History (in millions of dollars)

FY	$	FY	$	FY	$	FY	$	FY	$
1976	92	1991	328	1997	283	2003	337	2009	390
1980	300	1992	350	1998	283	2004	335	2010	420
1984	275	1993	357	1999	300	2005	331	2011	404
1988	306	1994	400	2000	304	2006	327	2012	348
1989	309	1995	400	2001	329	2007	349		
1990	317	1996	278	2002	329	2008	351		

Source: Table prepared by the Congressional Research Service.

FY1997-FY2001

The phase-out of the LSC envisioned by the House budget resolution did not occur. Instead, between FY1996 and FY2001, LSC funding was gradually increased. For FY1997, Congress funded the LSC at $283 million (P.L. 104-208).

For FY1998, Congress again funded the LSC at $283 million (P.L. 105-119). For FY1999, Congress funded the LSC at $300 million (P.L. 105- 277). For FY2000, Congress funded the LSC at $305 million, but also included a provision in the legislation that mandated a 0.38% government-wide rescission of discretionary budget authority for FY2000. The funding for the LSC for FY2000 was thereby decreased to $304 million (P.L. 106-113).

For FY2001, the Clinton Administration requested $340 million for the LSC. The Clinton Administration had requested $340 million every year since FY1997, in an effort to partially restore the 1996 cutback in funding. P.L. 106-553 included $330 million for LSC for FY2001, and was signed by President Clinton on December 21, 2000. P.L. 106-554 mandated a 0.22% government-wide rescission of discretionary budget authority for FY2001 for almost all government agencies. Thus, the $330 million appropriation for LSC for FY2001 was reduced to $329.3 million.

FY2002-FY2005

For FY2002 through FY2005, the Bush Administration requested $329.3 million in annual appropriations for the LSC. In carrying out the LSC's vision of an effective and efficient statewide system of delivering legal services to the poor, grantees had been merging and reconfiguring their legal services programs to better use every federal dollar allocated to them.[10] The House report (H.Rept. 107-139) indicated concern about the LSC overruling, without appeal, certain configurations implemented by grantees via the state planning process. The House report directed the LSC to review the state planning process and report back to the committee with a proposal that outlined the reconfiguration standards and the process for states to appeal LSC's decisions. P.L. 107-77 included $329.3 million for LSC for FY2002.

For FY2003, Congress funded the LSC at $336.6 million (P.L. 108-7); this funding level included a $9.5 million allotment to offset decennial Census funding reallocations (i.e., to partially compensate some service areas for smaller LSC funding levels for FY2003 than the area received for FY2002 as a result of the change in state poverty populations based on census data for 2000), and a mandated 0.65% government-wide rescission.

For FY2004, Congress funded the LSC at $335.3 million (P.L. 108-199); this funding level included a 0.59% across-the-board government-wide rescission and an additional 0.465% uniform rescission applicable only to funding for the Commerce, Justice, State, and Related Agencies appropriation (which included the LSC).

For FY2005, Congress funded the LSC at $330.8 million (P.L. 108-447); this funding level included a provision that allowed the LSC to spend up to $1 million of prior-year funding balances for a school student loan repayment pilot program, a 0.8% across-the-board government-wide rescission, and an additional 0.54% uniform rescission applicable only to funding for the Commerce, Justice, State, and Related Agencies appropriation (which included the LSC).

FY2006-FY2008

For FY2006, the Bush Administration requested $318.3 million for the LSC. P.L. 109-108 included $330.8 million for the LSC for FY2006—the same amount originally passed by the House, instead of $358.5 million, as passed by the Senate. P.L. 109-108 also included a general rescission equal to 0.28% of funding for the Science, State, Justice, Commerce, and Related Agencies appropriation (which includes the LSC). P.L. 109-148 included a 1% government-wide rescission on discretionary programs. Thus, the LSC appropriation for FY2006 was lowered to $326.6 million.

For FY2007, the Bush Administration requested $310.9 million for the LSC. P.L. 110-5 included language that specified that the LSC would be funded at $348.6 million for FY2007. P.L. 110-5 incorporated the fourth continuing resolution for FY2007 (H.J.Res. 20), which included provisions to fund most of the government agencies, including the LSC, through FY2007.

For FY2008, the Bush Administration requested $311 million for the LSC. The Administration's budget request included $289 million for basic field programs and requires independent audits; almost $13 million for management and administration; $5 million for client self-help and information technology; and $3 million of the Office of the Inspector General.

For FY2008, the Senate Appropriations Committee recommended $390 million for the LSC (S. 1745), a $41.4 million increase above the FY2007 LSC appropriation, and $79.1 million above the Administration's FY2008 budget request for the LSC. During the Senate debate on the bill (H.R. 3093), an amendment by Senator Bingaman was passed to permit LSC-funded legal services programs to provide legal assistance to "H2B" workers—temporary foreign workers employed in the forestry industry—in matters directly related to their employment. LSC-funded programs are currently prohibited from serving H2B workers. The Senate-passed bill provided $390 million for the LSC for FY2008.

For FY2008, the House Appropriations Committee recommended $377 million for the LSC, a $28.4 million increase above the FY2007 LSC appropriation, $66.1 million above the Administration's FY2008 budget request for the LSC, and $13 million below the Senate-passed bill. The House-passed bill (H.R. 3093) included $377 million for the LSC for FY2008.

Pursuant to a continuing appropriations resolution (H.J.Res. 52), enacted September 29, 2007, the LSC operated at FY2007 funding levels through November 16, 2007 (P.L. 110-92). Pursuant to a second continuing appropriations resolution in the FY2008 Department of Defense appropriation (H.R. 3222), enacted November 13, 2007, the LSC operated at FY2007 funding levels through December 14, 2007 (P.L. 110-116). Pursuant to a third continuing appropriations resolution (H.J.Res. 69), enacted December 14, 2007, the LSC operated at FY2007 funding levels through December 21, 2007 (P.L. 110-137). Pursuant to a fourth continuing appropriations resolution (H.J.Res. 72), the LSC operated at FY2007 funding levels through December 31, 2007 (P.L. 110- 137).

P.L. 110-161, the Consolidated Appropriations Act, 2008 (H.R. 2764—enacted December 26, 2007), included $350.5 million for the LSC for FY2008. This amount is $1.9 million above the FY2007 appropriation for the LSC and $39.6 million above the Administration's FY2008 budget request for the LSC. However, it is below the amounts that were passed by the House and the Senate. The FY2008 appropriation for the LSC includes $332.4 million for basic field programs and required independent audits, $12.5 million for management and administration, $2.1 million for client self-help and information technology, $3.0 million for the Office of the Inspector General, and $0.5 million for loan repayment assistance. According to the LSC, pursuant to P.L. 110-161, LSC-funded legal services programs can now provide limited representation to temporary forestry workers.

FY2009

For FY2009, the Bush Administration requested $311.0 million for the LSC.[11] The Administration's budget request included $290.1 million for basic field programs and required independent audits; $12.8 million for management and administration; $5.0 million for client self-help and information technology; and $3.0 million for the Office of the Inspector General.

For FY2009, the House Appropriations Committee approved $390 million for the LSC. The House committee-approved draft bill provided 11% more than the FY2008 LSC appropriation and 25% more than the FY2009 request for the LSC. It included $367 million for basic field programs and required independent audits, $16 million for management and administration, $3 million for client self-help and information technology, $3 million for the Office of the Inspector General, and $1 million for loan repayment assistance.

For FY2009, the Senate Appropriations Committee, like the House committee, also approved $390 million for the LSC. However, the Senate committee bill (S. 3182) included $369 million for basic field programs and required independent audits, $13 million for management and administration, $3.8 million for client self-help and information technology, $3.2 million for the Office of the Inspector General, and $1 million for loan repayment assistance.

P.L. 110-289, the Housing and Economic Recovery Act of 2008 (enacted July 30, 2008), included a provision that provides $30 million for pre-foreclosure and legal counseling through a new grant program. Under the new program, the Neighborhood Reinvestment Corporation, a congressional chartered nonprofit organization, is required to make grants to housing counselors to hire LSC attorneys to assist homeowners who have legal issues directly related to the homeowner's foreclosure, delinquency, or short sale.[12]

P.L. 110-315, the College Opportunity and Affordability Act of 2008 (enacted August 14, 2008), included a provision that authorizes $10 million for the US Department of Education to distribute as loan repayment assistance grants (up to $6,000 per year, $40,000 for a lifetime) to full-time civil legal aid lawyers who agree to remain employed as such for at least three years.[13] Although the loan repayment program was authorized, funding for the program has not yet been appropriated.

P.L. 110-329, the Consolidated Security, Disaster Assistance, and Continuing Appropriations Act, 2009 (enacted September 30, 2008), among other things, required that the LSC continue to operate at FY2008 funding levels (i.e., $350.5 million) until March 6, 2009, or until LSC's regular FY2009 appropriation is enacted.

P.L. 111-8, the Omnibus Appropriations Act, 2009 (enacted March 11, 2009), includes $390.0 million for the LSC for FY2009. This amount is $39.5 million above the FY2008 appropriation for the LSC and $79.0 million above the Bush Administration's FY2009 budget request for the LSC. The FY2009 appropriation for the LSC includes $365.8 million for basic field programs and required independent audits, $16.0 million for management and administration, $3.0 million for client self-help and information technology, $4.2 million for the Office of the Inspector General, and $1.0 million for loan repayment assistance.

FY2010

For FY2010, the Obama Administration requested $435 million for the LSC.[14] This amount is $45 million (11.5%) above the FY2009 appropriation of $390 million for the LSC. The Administration's budget request included $410.4 million for basic field programs and required independent audits; $17 million for management and grants oversight; $3.4 million for client self-help and information technology; $3.2 million for the Office of the Inspector General; and $1 million for loan repayment assistance. The Obama Administration also proposed that LSC restrictions on class action suits and attorneys' fees be eliminated.

For FY2010, the House Appropriations Committee approved $440 million for the LSC (H.Rept. 111-149). The House bill (H.R. 2847) provides almost 13% more than the FY2009 LSC appropriation and 1% more than the Administration's FY2010 budget request for the

LSC. The House approved $440 million for the LSC on June 18, 2009. The House voted to continue existing limitations on the use of LSC funds (and non-LSC funds) except for the restriction on the ability of LSC-funded programs to collect attorneys' fees. The House bill also included funds for a loan repayment assistance program to help legal services programs recruit and retain talented attorneys.

For FY2010, the Senate Appropriations Committee approved $400 million for the LSC (S.Rept. 111-34). The Senate version of the bill (H.R. 2847) provides about 3% more than the FY2009 LCS appropriation and 8% less than the Administration's FY2010 request for the LSC. The Senate passed H.R. 2847 on November 5, 2009. The Senate-passed version of the bill included $400 million in funding for the LSC and would continue existing limitations on the use of federal funds but would eliminate the restrictions on the use of nonfederal funds except in litigation involving abortion and cases involving prisoners.[15] The conference agreement on H.R. 3288 (consolidated appropriations for 2010—H.Rept. 111-366), which includes $420 million for the LSC for FY2010, was passed by the House on December 10, 2009, and by the Senate on December 13, 2009.

P.L. 111-117, the Consolidated Appropriations Act, 2010 (enacted December 16, 2009), includes $420.0 million for the LSC for FY2010. The FY2010 appropriation for the LSC includes $394.4 million for basic field programs and required independent audits, $17.0 million for management and administration, $3.4 million for client self-help and information technology, $4.2 million for the Office of the Inspector General, and $1.0 million for loan repayment assistance. P.L. 111-117 continues existing limitations on the use of LSC funds (and non-LSC funds) except for the restriction on the ability of LSC-funded programs to collect attorneys' fees.

FY2011

For FY2011, the Obama Administration requested $435 million for the LSC.[16] This amount is $15 million (3.6%) above the FY2010 appropriation of $420 million for the LSC. The Administration's budget request included $407 million for basic field programs and required independent audits, $20 million for management and grants oversight, $3 million for client self-help and information technology, $4 million for the Office of the Inspector General, and $1 million for loan repayment assistance. The Obama Administration also proposed that LSC restrictions on class action suits and attorneys' fees be eliminated.

On July 22, 2010, the Senate Appropriations Committee approved $430 million for the LSC for FY2011 (S.Rept. 111-229; S. 3636), which represents a 2.4% increase over FY2010 funding and a 1.1% decrease below the Administration's budget request. The Senate Appropriations Committee recommendation for the LSC provided $401.7 million for basic field programs, to be used for competitively awarded grants and contracts; $20.0 million for management and administration; $3.0 million for client self-help and information technology; $4.3 million for the Office of the Inspector General; and $1.0 million for loan repayment assistance.

The Senate Appropriations Committee report stipulated that implementation of the recent recommendations of the Government Accountability Office (GAO) and the LSC Inspector General for the LSC must be a priority of the LSC. In addition, the Senate Appropriations Committee bill continued existing limitations on the use of federal funds, but lifted restrictions on the use of nonfederal funds except in litigation involving abortion or litigation on behalf of prisoners.

Although the House Appropriations Subcommittee approved a $440 million FY2011 budget for the LSC on June 29, 2010, the full House Appropriations Committee did not act on the proposal. Neither the full Senate or House passed a regular appropriations bill that included funding for the LSC for FY2011 during the 111th Congress. Instead, several continuing resolutions were passed.[17]

On April 14, 2011, H.R. 1473, the Department of Defense and Full-Year Continuing Appropriations Act, 2011, was passed by the House and Senate. It was signed into law (P.L. 112- 10) by President Obama on April 15, 2011. P.L. 112-10 included funding of $405 million for the LSC for FY2011. However, the act also included a 0.2% across-the-board rescission. So, the funding for the LSC for FY2011 is about $404.2 million ($404,190,000).

FY2012

For FY2012, the Obama Administration requested $450.0 million for the LSC.[18] This amount is $45.8 million (11.3%) above the FY2011 appropriation of $404.2 million for the LSC. The Administration's FY2012 budget request included $420.2 million for basic field programs and required independent audits, $19.5 million for management and grants oversight, $5.0 million for client self-help and information technology, $4.4 million for the Office of the Inspector General, and $1.0 million for loan repayment assistance. The Obama Administration also proposed that LSC restrictions on class action suits and attorneys' fees be eliminated.[19]

On July 20, 2011, the House Committee on Appropriations recommended $300 million for the LSC for FY2012 (H.Rept. 112-169; H.R. 2596). This amount is 33.3% less than the Administration's FY2012 budget request and 25.8% less than the FY2011-enacted amount. The committee also encouraged the LSC Inspector General to conduct annual audits of LSC grantees to make sure that they are not using LSC funds in violation of the prohibition against engaging in political activities or any of the other restrictions on LSC activities. The committee recommended that funds be withdrawn from any LSC grantee found to be engaging in political activity.

On September 15, 2011, the Senate Committee on Appropriations recommended $396.1 million for the LSC for FY2012 (S.Rept. 112-78; S. 1572). This amount is 32.2% more than the amount recommended by the House Committee on Appropriations, 12.0% less than the Administration's FY2012 budget request, and 2.0% less than the FY2011-enacted amount. The Senate Committee on Appropriations' recommendation for the LSC for FY2012 included $370.5 million for basic field programs and required independent audits, $17.0 million for management and grants oversight, $3.4 million for client self-help and information technology, $4.2 million for the Office of the Inspector General, and $1.0 million for loan repayment assistance. The committee also (1) directed the LSC to continue its collaboration with the Department of Justice to conduct a national study of the cost-effectiveness of a legal services program patterned after existing state models; (2) encouraged the LSC to have its grantees improve and/or increase private attorney pro bono participation; and (3) directed LSC to conduct a study of the implementation and costs of a legal aid fellowship program that would provide incentives for retirees and/or recent law school graduates to commit to working in legal services programs for a specified period of time. The committee also recommended that all the restrictions on the use of *private funds* for the LSC, except those associated with abortion-related cases and representation of prisoner cases, be eliminated.[20] The restrictions on the use of public funds for the LSC would remain in effect.

On November 1, 2011, the Senate passed a bill (H.R. 2112) that included funding of $348 million for the LSC for FY2012. On November 17, 2011, both the House and the Senate passed the conference report on H.R. 2112 (H.Rept. 112-284). Among other things, it funded the LSC at $348 million for FY2012. The conference report included the existing restrictions on LSC activities. H.R. 2112 (the Consolidated and Further Continuing Appropriations Act, 2012) was signed into law (P.L. 112-55) by President Obama on November 18, 2011.

The FY2012 appropriation for the LSC, $348 million, is 13.9% less than the FY2011 LSC appropriation, 22.7% less than the Administration's budget request, 16% more than the House committee's recommendation, and 12.1% less than the amount passed by the Senate. The FY2012 appropriation for the LSC included $322.4 million for basic field programs and required independent audits, $17.0 million for management and grants oversight, $3.4 million for client self-help and information technology, $4.2 million for the Office of the Inspector General, and $1.0 million for loan repayment assistance. It also included the existing restrictions on LSC activities.

FY2013

For FY2013, the Obama Administration requested $402.0 million for the LSC.[21] This amount is $54.0 million (15.5%) above the FY2012 appropriation of $348.0 million for the LSC. The Administration's FY2013 budget request includes $376.8 million for basic field programs and required independent audits, $17.0 million for management and grants oversight, $3.0 million for client self-help and information technology, $4.2 million for the Office of the Inspector General, and $1.0 million for loan repayment assistance. The Obama Administration also proposed that LSC restrictions on class action suits and attorneys' fees be eliminated.[22]

On April 19, 2012, the Senate Committee on Appropriations recommended $402 million for the LSC for FY2013 (S.Rept. 112-158; S. 2323). This amount is the same as the Administration's FY2013 budget request and 15.5% more than the FY2012-enacted amount. S. 2323 would delete restrictions concerning the use of non-federal funding for LSC activities except for activities regarding class action law suits; abortion litigation; and litigation on behalf of federal, state, or local prisoners.

On April 26, 2012, the House Committee on Appropriations recommended $328 million for the LSC for FY2013. This amount is 18.4% less than the amount recommended by the Senate Committee on Appropriations and the Administration's FY2013 budget request, and 5.7% less than the FY2012-enacted amount. The committee also encouraged the LSC Inspector General to conduct annual audits of LSC grantees to make sure that they are not using LSC funds in violation of the prohibition against engaging in political activities or any of the other restrictions on LSC activities.

The committee recommended that funds be withdrawn from any LSC grantee found to be engaging in political activity. In addition, the committee included a technical change to the allocation formula for basic field grants. Currently the allocation for LSC grantees in each geographic area is based on poverty statistics from the "most recent decennial census."

The Census Bureau has since stopped collecting poverty data in the decennial census and instead collects those data in the American Community Survey (ACS). The committee recommended that the formula be altered to reflect this shift.

Since ACS data are released more frequently, the committee recommendation allows reallocation of LSC funding every three years. On May 10, 2012, the House passed the FY2013 CJS Appropriations bill (H.R. 5326). which included $328 million for the LSC as well as the revised Census Bureau language.

It also included the existing restrictions on LSC activities. One House amendment that would have eliminated all funding for the LCS and another House amendment that would have cut the funding for the LSC to $200 million for FY2013 were rejected.

It is important to note that since FY1996, all of the LSC appropriations laws have included language stipulating the provisions restricting the activities of LSC grantees enacted in previous LSC appropriations laws.[23] (See the earlier section titled "Restrictions on Activities.") *Table 2* shows LSC appropriations for FY2003-FY2012, by component of funding.

Table 2. LSC: Funding for Program Components, FY2003-FY2012 (in millions of dollars)

LSC Program Components	FY2003	FY2004	FY2005	FY2006	FY2007	FY2008	FY2009	FY2010	FY2011	FY2012
Basic field programs	308.0	316.4	312.4	308.4	330.8	332.5	365.8	394.4	378.6	322.4
Management and administration	13.2	13.0	12.8	12.7	12.7	12.5	16.0	17.0	17.0	17.0
Client self-help and information technology	3.4	1.3	1.3	1.2	2.1	2.1	3.0	3.4	3.4	3.4
Office of the Inspector General	2.6	2.6	2.5	2.5	3	3	4.2	4.2	4.2	4.2
Offset for census-based reallocations	9.4	1.8	1.8	1.8	0	0	0	0	0	0
Student loan repayment program	0	0	0	0	0	0.5	1.0	1.0	1.0	1.0
Total	336.6	335.3	330.8	326.6	348.6	350.5	390.0	420.0	404.2	348.0

Source: Table prepared by the Congressional Research Service.

Note: These data reflect appropriations after all rescissions; numbers may not add to total due to rounding.

DISTRIBUTION OF LSC FUNDS AND NON-LSC RESOURCES

LSC funds appropriated for basic field programs are distributed to the states and jurisdictions on a per capita basis, according to US Census Bureau data[24] on the number of "poor" persons in each service area.[25] Grantees within each state or jurisdiction then compete among themselves for funding.

In the 2010 decennial census, the Census Bureau did not use the "long form" and did not collect data on personal income. In lieu of the "long form," the Census Bureau developed the American Community Survey (ACS), an ongoing survey that provides data every year on income and benefits, family and relationships, and other kinds of data, which provides a more timely picture of poverty and other demographic information. Due to these changes in the data sets obtained by the 2010 decennial census, LSC funding can no longer be distributed according to the provisions of the current appropriations act that funds the LSC. On September 19, 2011, the LSC Board recommended that (1) the determination of the number of individuals in poverty in each geographic area would be made by the US Census Bureau, without any reference to the decennial census as the basis for that determination; (2) LSC funding would be reallocated among geographic areas every three years based on updated poverty population determinations by the Census Bureau; and (3) the first reallocation would be phased in over two years, in FY2013 and FY2014.[26]

Although the LSC is the largest single source of funding for the civil legal services system in the United States, it is not the only source of funding. Local legal services programs supplement their LSC grants with funds from a variety of governmental and private sources. Non-LSC funding sources include state and local grants; state Interest on Lawyers' Trust Accounts (IOLTAs) programs;[27] federal programs such as the Title XX Social Services Block Grant, the Older Americans Act, the Violence Against Women Act, and Community Development Block Grants; and private grants from entities such as the United Way, foundations, and national, state, and local bar associations. In addition, private attorneys accept referrals to provide legal services to the poor, primarily through LSC-funded pro bono programs.[28]

As shown in *Table 3,* in 2010 LSC funding accounted for about 44% of the $960.1 million spent in the United States for civil legal services for the poor.[29]

Table 3. Funding for LSC and Non-LSC Programs, by Jurisdiction, FY2010

State	LSC Funding	Number of LSC Programs	Non-LSC Funding	Total Funding	LSC Funding as % of Total
Alabama	8,814,222	1	1,445,748	10,259,970	85.9
Alaska	1,546,778	1	1,459,237	3,006,015	51.5
Arizona	11,756,833	3	4,835,009	16,591,842	70.9
Arkansas	4,699,078	2	2,016,989	6,716,067	70.0
California	54,851,018	11	51,356,978	106,207,996	51.6
Colorado	4,252,999	1	10,935,939	15,188,938	28.0
Connecticut	2,991,490	1	368,432	3,359,922	89.0
Delaware	751,959	1	373,154	1,125,113	66.8
District of Columbia	1,297,599	1	550,848	1,848,447	70.2
Florida	22,769,563	7	23,260,743	46,030,306	49.5
Georgia	11,119,458	2	12,862,816	23,982,274	46.4
Hawaii	1,970,833	1	6,834,870	8,805,703	22.4
Idaho	1,692,506	1	809,779	2,502,285	67.6

State	LSC Funding	Number of LSC Programs	Non-LSC Funding	Total Funding	LSC Funding as % of Total
Illinois	13,949,562	3	17,700,826	31,650,388	44.1
Indiana	6,107,097	1	3,016,859	9,123,956	66.9
Iowa	2,798,162	1	5,667,723	8,465,885	33.1
Kansas	2,772,618	1	4,860,656	7,633,274	36.3
Kentucky	7,171,940	4	11,676,115	18,848,055	38.1
Louisiana	9,572,424	4	5,506,311	15,078,735	63.5
Maine	1,750,628	1	4,924,434	6,675,062	26.2
Maryland	4,675,004	1	21,699,268	26,374,272	17.7
Massachusetts	6,640,767	4	1,926,837	8,567,604	77.5
Michigan	11,453,660	6	14,717,689	26,171,349	43.8
Minnesota	4,383,921	5	12,659,169	17,043,090	25.7
Mississippi	6,254,734	2	1,681,420	7,936,154	78.8
Missouri	6,854,591	4	14,145,757	21,000,348	32.6
Montana	1,727,352	1	1,684,173	3,411,525	50.6
Nebraska	1,781,836	1	3,482,961	5,264,797	33.8
Nevada	2,798,007	1	648,495	3,446,502	81.2
New Hampshire	829,919	1	121,814	951,733	87.2
New Jersey	7,774,018	6	33,240,956	41,014,974	19.0
New Mexico	4,469,353	1	2,346,083	6,815,436	65.6
New York	31,808,736	7	70,247,696	102,056,432	31.2
North Carolina	12,283,849	1	12,569,562	24,853,411	49.4
North Dakota	1,172,266	1	1,112,034	2,284,300	51.3
Ohio	12,766,747	6	38,890,890	51,657,637	24.7
Oklahoma	6,398,976	2	5,765,933	12,164,909	52.6
Oregon	4,375,105	1	5,209,861	9,584,966	45.6
Pennsylvania	14,230,903	8	23,785,419	38,016,322	37.4
Rhode Island	1,281,756	1	2,848,513	4,130,269	31.0
South Carolina	5,842,644	1	4,068,159	9,910,803	59.0
South Dakota	2,223,345	2	1,112,084	3,335,429	66.7
Tennessee	8,528,612	4	15,187,110	23,715,722	36.0
Texas	34,899,576	3	32,143,665	67,043,241	52.1
Utah	2,451,988	1	2,040,879	4,492,867	54.6
Vermont	671,957	1	70,173	742,130	90.5
Virginia	7,256,407	6	14,187,479	21,443,886	33.8
Washington	7,722,425	1	14,812,631	22,535,056	34.3
West Virginia	3,378,270	1	5,137,430	8,515,700	39.7
Wisconsin	5,559,183	2	6,662,651	12,221,834	45.5
Wyoming	782,736	1	87,048	869,784	90.0
Guam	412,650	1	832,933	1,245,583	33.1
Micronesia	1,899,007	1	595,293	2,494,300	76.1
Puerto Rico	19,785,465	2	4,291,993	24,077,458	82.2
Virgin Islands	377,442	1	1,202,397	1,579,839	23.9
Total (states and DC)	395,915,410	131	534,757,305	930,672,715	42.5
Total (states, DC, and territories)	418,389,974	136	541,679,921	960,069,895	43.6

Source: Table prepared by the Congressional Research Service, using data from the Legal Services Corporation, Legal Services Corporation Fact Book 2010, June 2011, This report can be found at https://grants.lsc.gov/ Easygrants_Web_LSC/ Implementation/Modules/Login/Controls/ PDFs/ Fact_Book_2010.pdf.

End Notes

[1] Center for Law and Social Policy. Securing Equal Justice for All: A Brief History of Civil Legal Assistance in the United States, by Alan W. Houseman and Linda E. Perle, Revised January 2007, p. 19, http://www.clasp.org/admin/ site/publications/files/0158.pdf. See also President Nixon, Special Message to the Congress Proposing Establishment of a Legal Services Corporation, May 5, 1971, http://www.presidency. ucsb.edu/ws /index.php?pid =2998.

[2] In 2009, 125% of the federal poverty guidelines was $27,563 for a household of four (higher in Alaska and Hawaii).

[3] This system supplanted the previous system of presumptive refunding for LSC grantees. The LSC is prohibited from granting any preference to current or previous grantees of LSC funds (§503(e) of P.L. 104-134, enacted April 26, 1996).

[4] Legal Services Corporation. State Planning—A Five Year Overview, 2005, pp. 1-7, http:// www.lsc.gov/pdfs/ 030194_sp5yrrprt.pdf.

[5] Ibid., p. 8.

[6] For additional information, see CRS Report R40679, Legal Services Corporation: Restrictions on Activities. Note: The prohibition against claiming or collecting attorneys' fees was eliminated by Section 533 of P.L. 111-117 (the Consolidated Appropriations Act, 2010).

[7] Legal Services Corporation, Legal Services Corporation Fact Book 2010, June 2011, https://grants.lsc.gov/ Easygrants_Web_LSC/Implementation/Modules/Login/Controls/ PDFs/Fact_Book_2010.pdf

[8] Testimony before the House Judiciary Committee Subcommittee on Commercial and Administrative Law Submitted by LSC President Helaine M. Barnett, March 31, 2004, http://www.lsc.gov/government/ testimony_detail_T116_R2.php.

[9] Legal Services Corporation, "Documenting the Justice Gap in America—The Current Unmet Civil Legal Needs of Low-Income Americans," September 2005, available at http://www.lsc.gov/press/documents/ LSCJusticeGap_FINAL_1001.pdf. See also Legal Services Corporation, "Documenting the Justice Gap in America— The Current Unmet Civil Legal Needs of Low-Income Americans," September 2009, available at http://www.lsc.gov/ pdfs/documenting_the_justice_gap_in_america_2009.pdf.

[10] Legal Services Corporation, A Special Report to Congress, State Planning & Reconfiguration, September 2001, pp. 2-3, 10.

[11] Each year the LSC submits its own budget request to Congress. In most years, the LSC budget request is significantly higher than the amount that appears in the President's annual budget. For FY2009, the LSC requested an appropriation of $471.4 million, a 52% increase over the President's budget request of $311 million for the LSC. The reasons cited for the significant increase included legal problems of existing and new clients stemming from the recent crises in the mortgage and housing industries, the ongoing impact of natural disasters, and widespread domestic violence, along with recent LSC findings that there is significant unmet need among America's poorest populations with regard to civil legal assistance.

[12] See Sections 2305 and 2401 of P.L. 110-289.

[13] See Section 431 of P.L. 110-315.

[14] Each year the LSC submits its own budget request to Congress. In most years, the LSC budget request is significantly higher than the amount that appears in the President's annual budget. For FY2010, the LSC requested an appropriation of $485.1 million, an 11.5% increase over the President's budget request of $435 million for the LSC. The reasons cited for the significant increase included legal problems of existing and new clients stemming from the recent crises in the mortgage and housing industries, the ongoing impact of natural disasters, and widespread domestic violence, along with recent LSC findings that there is significant unmet need among America's poorest populations with regard to civil legal assistance.

[15] S.Rept. 111-34 (page 143) deletes Section 504(d) of P.L. 104-134 (pertaining to the use of nonfederal funds for activities prohibited by the LSC), but also stipulates that no funds (federal or nonfederal) can be used for activities specified in Section 504(a)(14) or Section 504(a)(15) of P.L. 104-134 (respectively, these two sections pertain to abortion litigation and litigation involving persons incarcerated in a federal, state, or local prison).

[16] Each year, the LSC submits its own budget request to Congress. In most years, the LSC budget request is significantly higher than the amount that appears in the President's annual budget. For FY2011, the LSC requested an appropriation of $484.9 million, an 11.5% increase over the President's FY2011 budget request of $435 million for the LSC. The reasons cited for the significant increase included legal problems of existing and new clients stemming from the recent crises in the mortgage and housing industries, the ongoing impact of

natural disasters, and the economic downturn, along with recent LSC findings that there is significant unmet need among America's poorest populations with regard to civil legal assistance.

[17] There were seven temporary appropriations for the LSC for FY2011: (1) P.L. 111-242 (H.R. 3081) continued appropriations for the LSC at the FY2010 enacted level (i.e., $420 million) until December 3, 2010; (2) P.L. 111-290 (H.J.Res. 101) continued appropriations for the LSC at the FY2010 enacted level until December 18, 2010; (3) P.L. 111-317 (H.J.Res. 105) continued appropriations for the LSC at the FY2010 enacted level until December 21, 2010; (4) P.L. 111-322 (H.R. 3082) continued appropriations for the LSC at the FY2010 enacted level until March 4, 2011; (5) P.L. 112-4 (H.J.Res. 44) continued appropriations for the LSC at the FY2010 enacted level until March 18, 2011; (6) P.L. 112-6 (H.J.Res. 48) continued appropriations for the LSC at the FY2010 enacted level until April 8, 2011; (7) P.L. 112-8 continued appropriations for the LSC at the FY2010 enacted level (i.e., $420 million) until April 15, 2011.

[18] Each year, the LSC submits its own budget request to Congress. In most years, the LSC budget request is significantly higher than the amount that appears in the President's annual budget. For FY2012, the LSC requested an appropriation of $516.550 million, a 14.8% increase over the President's FY2012 budget request of $450 million. The reasons cited for the significant increase included legal problems of existing and new clients stemming from the economic downturn and slow recovery, continued crises in the mortgage and housing industries, and the ongoing impact of natural disasters, along with recent LSC findings that there is significant unmet need among America's poorest populations with regard to civil legal assistance.

[19] The restriction on attorneys' fees was eliminated pursuant to P.L. 111-117 (§533). For further information, see CRS Report R40679, Legal Services Corporation: Restrictions on Activities, by Carmen Solomon-Fears.

[20] According to the Senate committee report (S.Rept. 112-78, pp. 123-124), the recommendation that would in effect allow LSC grantees to use private sources of funding for LSC activities (with the exceptions mentioned above) that cannot be funded with public sources of funds is intended to "level the playing field between legal aid attorneys and their counterparts in the private sector and open potentially crucial sources of additional revenue to legal aid providers in a year in which State and private funding sources are decreasing."

[21] Each year, the LSC submits its own budget request to Congress. In most years, the LSC budget request is significantly higher than the amount that appears in the President's annual budget. For FY2013, the LSC requested an appropriation of $470.0 million, a 16.9% increase over the President's FY2013 budget request of $402 million. The reasons cited for the significant increase included legal problems of existing and new clients stemming from the slow recovery, continued crises in the mortgage and housing industries, the decline in non-LSC resources available for legal services programs, and the ongoing impact of natural disasters, along with recent LSC findings that there is significant unmet need among America's poorest populations with regard to civil legal assistance.

[22] The restriction on attorneys' fees was eliminated pursuant to P.L. 111-117 (§533). For further information, see CRS Report R40679, Legal Services Corporation: Restrictions on Activities, by Carmen Solomon-Fears.

[23] Although the authorizing statute contains some restrictions on LSC activities, many more restrictions were added by P.L. 104-134 in 1996. Other restrictions and modifications or clarifications were added in 1997 (P.L. 105-119) and 1998 (P.L. 105-277). All LSC appropriation laws enacted after 1996 have included language referencing the restrictions in prior appropriation laws.

[24] Until recently, the distribution of LSC funds was based on census data that used the most recent decennial census. However, the distribution of LSC funding for 2010, 2011, and 2012 has continued to be based on census data from the year 2000.

[25] In other words, if a specific state has 12% of the US poverty population, that state generally would receive about 12% of the LSC funding amount allocated for local legal services programs.

[26] As mentioned earlier, H.R. 5326 as passed by the House included revised Census Bureau language that does not mention the decennial census.

[27] These funds represent interest earned on sums deposited by clients with attorneys for short periods of time.

[28] In 2010, approximately 36,000 private attorneys accepted referrals to help LSC clients.

[29] Legal Services Corporation, Legal Services Corporation Fact Book 2010, June 2011, https://grants.lsc.gov/ Easygrants_Web_LSC/Implementation/Modules/ Login/Controls / PDFs/Fact_Book_2010.pdf.

In: Indigent Defense
Editors: Betty Nichols and Jeff Weaver

ISBN: 978-1-62257-441-4

Chapter 3

EXPERT WORKING GROUP REPORT: INTERNATIONAL PERSPECTIVES ON INDIGENT DEFENSE*

U.S. Department of Justice

AUTHORS' NOTE

The group of experts that assembled in late January 2011 came well prepared to discuss the international and domestic practice of criminal indigent defense and the research needed to improve it. As the co-organizers and rapporteurs for the group, we would like to thank all of the attendees for taking time out of their busy schedules and arriving ready to engage the issues.

Without their willingness to participate in open and frank discussions, this meeting would not have been the success it was. We also hope the convening expanded and strengthened the network of international experts working on criminal legal aid. We would like to thank our colleagues at the Access to Justice Initiative (ATJ) and the National Institute of Justice (NIJ), specifically, Deborah Leff, Deputy Counselor for Access to Justice, for her guidance and tireless support throughout the planning of this meeting, and Edwin Zedlewski, the recently retired Director of the International Center at NIJ, for his commitment to our efforts and for ensuring that this convening happened.

We also thank Maureen McGough, Lynn Overmann, Melanca Clark, Karen Lash and Daniel Olmos for all of their assistance in planning and preparing for the meeting and for serving as facilitators for the very important breakout group sessions, and Jonathan Luckett and Matthew Baker for their assistance in locating citations for this report. Please note that this chapter does not attribute any comments made during the working group to individual participants. While the chapter is primarily a summary of the proceedings, in some instances we have included participants' statements unedited.

---

* This is an edited, reformatted and augmented version of the U.S. Department of Justice publication, NCJ 236022, dated September 2011.

For more information on the Access to Justice Initiative and its work on indigent defense, please visit http://www.justice.gov/atj/. For more information on the National Institute of Justice and its work in the field of wrongful convictions, please visit http://www.nij.gov.

Maha Jweied,
Senior Counsel, Access to Justice Initiative

Miranda Jolicoeur,
former International Liaison and Research Analyst,
National Institute of Justice

INTRODUCTION

The vast majority of criminal defendants in the United States are too poor to afford a lawyer, yet adequate funding and resources for defense counsel remains an elusive goal. The U.S. Department of Justice (the Department) seeks effective, evidence-based solutions to problems in indigent defense so that the nation can deliver on its constitutionally guaranteed promise to provide legal representation to people accused of crime who cannot afford it.

In January 2011, the Department‘s Access to Justice Initiative (ATJ) and National Institute of Justice‘s (NIJ) International Center jointly convened an Expert Working Group (EWG) on *International Perspectives on Indigent Defense* to explore domestic and international practices in indigent defense.

That the convening started on the same day that the Governor of Massachusetts announced his plans to overhaul the commonwealth‘s public defender system was only further evidence of the importance of identifying the best approaches to the delivery of defender services.[1]

The 40-person EWG consisted of leading experts drawn from multidisciplinary communities, including domestic and international practitioners, researchers, government officials and advocates from nine countries.[2] The goals of the workshop were to:

- Help suggest federal priorities on indigent defense;
- Help identify research in the field of indigent defense;
- Learn about alternative and best practices in the provision of defender services for the poor from the United States and around the globe;
- Consider the transferability of successful international practices to the United States; and
- Forge sustained American and international collaborations in the field of criminal legal aid.

Over a day and a half, participants were led in a facilitated discussion around the following six panels:

- The state of indigent defense in the United States generally;
- Costs associated with being indigent in the criminal justice system;

- Improvements to the provision of defender services for the poor;
- Improvements to the provision of defender services for juveniles;
- The intersection of indigent defense and immigration; and
- Indigent defense in indigenous communities.[3]

At the conclusion of the facilitated discussions, participants were divided into five breakout groups to identify specific, actionable recommendations for ATJ and NIJ. These breakout groups aligned with the panel topics of the convening and were organized to consider *costs* of being indigent, *general improvements* to the criminal justice system, improvements for *juveniles*, special considerations for *immigrants* and special considerations for *indigenous communities*.

The breakout groups were asked to create recommendations to advance ATJ's and NIJ's efforts to set federal priorities in indigent defense, identify research gaps in the field and identify international practices that should be assessed for transferability to the United States.

This chapter provides an overview of the EWG's discussions and includes the breakout groups' recommendations following the summary of the corresponding panel presentations.

ATJ and NIJ were pleased they could foster a new level of cooperation between domestic and international researchers and practitioners in the field of criminal legal aid. Although the level of participation in the EWG is a measure of this new cooperation, so too are the many contacts that have continued after the meeting.

This chapter provides the federal government and the indigent defense community with recommendations that can help steer the direction of indigent defense research and potential reform strategies for years to come.

The authors have included an appendix summarizing the international practices identified in the workshop.[4] No effort has been made to assess whether these practices can or should be transferred to the United States. It is the hope of the authors that assessments of the transferability of some of these practices can be produced in the months ahead.

FRAMING THE ISSUE: THE STATE OF INDIGENT DEFENSE IN THE UNITED STATES

The EWG began with a general discussion on the state of indigent defense in the United States. Participants discussed various problems in the delivery of effective defender services for the poor with the following themes dominating the discussion:

- Underfunding and the overdependence on judges and politicians who control budgets;
- Costs associated with remedying cases with ineffective assistance of counsel;
- Lack of federally enforceable standards on the delivery of defender services for the poor;
- Excessive caseloads, including the impact of defending misdemeanors;
- The impact of race on outcomes for clients;
- Lack of access to experts, interpreters and other crucial resources; and
- Prosecutorial and police misconduct.

The problem of *limited funding* for public defender offices was a significant concern for the EWG. One participant noted that funding given to state and local agencies often lacks transparency, oversight and accountability. She also noted that due to excessive caseloads, public defenders often struggle to meet their clients even once before trial.

Another participant discussed the *costs* associated with ineffective assistance of counsel, including the costs associated with reversing wrongful convictions.[5] These are often greater than the costs associated with providing adequate counsel in the first instance. She cited the case of Roberto Miranda, who was wrongfully convicted of first-degree murder in Nevada and on appeal, secured a reversal of his conviction and a $5-million judgment against the state.[6] The cost of this reversal and judgment was more than what the cost would have been had Mr. Miranda been assigned competent defense counsel from the outset of the case. Moreover, when factoring in the substantial administrative resources that were expended to adjudicate his claim of constitutionally inadequate counsel, the monetary costs exceeded the $5 million judgment.

One expert discussed cost-savings research from Michigan where the appellate defender office was able to document the cases of criminal defendants that were sentenced to more time than was appropriate because of the inability of defense counsel to effectively navigate the complex sentencing scheme.[7] The white paper computed the cost of that additional time served and compared it with what the cost would have been had the defendant received an adequate defense, which could have identified and challenged the errors in sentencing. It was suggested that producing similar studies would be effective in supporting costs associated with defender services, especially given the recent publicity surrounding efforts to reduce prison populations.

Participants also stressed the necessity of *establishing enforceable defense standards* on delivery systems for the legal representation of the poor, which was discussed over the course of the entire workshop. The 2003 NIJ-funded National Legal Aid and Defender Association study demonstrated that standards could have a dramatic impact on quality in the system, but that standards, in the infrequent instances in which they are adopted or imposed, are rarely enforced.[8]

A participant also discussed the effectiveness of public defense pilot programs in Washington State that were developed with limited appropriations.[9] The independent evaluations of these programs demonstrate they reduced incarceration rates and increased deferred prosecutions.[10]

The EWG also discussed the potential advantages of creating a federal ombudsman office, which could receive individual complaints of ineffective defense and could have the power to investigate and recommend relief.[11] Participants noted that the American Bar Association (ABA) supports the creation of independent boards, commissions and ombudsman offices.[12] South Africa‘s Office of the Public Protector was mentioned as a particularly successful model worthy of study. One participant described efforts in Eastern Europe to emulate the South African office noting its effectiveness as an institution created by, accountable to, and ultimately funded by parliament. (*See* Appendix A, International Practices, South African Ombudsman Model).

The EWG also discussed the impact on *caseloads* of the 1972 Supreme Court decision of *Argersinger*, which required public defender offices to represent individuals in cases involving misdemeanors.[13] In 2007, the Department‘s Bureau of Justice Statistics (BJS) released two studies on state and county-based local defender offices that confirmed that the caseload crisis in indigent defense is worsening and that misdemeanors are a major factor in increasing caseloads.[14] The study found that 15 of 19 state public defender systems reported caseloads above national standards. In fact, between 1999 and 2000, public defender caseloads increased by 20%, while staffing increased by only four percent.[15] And 73% of county public defenders exceeded national caseload standards.[16] The studies found that 43% of state caseloads and 56% of county cases were misdemeanors or low-level infractions.[17]

The EWG also discussed the impact of *race* on the United States criminal justice system. One policy expert stressed that the earliest efforts to improve access to counsel were to alleviate the disparities in the criminal justice system between white and African-American defendants.

She noted that communities of color, including the African-American community, often experience the criminal justice system as discriminatory, where at each stage in a criminal proceeding, there are unique experiences faced by individuals of color: racial profiling, prosecutorial discretion being exercised to punish defendants of color more harshly and underrepresentation of minorities on juries. She stressed that these factors significantly contribute to higher rates of arrests and incarceration of African Americans than their representation in the U.S. population.[18] Black men are imprisoned at a rate of 6.5 times the rate of white men.[19] She linked this reality to the fact that many of the African Americans in the criminal justice system are poor and suffer from inadequate defender services. She noted that these individuals often feel alienated from the criminal justice system because it is managed predominantly by white prosecutors, public defenders and judges. This reality creates racially disproportionate collateral consequences in the criminal justice system, such as the increased need for foster care for black families and the denial of the right to vote to formerly incarcerated black men.[20]

Another important issue discussed by the EWG was the impact of the lack of *resources,* such as experts, interpreters and social workers, for poor defendants.

The participants discussed how defender offices are often good models and are usually successful at bringing together the needed resources to provide holistic defense to poor clients. One participant described the Criminal Defense Consortium of Cook County, Illinois, which was created 35 years ago as an alternative to the Cook County Public Defender Office. This consortium of six community-based neighborhood offices was funded by the Department in the 1970s and approached defender services from a holistic perspective using attorneys, investigators and social workers to care for all the legal needs of clients.[21]

The impact of *prosecutorial* and *police misconduct* was also considered by the EWG. Participants discussed the case of Chicago Police Department Detective and Commander Jon Burge, who was convicted of torturing over 200 criminal suspects and forcing confessions while serving as a police officer between 1972 and 1991.[22]

Participants discussed the effectiveness of the defender community in Chicago in helping to secure justice for these individuals, many of whom were indigent. One participant noted that due in part to the Burge investigation, former Illinois Governor George Ryan instituted a death penalty moratorium in Illinois.

Another participant remarked that the Burge case provides an important lesson for public defenders on the use of international law and procedure. When the investigation was delayed, a petition was filed by victims and human rights lawyers to the Inter-American Commission on Human Rights requesting a hearing both on the facts of the case and on the delay, which was instrumental in creating the political pressure necessary to push the investigation into federal court more quickly.[23]

Many participants agreed that the fact that indigent defendants are a politically weak constituency contributed to these problems. Public defenders and their allies need to continue their advocacy on behalf of this population when new approaches in criminal justice are being developed.

One participant cautioned that recent trends in criminal justice, such as restorative justice and the creation of special courts, do not always serve the interests of poor defendants and public defenders must monitor these efforts appropriately. At the conclusion of the panel presentations, participants discussed their goals for the workshop and provided recommendations to improve indigent defense generally. These included:

- *Increase Federal Funding for Defender Services.* The Department should increase funding for defender services and assess how funding for indigent defense is distributed through the Edward Byrne Memorial Justice Assistance Grant (Byrne JAG) Program.[24]
- *Pass the Justice for All Act.* Congress should pass and fully fund the Justice for All Reauthorization Act of 2010,[25] which includes enforcement authority for the Department's Civil Rights Division to address patterns and practice of constitutional failings in indigent defense systems, provides additional training and technical assistance to help states improve their systems and imposes a comprehensive planning requirement for the Byrne JAG Program which will require that defenders are included in the planning process.
- *Increase Federal Funding for Evidence-Based Research.* The federal government should fund evidence-based research on the delivery of legal services for the poor, including a review of international efforts to look at the impact of different models and levels of representation. Participants noted that evidence-based research is necessary because it is most effective in persuading special interest groups who do not support increased or enhanced defender services.
- *Require Better Data Collection.* The Department should collect data to better understand how effective representation can lead to safer and healthier communities, a fairer society and cost-savings by preventing unreasonable, ineffective or unnecessary incarceration. Participants suggested that the Department use its grant solicitation process to gather data on state and local indigent defense spending. One participant mentioned the strains felt by public defender offices in collecting data and suggested that the federal government fund software and technology improvements to assist these offices with case management and tracking as a way to address this problem.
- *File Amicus Curiae Briefs.* The Department should assist state and local defenders through the filing of amicus curiae briefs in support of legal positions taken by defenders and indigent criminal defendants in lawsuits challenging the delivery of legal services in criminal cases.
- *Fund Studies on Ombudsman Offices.* The Department should fund studies on the success of ombudsman offices that oversee complaints related to public defender issues to assess whether to establish a federal ombudsman office. Participants

suggested that the Department fund studies on how these types of offices are created and their effectiveness.

- *Launch Effective Public Relations Campaign.* The federal government should launch a public relations campaign publicizing the results of indigent defense research to help change public perception on the need for criminal defense. Participants noted that publicizing exonerations has helped increase awareness of the potential for wrongful convictions. Similarly, they noted the importance of educating judges and prosecutors (and defenders) about client-based indigent defense systems and their benefits. Participants stressed the need to assess the points of view of judges and prosecutors to map a strategy to create support for reform and change that is beneficial for indigent defendants.
- *Study the Effectiveness of Standards for Criminal Defense.* The Department should study the effects of implementing and enforcing standards on criminal defense, which have been in existence for nearly forty years.[26]
- *Increase Federal Funding for Research Specifically to Examine Costs.* The Department should fund research to examine the amount states are spending on indigent defense, corrections, law enforcement and prosecution. Potential research questions include: How much is the federal government giving the states through various grants? What are the disparities in funding?

It should be noted that all of these recommendations were repeated in some fashion at different points in the convening.

COSTS ASSOCIATED WITH BEING INDIGENT IN THE CRIMINAL JUSTICE SYSTEM

The next session explored the economic and non-economic costs associated with incarcerating and sentencing low-income individuals convicted of crimes.

Participants discussed the high incarceration rate in the United States, how delinquent youth are handled across systems, the impact of race, the impact of profit motive and the consequences of plea bargaining. The EWG focused on how poverty amplifies these issues and the costs associated with sentences such as the death penalty.

Rates of Incarceration

One researcher provided an overview of the incarceration rate in the United States, which is the highest in the world. Since the mid-1970s, the rate of incarcerating individuals in the United States has increased by well over 300 percent, from around 170 per 100,000 population to 750 per 100,000 population.[27] It was also reported that smaller, but similar changes have taken place in Australia, New Zealand and the United Kingdom.

But divergent trends also exist. Canada‘s prisoner rates have remained more or less constant, while several Western European countries, such as Germany, France, Switzerland and Belgium, have rates below 100 per 100,000 population.[28] And the Nordic countries —

Finland, Denmark, Norway and Sweden — have low rates which vary between 60 and 75 per 100,000 population.[29]

The EWG discussed the reasons for the difference in these rates. One expert argued that the difference could not be explained by rates of crime or victimization in the United States, but suggested it could be the result of weak social welfare policies. In countries with lower rates of incarceration, the disparities in wealth tend to be lower and social welfare programs tend to be more widely available. Therefore, political culture, including trust in government, might explain part of this disparity. But the expert stressed that this would not account for the whole of the disparity between the United States and other Western countries. Instead, it was suggested that the punitive nature of the American public, as well as issues related to race, ethnicity and social discrimination might account for these differences.

As to race, the EWG discussed the disparities in the rate of incarceration based on the race of the offender. A researcher suggested that —ethnic fractionation," or the amount of ethnic diversity in a given society, is often cited as an explanation for differences in incarceration rates, but suggested that in his view political reasons often explain these differences.

The EWG discussed the differences in incarcerating juveniles across jurisdictions. One expert noted that in Finland, there are around five children aged 15 – 17 in prison, as compared to approximately 120 children in the 1970s.[30] This is generally attributed to changes in the child welfare system, including increased efforts to restrict custodial sentences for juveniles.

Another researcher noted that data related to juvenile justice systems in European institutions are often incomplete given the variations in methods used to detain children, such as detention centers, prisons, residential settings and children's homes. For example, placing children in detention centers in the Netherlands has significantly decreased during the past three years, but many of these children are now placed in other facilities while continuing to be deprived of their liberty.[31] So, in fact, the number of children in the criminal justice system continues to increase. The EWG agreed that the careful collection of such data is necessary to draw accurate conclusions.

The group discussed whether the fact that the United States uses private prison corporations might contribute to the fact that the United States has the highest rate of incarceration. It was confirmed by one expert that private prisons are not used anywhere else in the world on the same scale as in the United States. For example, there are no private prisons in Scandinavia, as this would be considered unconstitutional. And while the United Kingdom has some prisons managed by private organizations, these schemes operate in a manner to financially reward a reduction in recidivism.[32] Therefore, studying the use of private prisons would be an important contribution to understanding the unique situation in the United States.

The EWG also discussed the effect of plea bargaining on prison populations. One researcher noted that about 10 – 15 years ago in South Africa, many in that criminal justice community argued that plea bargaining was not available. But research revealed that it was in fact available to defendants with means, who were usually white. As a result of that research and the publicity it generated,[33] the South African Law Reform Commission began to provide trainings to attorneys on how to plea bargain effectively. Interestingly, in Finland there is no plea bargaining, but there are sentencing rules to guide the judge, including criteria for mitigating and aggravating factors such as those related to equity or mercy. Similarly, in the

United Kingdom, there is no plea bargaining, but a defendant can ask for an early indication from the judge as to whether the sentence would be custodial or noncustodial. A defendant can also have a —basis of a plea," where the prosecution and defense stipulate to the core agreed facts, but judges do not have to accept this. Defendants can receive discounts in sentences for early pleas and sentences are generally reduced by a third if defendants plead guilty at the first hearing. The government is considering increasing that to half if defendants plead at the earliest stage, i.e., at the police precinct.

Measuring Costs

The EWG also discussed the process of measuring costs associated with indigent defense. One participant cited a number of studies produced by the Open Society Justice Initiative (OSJI), which examined the cost of detentions in Mexico and Argentina.[34] These studies looked at costs to the state, the individual, the family and the community.

OSJI is also studying the defender systems in Sierra Leone, Ukraine and Indonesia and identified socioeconomic arguments that could be ripe for measurement.[35] In Sierra Leone, OSJI is piloting the use of community-based paralegals to provide legal advice at police stations. Community-based paralegals can be trained and employed more cheaply than trained lawyers.[36] They can also create cost-savings to the community by decreasing the length of pre-trial detention of individuals who would not otherwise obtain legal counsel.[37] (*See* Appendix A, International Practices, Community-based Paralegals in Africa.)

Another participant noted the development of access to justice measurements at institutions like the University of Tilburg in the Netherlands. Such efforts have begun to measure the private costs that people spend on justice, the quality of the procedure and their perceptions of outcomes.[38] The methodology is being tested in a variety of countries and is also being applied to victims of crime. Ultimately, finding how people think about and perceive justice, including its costs, can lead to better assessments of different models.

Participants turned to discussions on the measuring of costs in a statewide public defender office through the development of caseload standards and the impact of austerity measures on criminal legal aid in England and Wales, where the criminal and civil legal aid schemes have historically been considered strong.

Developing Caseload Standards in Maryland

The EWG next discussed the importance of alleviating high caseloads through better management and staffing of public defender offices. One researcher detailed a 2005 attorney and staff workload assessment of the Maryland Office of the Public Defender (OPD) by the National Center for State Courts (NCSC). [39]

OPD was tasked by the Maryland Legislative and Executive branches to develop caseload standards in order to establish its operating budget. To accomplish this task, OPD worked with NCSC to design a study to measure OPD's attorney and staffing assignments to assess its workload to ensure that the state fulfilled —its constitutional obligation to provide effective assistance of counsel.[40] NCSC designed a project that (1) compiled and inventoried the cases opened by OPD, (2) measured the amount of time that attorneys and staff spent on cases, (3) collected data on sufficiency of time to complete cases through surveys of attorneys and staff, (4) conducted site visits of OPD district offices, (5) convened focus groups of circuit court attorneys district court attorneys, juvenile court attorneys and statewide division attorneys and staff and (6) assigned recommended case weights that were ratified by the OPD Advisory Committee.[41] This project helped to establish recommended caseloads for OPD and importantly, the work had the support of the Maryland General Assembly and the Governor who understood that improving resources for defenders would benefit the criminal justice system.[42]

At the end of the assessment, NCSC found that the public defender office needed about 125 additional attorneys and about 69 additional staff members.[43] In 2003, the Maryland General Assembly and Governor endorsed a plan to provide additional staff to OPD over three consecutive years to address the excessive caseloads that prompted the study in the first place. Thus, in 2005 and 2006, OPD was already slated to hire an additional 62 attorneys and about 69 additional staff, partially meeting the need identified by the NCSC study.[44] The study helped educate policy makers about the overall need and made a stronger case for increasing OPD staffing levels. But as one researcher noted excessive caseloads still remain a problem for OPD —and as reported in the most recent OPD annual report available online, in FY 2008, OPD was "42% compliant (5 of 12 Districts) with Circuit Court caseload standards; 25% compliant (3 of 12 Districts2 with District Court caseload standards; and 42% compl i ant with Juvenile caseload standards." [45]

The EWG noted that implementing recommendations to improve offices like OPD often depends on funding considerations and collecting this data is an important first step in making the best case. The ABA's Standing Committee on Legal Aid and Indigent Defense (SCLAID) collected and posted data from all 50 states and the District of Columbia.[46] Maintaining this information is important and participants agreed that finding such data was much easier when it was collected from a central state agency as opposed to municipalities and local jurisdictions.

Both the practitioners and researchers of the EWG also agreed that basic terms such as "case" and "caseload" must be defined consistently across systems and amongst the prosecutor and defender communities to create better comparative data and to assess inefficiencies in resources.

The EWG discussed the impact of plea bargaining on lightening caseloads and whether there is a tendency to plea bargain away cases because of difficulty in the case or under-staffing. A need for better case management systems in public defense systems and in the courts was identified, which could collect data to assess reasons for case closures.

Many participants discussed the need to build quality of representation into workload studies, as was done in NCSC's assessment of OPD. One participant suggested that this could be accomplished by using the established standards on the delivery of defender services when assessing the effectiveness and quality of representation.

The Impact of Austerity Measures on the Legal Aid Scheme in England and Wales

The EWG discussed the criminal legal aid scheme in England and Wales and the impact of proposed austerity measures currently under consideration. The American members of the EWG were particularly interested in understanding the criminal legal aid scheme in the United Kingdom (and expressed similar interest in the United Kingdom's civil legal aid scheme) given the shared common law traditions between the two countries.[47]

As in the United States, criminal defendants in England and Wales have a right to a lawyer, paid for by the state and can choose to retain a private attorney if they can afford one.

In England and Wales, the legal profession is divided between solicitors and barristers—and each have a role in the provision of legal aid on both the defender and prosecutor sides. Lawyers who seek to perform publicly funded work as defense counsel or as prosecutors enter into a competitive process for such contracts, which often leads to highly qualified and experienced attorneys being engaged in the process. Moreover, defense attorneys and prosecutors are compensated at roughly the same levels. It should be noted that while this compensation is generally an adequate salary, it is often less than what can be earned in the private sector.

In the context of criminal legal aid, solicitors can represent defendants in the lower courts, while barristers along with solicitors represent defendants in more serious cases in the Crown Court.[48] Interestingly, barristers also serve as prosecutors and the private bar performs the vast majority of this work, with a percentage handled by public prosecutors employed by the Crown Prosecution Service.[49]

When serving as defense counsel, the barrister‘s paramount duty is to the court and proper administration of justice with a secondary duty to the defendant, although defense counsel is charged with securing an acquittal for her client. When serving as a prosecutor in a criminal trial, the barrister‘s role is to present the case fairly and impartially, not to secure a conviction.

Since the 1940s the state has funded the most vulnerable in society in cases involving crimes or family disputes.[50] One participant noted that as a policy matter, the government of the United Kingdom has supported the need for proper defense. In fact, as a signatory to the European Convention on Human Rights, the United Kingdom has acknowledged legal aid as a human right.[51]

The government‘s commitment to funding both criminal and civil legal aid is often cited as an exemplar of state funded legal aid schemes. While legal aid in the United Kingdom is not administered centrally across all four of its constituent countries, funding for legal aid in England and Wales is run by the independent Legal Services Commission.[52] In 2010, the budget for civil and criminal legal aid exceeded £2 billion or approximately $3 billion, but by the 2014-15 funding year, as a result of austerity measures put in place by the government across all agencies, the Ministry of Justice‘s budget (where legal aid resides) will be cut by 23 percent.[53] Thus, legal aid in England and Wales will have to undergo some substantial changes.

Before reforms are implemented, the government is required to perform a mandatory impact assessment, including their impact on ethnic minorities and indigent defendants. The government will also attempt to quantify the economic impact of cutting funds for advocates.[54]

These assessments are considering the following questions:

- What are the fundamental concerns that justify state-funded legal representation? For example, violence, loss of liberty, the welfare of children, the loss of a dwelling?
- Should means-testing be introduced for criminal legal aid?
- How can the Government introduce more efficient and competitive systems for distribution of legal aid?
- How can criminal trials be more cost efficient?

- Should family disputes (e.g., concerning access to children) be resolved by judges, or could they be better and (more cheaply) resolved through mediation?

The government had also been considering how to reduce the prison population. In December, the Ministry of Justice issued a proposal to reduce its current prison population of 85,000 by 3,000 in four years,[55] which could result in substantial cost-savings. But in June 2011, the Ministry of Justice abandoned this proposal.[56] Predicting this outcome, one participant noted that the pressure on cutting legal aid funding will intensify.

In an effort to reduce civil legal aid costs, the government is preparing to overhaul civil justice to make the pursuit of claims cheaper and is seeking to introduce new forms of private funding like U.S.-style contingency fee agreements.[57] In late June, the government unveiled its Legal Aid, Sentencing and Punishment of Offenders Bill, which upon enactment will implement many of these changes.[58]

Broader concerns include whether cuts i n legal aid will seriously impair access to justice and whether in practice downgrading legal aid will cause "ripple" effects (and costs) through the administration of justice.

The Death Penalty

The EWG concluded the discussion of costs with an examination of the death penalty in the United States, which is a unique practice among Western and commonwealth countries. One expert noted that while there is a growing cultural distaste for executions, there is a political inability to abolish death sentencing, which has resulted in a capital legal process in the United States that is cumbersome, slow and extremely expensive.

One expert cited the Brian Nichols courthouse shootings as an example of the inefficiencies in capital cases. That one case in Georgia drained both the financial and political resources of a newly launched statewide public defender system that had taken many years of effort to create. [59]

He further noted that in federal death penalty cases that reach trial, median defense costs now approach nearly half a million dollars per defendant, and federal cases where substantially less money is spent on the defense have been shown to have a much higher likelihood of ending in a death sentence.[60] Most state courts (where the vast majority of such cases are prosecuted) compensate defense counsel for death penalty cases at rates lower than the federal courts, and the death-sentencing rates of many of these jurisdictions are much higher.[61]

The EWG also discussed the usefulness of research examining the outcomes of capital cases as compared to the amount of money spent and the independence of the defense. Examining these correlations would help assess whether life or death in the American capital punishment system turns on the level of these resources and their allocation, and how lawyers are appointed, trained and organized in capital cases. One participant gave as an example the action taken by Virginia, which historically has had the second highest execution rate in the United States behind Texas. About three years ago, the commonwealth added regional defender offices to handle the majority of its capital cases. Interestingly, since that time, Virginia has not sent anyone to death row.[62]

These new offices have been economical and carry a degree of independence,[63] which has been recognized as very important both by the ABA's Ten Principles of a Public Defense Delivery System[64] and by the U.S. Supreme Court.[65]

The expert suggested that by abandoning the death penalty as a viable sentence, the cost-savings to the defense system would be tremendous and the savings could be placed back into defender services to improve the quality of defense for all defendants, regardless of potential sentence. He noted a need for further research to test the relationship between a jurisdiction's indigent defense practices and its rates of death sentences and executions. Another participant suggested that research should be conducted to determine whether states which have eliminated the death penalty use the savings from not carrying out the sentence to provide better defender services.

The great expense associated with death penalty cases stems at least in part from the Supreme Court's insistence on especially high levels of accuracy and fairness in the process by which the death penalty is imposed in any given case. While this insistence has flagged at times over the 35 years of the modern use of capital punishment, recent exonerations of death row inmates appear to have renewed judicial and public support for special care in death penalty litigation.

The group agreed that absent a comparable focus on the quality of indigent defender services for non-capital cases, providing adequate resources to the relatively few death penalty cases may have the effect of further impoverishing the criminal defense system as a whole. It was suggested that such imbalances should be recognized as a previously unnoticed cost of the death penalty in the United States.

Recommendations

The breakout group on costs provided the following recommendations:

1. *Increase Federal Funding for Defender Services.* The Department should increase funding for defender services and assess how funding for indigent defense is distributed through the Byrne JAG Program.
2. *Establish a Federal Clearinghouse.* The Department should establish a federal clearinghouse or center to promote quality indigent defense, best practices and promising approaches.
3. *Fund Studies on the Effectiveness of Standards for Criminal Defense.* The Department should fund studies on the cost of implementing national indigent defense standards together with the cost savings that could result from that implementation.
4. *Study Incarceration Rates across States.* Based on the compelling discussion of disparities in incarceration rates across countries, the Department should perform a study comparing the states with the lowest incarceration rates to the states with the highest rates and identify possible reasons for these differences.
5. *Fund Research on the Effect of Timing of Appointment of Counsel.* Given the lack of information about the attendant fiscal implications, the Department should fund research on the economic impact of the timing of when counsel enters a case from the earliest stage of a criminal investigation (i.e., at the police station during interrogation) on the criminal justice system.

6. *Fund Studies on Recidivism.* The Department should fund studies on the types of charges which generate the highest levels of recidivism and whether incarceration or length of incarceration associated with particular charges (such as non-violent drug offenses) actually increases recidivism.
7. *Fund Research on the Opportunities to Retrain Correctional Personnel.* Should efforts to lower rates of incarceration be successful, correctional personnel would suffer a loss in job opportunities. Therefore, the Department should fund research to assess which careers correctional personnel can transition to most easily.

IMPROVEMENTS TO THE PROVISION OF DEFENDER SERVICES FOR THE POOR

In the next session, the EWG considered innovations that have improved the provision of defender services to low-income individuals both domestically and abroad.

Discussion focused on the benefits and costs of more fully integrating private attorneys into the defense bar as in the United Kingdom, possible lessons which could be learned from recent developments in Eastern and Central Europe, the American holistic defense model and the variety of approaches for the provision of defender services taken by the international criminal tribunals.

The Role of the Private Bar in the Delivery of Defender Services

One expert encouraged the development of programs in which private lawyers are substantially involved in delivering indigent defense services in the United States, similar to the system in place in the United Kingdom. The ABA has recognized the need for the involvement of the private bar and has taken the position that public defender offices should only be established when a sufficient number of cases justify these programs.[66] He asserted that without involving the private bar, legal challenges to caseloads will remain a constant. Also, competition introduced through the private bar creates incentives to perform strong representation in order to gain more client referrals, as is the case in England.[67]

In response to this proposal, the EWG discussed the necessity of providing good monitoring, training and certification processes for private bar members. The San Mateo County Bar Association was highlighted as an organization that effectively trains private bar members to represent indigent criminal defendants through its Private Defender Program.[68]

The EWG also discussed the impact of private bar members who become involved in indigent defense. Private bar members can be effective lobbyists to improve access to quality counsel from the earliest instance in a case and can speak against regressive legislation, such as those concerning the death penalty. But it was noted that private bar members are sometimes limited by the interests of their other clients or by their preference to avoid unpopular causes.

Some practitioners noted that private bar members may be willing to provide monetary contributions or pro bono representation, but in general may not be willing to advocate for legislative change. One notable exception is in Massachusetts, where the Committee for

Public Counsel Services, a 15-member committee which oversees the provision of defender services for the poor, has successfully included private attorneys who help to advocate for meaningful change.

The federal defender system was also suggested as a model. It typically has better funding and better private panel representation so that when the federal defender appoints or designates a panel lawyer to handle a case, the client receives effective representation. Moreover, the federal defender office can serve as a resource for private panel attorneys assigned to federal cases, which was cited as one of the reasons the Federal Defender Office for the District of Alaska was created.

In the Eastern European context, moving public defenders into a stronger alliance with the private bar has shifted dynamics such that defenders have begun to feel a stronger connection to the profession and thus guided by ethical responsibilities and standards – improving representation.

The EWG noted two issues concerning the use of private bar members as counsel to indigent defendants: (1) ensuring quality control; and (2) appropriately distributing cases between the private bar and public defender community. Therefore, public-private partnerships, where public defender offices work with private attorneys, and the use of pro bono services in this field should be examined anew to assess these concerns.

Criminal Legal Aid in Central and Eastern Europe

The EWG discussed efforts in the European Union and Central and Eastern Europe over the past decade to reform the criminal legal aid system. In 2003, the European Commission, in an effort to establish minimum procedural safeguards for defendants in criminal proceedings within the European Union, issued a statement that while all the rights needed to ensure a fair trial are important, some rights are so fundamental that they should be given priority status.[69] The first priority was the right to legal advice and assistance. If accused individuals have no lawyer, they are less likely to be read their rights and therefore to have those rights respected. This right was deemed necessary to the protection of all other rights. But in 2007, the Commission's work in this area was stopped as it was opposed by several member states.[70] Private advocacy groups decided to carry on this work and provided evidence which documented the degree to which defense rights were provided in practice by member states.[71]

These organizations argued that effective criminal defense is an integral aspect of the right to a fair trial and that it requires not only the right to competent legal assistance, but also legislative support, an organizational structure and a robust legal and professional culture. However good the assistance of counsel is, it will not be enough if the other essential elements are missing.

In the 2008 European Court of Human Rights decision of *Salduz v. Turkey*, the court held that Article 6.1 of the European Convention on Human Rights requires a lawyer to be present from the first time a suspect is interrogated by police, unless it is demonstrated that there are compelling reasons to restrict the right.[72] Prior to *Salduz*, most of the countries in Europe had not recognized this right or if they had, it was not put into practice. As a result of this decision, a number of countries have begun to introduce reforms to implement this requirement. For example, France and Scotland have begun the practice of providing legal advice in police stations during and even before a suspect's first interrogation. Currently the European Union is implementing its criminal justice agenda aimed at adoption of legislative measures for strengthening rights of defendants in criminal proceedings, which includes guaranteeing the right of a suspect to speak with a lawyer.[73]

A participant noted that the right to an attorney during an investigation has been recognized in the United States for decades and thus can serve as a model for European countries' efforts as they establish this practice.

Holistic Defense

The EWG next considered holistic approaches to defense – that is, the use of community-based offices which employ a diverse group of professionals (e.g., criminal defense lawyers, investigators, social workers and civil legal service providers) to assist clients with legal and in many cases extra-legal needs. Such a model considers the needs of clients beyond the individual criminal case, with an eye towards addressing the problems that may have led to the individual's arrest including drug addiction or mental health issues. Holistic defender offices, with strong ties to the communities in which they are located and serve, are often advocates for systemic reforms in the criminal justice system that can help break the cycle of arrest and incarceration that have particularly burdened low-income and minority communities.

It was noted that the holistic defender offices are often considered to be more expensive than other types of defender offices. However, overhead costs may be lowered by bringing all services under one roof, and there is some evidence to suggest that clients of holistic defender offices have lower incarceration and recidivism rates as compared to those served by traditional offices.[74] Additional research is needed to effectively evaluate the costs and savings of these offices.

Defender Services in the International Criminal System

The EWG also considered the approaches to the provision of defender services in the international criminal system. One participant provided an overview of the development of defender services in the post-Nuremberg era of international criminal law. He provided an overview of all of the more recently created international tribunals and courts and the evolving placement of the defense unit within these bodies.[75]

Starting with the ad hoc United Nations tribunals for the former Yugoslavia and Rwanda, he explained that the defense unit is separate from the other workings of the tribunals.[76] In these two institutions, the tribunals simply maintain a roster of defense attorneys who have met basic criteria, from which an accused can choose, and who will be compensated from the tribunals'operating budgets. The more recent international courts have refined this approach and the International Criminal Court,[77] the Special Court for Sierra Leone[78] and the Extraordinary Chambers in the Courts of Cambodia[79] have all been formed with an independent defense institution located within the court. These offices certify the defense counsel who can appear before these courts and administer payment of counsel and their teams. These offices also provide limited oversight of case management. And courts monitor action plans to ensure that the attorneys' fees being paid by these bodies are reasonable and appropriate.

The most recently created tribunal, the Special Tribunal for Lebanon, has similarly established an independent institution within the court for defender services, but with even more autonomy than the other courts described.[80] The head of this office is organizationally at the level of a court registrar, which is believed to strengthen the office and increase its independence. Again, defense attorneys must be certified to practice in this court and in fact, the certification process is even more rigorous than in the other courts—requiring applicants to pass an hour-long panel interview. While the case work of this court is still at the very earliest stages, it is envisioned that in addition to the defendant's lawyer, the defender services office of the tribunal will submit briefs on behalf of the accused to maximize the rights for the accused. However, it is unclear what will happen if defense counsel and the defender services office disagree on the theory of the case.

Recommendations

The breakout group on general improvements provided the following recommendations:

1. *Decriminalization.* The federal government should focus on decriminalizing certain conduct in order to decrease pressure on the system and the need for massive funding.
2. *Adopt Enforceable Standards for Criminal Defense.* The Department should create federal enforceable standards, based on the standards produced by the National Advisory Commission on Criminal Justice Standards and Goals, the National Legal Aid and Defender Association and the American Bar Association, which would improve the work of public defenders and outcomes for their clients.
3. *Increase Federal Funding for Cost-Savings Research.* The Department should fund research to study the economic impact of legal aid and public defender offices. Such research should examine the role and involvement of defense attorneys at different stages in a case.
4. *Study the Effects of Competition among the Defender Bar.* The Department should fund research to consider the impact of competition among the defender bar. Specifically, the research should examine involvement of the private bar and paralegals in the provision of services and how competition can be used to improve the system rather than create additional problems.
5. *Fund Research on the Changing Role of Public Defenders.* The Department should fund research to study the changing role of public defenders, including their workloads, responsibilities and expectations.

THE INTERSECTION OF INDIGENT DEFENSE AND IMMIGRATION

The EWG next discussed the collateral consequences of a criminal conviction for immigrants. The participants discussed the recent Supreme Court decision of *Padilla v. Kentucky* and how best to implement it. The group also discussed alternatives developed by the European regional human rights system and one of its member-states, Sweden.

Immigration Assistance for Indigent Defenders: The Requirements of Padilla

The EWG discussed the 2010 U.S. Supreme Court case of *Padilla v. Kentucky*,[81] which held that defense attorneys must inform their clients of the immigration consequences of a criminal conviction, if those consequences are clear (and, if not clear, that a conviction may have adverse immigration consequences). However, one participant remarked that a potential problem with *Padilla* is that it may never be implemented or followed if the resources required by the decision are not made available. Moreover, defense attorneys must have an adequate understanding of immigration law to know whether or not the immigration consequences are clear.

One expert suggested that *Padilla* could best be implemented through training, the distribution of written reference materials[82] and through consultations with immigration lawyers. He discussed three models that public defender offices could follow for providing and delivering immigration support:

- The *central model*, where an immigration expert is centrally located in the town, city or state and can provide training and reference materials and offer consultation to several different public defender offices.
- The *in-house model*, where the public defender office has an in-house immigration expert. (The EWG discussed this model in detail and a lengthier discussion follows below.)
- The *contract model,* where the public defender office contracts with a nonprofit immigration office to provide these services within a jurisdiction.

The EWG remarked that *Padilla* is legally significant because courts in the United States have resisted recognizing the legal significance of collateral consequences in criminal cases.[83] The group discussed the possibility that *Padilla* may open the door to a discussion about other collateral consequences in criminal cases, including those related to voting, access to entitlements, firearm ownership and professional certification. The group agreed that it is important for public defenders to be able to advise their clients of all collateral consequences, but this is often difficult without training. Participants also indicated a belief that advising on collateral consequences, especially in terms of immigration, should be factored into any defender workload analyses.

The EWG agreed that the NIJ-funded ABA National Study on the Collateral Consequences of Criminal Convictions is a good resource on this issue.[84] The project has catalogued an average of 700 statutes per state or territory that impose collateral consequences on people convicted of crimes.[85] In fact, the Attorney General has sent a letter to every state attorney general asking them to review these collateral consequences and decide which ones are truly necessary for public safety.[86]

The EWG agreed that *Padilla's* placement of the burden on defense counsel rather than on judges was the correct approach. Counsel are in the best position to know the citizenship status of defendants, and attorneys should assess the immigration consequences of any strategy in a criminal case from the very start.

Participants also felt that the advice covered by *Padilla* should include plea negotiation and post-plea advice because that would help clients to understand the process.

They also felt that it is important to be creative in terms of resources, specifically examining whether there are academic institutions, nonprofits or private immigration attorneys that will work with the public defender office to provide immigration services.

The EWG discussed the unresolved issues from *Padilla*, namely whether it extends to representation of juveniles and whether a defender is obligated to determine citizenship status of his or her clients. It was agreed that these were areas that would likely become clearer as the law continues to develop.

The opportunity for public defenders to exert pressure on judges in this area was discussed. One participant noted that some judges ask the immigration status of defendants on the record. Given the public policy arguments against that practice, she urged public defenders to intervene when judges ask these questions.

Additionally, she cautioned that defenders should continue to advise their clients on all matters, including immigration, even when judges attempt to offer such advice. She suggested that when defenders work with prosecutors, they should consider whether there could be a plea which would avoid deportation and still serve the interests of justice.

Participants agreed that there is an economic argument to *Padilla*. If clients get effective representation earlier on in their case, they are less likely to seek postconviction remedies for ineffective assistance of counsel, which can be quite costly.

They felt that if researchers could gather the data and evidence which could back these assertions, it could help encourage the deployment of resources that *Padilla* requires.

The group also discussed the need for adequate interpreter services in defender offices, which is often a necessity in cases involving immigrants. Participants noted that many courts incorrectly take the position that these costs should be passed on to the defendant.[87]

In-House Immigration Experts

The EWG discussed the use of in-house immigration experts at length. At the center of this discussion was the concept of community-oriented, holistic defense.

As in the general discussion of community-oriented defense, participants discussed the costs arguments associated with additional resources in a defender office that practices holistic defense—here, an immigration law expert. But again, participants agreed that the overall cost savings outweighed any initial outputs, such as an expert's salary. The costs saved in not having to train all defenders in the complexities of immigration law could offset the salary of an immigration law expert. Moreover, an immigration law expert can assess immigration issues far more efficiently than criminal defense attorneys.

But participants cautioned that such a model may not be appropriate for all settings. For example, it might not be cost-effective to hire a full-time immigration law expert for a small, rural office. Thus, immigration organizations that help to provide this expertise are equally important, and funding should be increased for these entities. Participants also suggested that factors such as the number of immigrant clients whom a defender office serves and the range of services provided could help determine whether an in-house expert is needed.

An alternative that was discussed was the use of immigration law fellows as in-house experts. For example, fellows like those employed by the Bronx Defenders, could help build a network of trained individuals who can work with both the civil legal aid community and the public defender community.

International Approaches to Immigration and Criminal Law

Participants discussed the expulsion and deportation of convicted criminals from the perspective of the European regional human rights system and under Swedish law. The European Court of Human Rights and Swedish law consider removal a deprivation of liberty, and, thus, balance a number of interests when determining whether to deport an immigrant who has committed a crime. A number of these provisions require the court to consider the length of stay in the country and the person's ties to the country, especially family ties. In Sweden, if a person has been legally in the country for longer than five years the court will not expel him or her, except under exceptional circumstances.[88] (*See* Appendix A, International Practices, Alternative Practices Related to Immigration and Indigent Defense.)

The EWG remarked that these are very different practices than what is in play in the United States. One participant noted that American immigration law does not consider deportation to be —punishment,|| nor in many cases does it allow for consideration of individualized circumstances, as in the examples from Europe. She pointed to the 1996 Illegal Immigration Reform and Immigrant Responsibility Act as the primary reason for this approach.[89] The law instituted mandatory detention and deportation of immigrants who committed any crime, ranging from a misdemeanor to a felony. The lack of discretion leads to mandatory deportation without consideration of such factors as military service, length of residency in the United States and whether children or other family members are U.S. citizens. This reality makes the *Padilla* decision all the more important—in order to serve their clients, defenders must consider these rigid and severe immigration consequences when developing strategy.

Recommendations

The breakout group on immigration provided the following recommendations:

1. *Fund Public Defender Offices that Provide Immigration Expertise.* The federal government should fund pilot projects of the various immigration defender models (e.g., in-house model, central model and contract model).
2. *Fund Long-Term Studies on the Different Immigration Public Defender Models.* The federal government should fund long-term studies to identify the cost effectiveness of the various public defender models that provide immigration expertise in light of *Padilla* and how they improve the efficiency of the justice system (by, for example, decreasing the resources needed for litigating ineffective assistance of counsel claims).
3. *Expand Legal Orientation Programs.* The federal government should expand legal orientation programs for individuals held in criminal or immigration custody, especially when they are detained in remote facilities. *Know Your Rights* presentations and direct representation (particularly for youth and the mentally disabled who are unlikely to be able to represent themselves even with such presentations) are extremely important and should be expanded.
4. *Adopt International Human Rights Standards.* The United States should ratify the Convention on the Rights of the Child, the American Convention on Human Rights and submit to the jurisdiction of the Inter-American Court of Human Rights to enable individuals to access international mechanisms for relief of human rights violations.

IMPROVEMENTS IN INDIGENT DEFENSE FOR JUVENILES

The EWG next discussed juvenile indigent defense in the United States and possible improvements to the system. Participants discussed international law and standards on children's rights, specifically the obligations imposed by the Convention on the Rights of the Child. Participants also discussed alternative and innovative practices occurring around the world in places struggling with a lack of resources for juvenile defense.

The State of Juvenile Justice in the United States

The EWG discussed the —kids for cash" scandal, a judicial corruption scandal involving juveniles in Luzerne County, Pennsylvania uncovered by the Juvenile Law Center.[90] In February 2011, former state Judge Mark Ciavarella was convicted of sending hundreds of children to a private detention center in return for payment from that facility. The fact that these juveniles waived their right to counsel allowed Judge Ciavarella's to easily overlook whether a child's plea was knowing and voluntary. This case received widespread, international attention. One participant noted that the reason for the particularly high publicity may have been due to the fact that the majority of the affected children were white.[91]

Whether every child should have an unwaivable right to counsel, as supported by the National Juvenile Defender Center and National Legal Aid and Defender Association principles, was discussed at length.[92] The consensus was that not only should children have such a right (or at least not be permitted to waive their right until they have had a meaningful consultation with a lawyer), they should have lawyers at all stages of delinquency proceedings.

The EWG also discussed whether states should presume that all juveniles are indigent. Pennsylvania is moving towards this presumption with a growing consensus that a child's right to counsel should not depend on his parents' determination of whether they can or should retain an attorney.

Another issue discussed was the reality of children being tried as adults. Article 37 of the Convention on the Rights of the Child (CRC) states that children who are under 18 should not be tried in the adult system.[93] However, in the United States, children are waived into the adult system and represented by defenders who have limited practice in representing children. The EWG expressed concerns that such defenders often do not have a background in adolescent development, have access to juvenile experts, know how to make use of public safety arguments and know how to keep the children in juvenile court. One of the challenges is to get nonjuvenile defenders to care about and understand these issues and not consider juvenile cases as —practice|| for their cases involving adults. One participant noted that research that compared the work of defenders representing adults to their efforts representing children would be informative.

Another participant noted that placing juvenile defense services in the adult public defender offices can create conflict issues. For example, at the conclusion of a criminal case, these offices often cannot represent these same clients in related family court proceedings necessary to reunify families because of conflicts' concerns. The EWG noted that specialized juvenile defender units in public defender offices, like the one that exists in the Philadelphia

Public Defender's Office, are a good model and not only ensure that the defenders have the expertise needed to represent juveniles, but also eliminates these conflicts' issues by insulating the attorneys who work on juvenile matters from others in the office.

One participant recommended that juvenile advocates should perform outreach to public defender agencies noting that many of these offices do not prioritize juvenile defense or recognize the need for specialized expertise.

Improving Juvenile Defense in the United States

The EWG next considered improvements to juvenile defense. One participant identified that a key component to the difficulties that exist in this field is the pressure for juvenile defenders to behave like counsel in child welfare matters. And while the lawyers and judges are often the same in the delinquency and dependency contexts, the rules, laws, duties, and standards of proof are different.

A positive development for improving juvenile defense has been the launch of the Juvenile Indigent Defense Action Network (JIDAN) in 2008.[94] JIDAN aims to develop and implement new solutions to improve indigent defense for juveniles and is an —issue-focused forum for the development and exchange of ideas and strategies across states, and for sharing practical information and expertise in support of reform.|| [95] It operates in eight states and works to improve access to counsel and to create juvenile defense resource centers.[96] The network is looking at issues of getting counsel at detention hearings, promoting legislation that establishes a presumption of indigence, ending routine, indiscriminate shackling of youth, creating developmentally friendly judicial colloquies, working with law schools on postdetention work and creating Web-based case management systems and collateral consequences checklists.

And like other individuals caught in the criminal justice system, juveniles can benefit tremendously from a holistic approach to solve the problems that created their delinquent behavior. In the juvenile setting, the more resources that are available to children at the beginning of their troubles, their chances of obtaining better long-term outcomes increases. Poor children and their families often are unable to advocate for themselves; therefore, juvenile representation should not be limited to delinquency issues. For example, children often need lawyers to obtain lawful entitlements, such as education services, mental health services, immigration-related services and housing.

In fact, many federal resources exist for children. The U.S. Department of Health and Human Services Administration for Children and Families funds programs that provide services for children and for families of children in abuse or neglect proceedings.

In addition, if children who manifest mental illness or substance abuse are identified at an early stage, delinquency issues might be prevented. Thus, it was suggested that community defenders should reach out to schools and provide training to school nurses and teachers to assist them in identifying these problems. Such training could help schools identify children who are at risk before behavioral problems take root and the children enter the criminal justice system. As a more sympathetic population, more help is available for children than for adults. Moreover, improvements for children in the criminal justice system can lead to improvements for the entire system. The EWG noted that this was a phenomenon found in many countries.

International Legal Standards: Legal Assistance for Detained Children

The EWG discussed international human rights standards and the importance of lawyers for juveniles in the international system. In particular, the EWG discussed the international obligation to provide legal and other appropriate assistance to children who are detained by a state under Article 37 of the CRC, which requires state parties to ensure:

a) No child shall be subjected to torture or other cruel, inhuman or degrading treatment or punishment. Neither capital punishment nor life imprisonment without possibility of release shall be imposed for offences committed by persons below eighteen years of age;
b) No child shall be deprived of his or her liberty unlawfully or arbitrarily. The arrest, detention or imprisonment of a child shall be in conformity with the law and shall be used only as a measure of last resort and for the shortest appropriate period of time;
c) Every child deprived of liberty shall be treated with humanity and respect for the inherent dignity of the human person, and in a manner which takes into account the needs of persons of his or her age. In particular, every child deprived of liberty shall be separated from adults unless it is considered in the child's best interest not to do so and shall have the right to maintain contact with his or her family through correspondence and visits, save in exceptional circumstances;
d) *Every child deprived of his or her liberty shall have the right to prompt access to legal and other appropriate assistance*, as well as the right to challenge the legality of the deprivation of his or her liberty before a court or other competent, independent and impartial authority, and to a prompt decision on any such action.[97]

The CRC recognizes the importance of lawyers, who can help juveniles challenge the legality of their detention and even identify alternatives to detention. And importantly, while the child is detained, the lawyer can significantly contribute to the overall objective of a juvenile justice intervention: reintegrating the child into society.[98] Indeed, lawyers serve as liaisons between children and their families in furtherance of Article 37(c)'s protection of a child's right to maintain contact with his family while detained, unless it runs counter to the best interests of the child.

Participants also noted that Article 37(d) recognizes a holistic approach in helping detained children by confirming a right to both legal *and* other appropriate assistance. While the standard has not been read to guarantee access to all important services for children, such as education, international experts noted that the standard is in line with the holistic approaches discussed during the course of the workshop. The EWG also discussed the applicability of Article 37 in immigration cases. The two leading European Court of Human Rights cases concerning the detention of immigrant minors concerned practice in Belgium.[99] While not concerning right to counsel, these cases concerned the use of detention for immigration purposes and the necessity of detaining minors in expulsion cases. These cases confirmed that the article's scope is broad and can serve as an important tool in immigration cases. (Article 5 of the European Convention on Human Rights, which concerns the deprivation of liberty, is another relevant provision in this context.) One researcher described the ABA's Rule of Law Initiative's (ABA ROLI) assessment methodology, which considers how to assess judges, lawyers and adherence to international conventions based on international standards. ABA ROLI developed a detention procedures assessment methodology, which allows individuals to examine resources on the right to counsel and detention procedures.[100] The assessments analyze the relevant laws and then look at practice using interviews and focus groups. It was suggested that this methodology and the reports completed to date could be useful in examining juvenile detention.[101]

The EWG stressed the need for the United States to ratify the CRC and emphasized its wide applicability.[102] One participant noted that the approximately 8,000 children who arrive unaccompanied in the United States and are detained pending an adjudication of their immigration status could benefit from the strong safeguards of Article 37—especially as it relates to the location of the detention facilities. Although the United States has become more responsive to the needs of these vulnerable children, the placement of the majority of these detention facilities within 250 miles of the United States southern border prevents many of these children from obtaining pro bono assistance. With the facilities located outside of most urban settings, there are not enough attorneys who are able to take on these children's cases pro bono.[103] The justification for the placement of these facilities near the border is that it eases the burden of transferring children between the U.S. Customs and Border Protection, which takes federal custody of the children, and the U.S. Department of Health and Human Services, which houses the children. Thus, if the CRC applied to these detained immigrant children, there would be increased pressure to place facilities in areas that could enable these children to access their right to counsel secured by Article 37.

Alternative Models for Juvenile Defense

One expert noted that the United States shares many of the same constraints and shortcomings as other countries in terms of access to justice for children who are in conflict with the law, but can learn much from the international community's efforts and should adopt international standards—like those flowing from the CRC.

He provided three common areas of concern for most countries and international responses that could provide guidance for the United States. The first is the lack of resources for juvenile defense. Generally, all legal aid systems are understaffed and all formal juvenile justice systems do not take sufficient advantage of informal dispute resolution and enforcement mechanisms as a means of addressing such resource shortfalls. Given that these resource constraints are unlikely to change in the near future, he suggested that new approaches that can augment resources to support the delivery of state-of-the-art services should be considered. Defender agencies are an integral part of this effort in many countries, such as in New Zealand and Canada. In other countries such as Malawi, Ghana, Uganda, Liberia and Sierra Leone, nonlawyers such as paralegals and community leaders are trained to deliver services to children in conflict with the law and to reduce recidivism. (*See* Appendix A, International Practices, Community-based Paralegals in Africa.) There may be certain tasks nonlawyers can perform in the United States without compromising the effectiveness of the representation of children in our juvenile courts.[104]

Another participant noted that in countries with very little resources for public defense, law school clinics are an important resource. More than offering a cost-saving alternative, these clinics can act as a service provider to communities with limited infrastructure. Legal clinics in South Africa funded by legal and were highlighted. (*See* Appendix A, International

Practices, Law School Clinics in South Africa.) But the EWG agreed that while it is important to think creatively in using alternative services, they should also proceed with caution because many public defender agencies might be tempted to use inexperienced lawyers, students or paralegals to handle juvenile cases.

The second common area shared across jurisdictions that the expert identified is the lack of due process protections and accurate fact-finding in juvenile cases. Because juvenile cases are often viewed as less "serious" than adult cases, and because in most jurisdictions, juvenile adjudications do not result in findings of "guilt," insufficient attention is paid to due process protections and accurate fact-finding.

The third area the expert identified is the over-institutionalization of youth. Formal juvenile justice systems rely too heavily on incarceration of youth, both pre- and post-trial and youth are often kept with adults in police stations, jails and prisons. He noted that other jurisdictions diverted children from juvenile courts to community-based mechanisms as a means of achieving better, more durable results while at the same time reducing pressure on juvenile courts.

In the context of learning from alternative practices in juvenile justice, the EWG also discussed the European Network of Ombudspersons for Children.[105] This network of 29 European countries provides important services for children, engages in lobbying efforts and shares information to encourage full implementation of the CRC's standards. It is an independent body that monitors the legal and systematic developments concerning children and provides independent monitoring at the local level. Like the South African Ombudsman discussed in Appendix A, these children-related offices can publicly scrutinize the government. It was suggested that such models be considered in the United States.

Recommendations

The breakout group on juveniles provided the following recommendations:

1. Issue Policy and Advisory Opinions. The Department should issue a range of policy positions or advisory opinions on juvenile justice to guide states to implement needed reforms, such as a general statement on the nature of juvenile defense, the inappropriateness of waiver of counsel by juveniles, the presumption of indigence of juveniles, the obligations of attorneys to their juvenile clients, the obligation to engage in holistic representation, the obligation for adequate resources for defense counsel and the recognition that the rights of adult defendants apply to juveniles.
2. Direct Grants Towards Innovations in Juvenile Defense. The Department should direct grants to catalyze innovation in juvenile defense and to force states to more evenly distribute federal funding throughout the criminal justice system. This should include grants to provide technical assistance for juvenile defenders and to increase data collection.
3. Fund Legal Representation for Unaccompanied Immigrant Children. The federal government should fund pilot projects to provide direct legal services for unaccompanied immigrant children in removal proceedings.
4. Fund Research on Holistic Defense and Diversion for Juveniles. The Department should fund research on the benefits of holistic representation for children, especially where positive youth development is incorporated. The Department should also fund

research on the cost effectiveness of diversion and decriminalization in the juvenile context.

5. Fund Research on Waiver of Counsel by Juveniles. The Department should fund research on waiver of counsel in juvenile cases. Research questions should include: Where are children waiving counsel and what are the rates of waiver? What are the outcome differences for jurisdictions that allow waiver as compared to those that do not? What are the benefits to public safety in providing juveniles with counsel? What are the cost savings for states when juveniles are represented?
6. Adopt International Human Rights Standards. The United States should ratify the United Nations Convention on the Rights of the Child and other international treaties addressing children and human rights, especially where the right to holistic defense is implicitly recognized.

INDIGENT DEFENSE IN INDIGENOUS COMMUNITIES

The EWG discussed the unique circumstances faced by indigenous communities in balancing traditional and Western forms of criminal justice. The group explored the recently enacted Tribal Law and Order Act and its possible effects on indigent defense in tribal communities, and discussed innovative partnerships between law schools and tribes like the Tribal Court Public Defense Clinic at the University of Washington. The EWG also examined restorative justice approaches as an alternative model to the adversarial criminal justice system and examined some of the practices of Canadian Aboriginal communities.

The Impact of the Tribal Law and Order Act on the Provision of Criminal Defense

One expert gave an overview of the recently enacted Tribal Law and Order Act (TLOA) and its effect on tribal justice systems.[106] The TLOA was intended to address a host of problems in the administration of justice in Indian Country, including lack of funding, the inability of tribes to prosecute serious offenses committed by Indians on tribal lands (and tribes' resulting inability to implement crime control at the tribal level), the complex web of overlapping jurisdictions and the perceived lack of accountability for crime in Indian Country at the federal level. The TLOA grew out of a desire of tribal governments to increase their autonomy and handle cases that would likely not be prosecuted federally. It should be noted that the TLOA does not impose more local control and jurisdiction over non-Indians, but it does put more accountability on the federal government to do its job in prosecuting those cases.

Historically, many criminal defense attorneys were opposed to allowing tribes to prosecute criminal cases because many tribes did not have the capacity to provide defender services. Section 202 of the TLOA accounts for this concern by allowing for enhanced sentencing only when tribal governments can provide substantive and procedural safeguards, including lawyers for indigent clients who face incarceration for more than one year.[107] For tribes that want to take advantage of enhanced sentencing, it also requires that they must guarantee that all defendants receive "effective assistance of counsel at least equal to that guaranteed by the United States Constitution,"[108] the judges presiding over these cases have sufficient legal training to preside over criminal matters and be licensed to practice law by a U.S. jurisdiction,[109] the tribes codify and publish their criminal codes, rules of evidence and rules of criminal procedure[110] and the tribal courts maintain a record (possibly an audio recording) of the criminal proceeding.[111]

Restorative Approaches to Improving Indigent Defense in Canadian Aboriginal Communities

The EWG next discussed the Canadian Aboriginal population which faces similar pathologies and challenges as the Native American population in the United States. In Canada, there are less active tribal law structures than in the United States. Criminal matters in Canadian Aboriginal communities are managed by Canadian Courts and virtually all criminal defense for Aboriginal individuals is handled by legal aid.[112]

One expert detailed the Canadian efforts to find new ways to approach justice problems in Aboriginal areas in order to minimize their contact with the Canadian criminal justice system. Canada has implemented a series of alternatives that exist on a continuum from local grassroots efforts to community-implemented restorative justice processes, even when dealing with extremely serious criminal offenses. (*See* Appendix A, International Practices, Restorative Justice for Aboriginal Communities in Canada.)

Court processes for Aboriginal people fall into three categories: (1) Gladue courts,[113] (2) indigenized courts,[114] and (3) itinerant courts.[115] Each has its strengths and each continues to be improved. To be effective, however, each system requires adequate training for court personnel, sufficient funding, oversight and safeguards for victims and their families.

One participant noted that these efforts can empower Aboriginal communities, which are often disenfranchised from the greater, Canadian criminal justice system. In many Aboriginal communities, the system appears too lenient because offenders who are convicted and incarcerated are often handled by a process that is removed from the Aboriginal community. Minimal efforts are made to engage the community in these mainstream processes, so it appears as if offenders have simply disappeared for a few years. When offenders return to the community at the completion of their sentence, it appears as if there was no accountability to the community at large. Thus, restorative justice processes not only provide an opportunity for communities to take responsibility for their own problems, but to allow for a process of healing.

Participants discussed the degree to which the indigenous legal system is driven by traditions and culture. They discussed the difficulties in trying to implement justice programs in cultures where there might be different views of justice. One participant noted that, like the United States, the Canadian government spent the first half of its history with Aboriginal peoples in an attempt to eradicate traditional processes. But as in the United States, Canada has started to change this approach and efforts to engage traditional responses to justice have increased. Given the relative newness of this approach, difficulties still exist and so the Canadian government is also working to refine its common law system to be more user-friendly to its indigenous community by employing more Aboriginal people in its courts.

Defender Services in U.S. Tribal Courts

The EWG next discussed the successes in providing effective defender services in tribal courts in the United States and focused on the Tribal Court Public Defense Clinic at the University of Washington. The clinic was formed in July 2002 out of an effort of the Tulalip Tribes to find an innovative way to provide public defender services in its court, which it was not obligated to do.[116] Today, the clinic partners with the Tulalip, Squaxin Island, Port Gamble S'Klallam and Puyallup Tribes to serve as the public defender in their courts.

The majority of the work of the clinic is with the Tulalip Tribal Court where the clinic has handled over 800 cases, with the assistance of four attorneys and 4-16 students each semester.[117] The clinic provides direct public defense to four tribal courts and as much indirect support to tribal public defenders as possible.[118] The clinic is a part of the Native American Law Center, which has met with delegations from Afghanistan about defender services within an indigenous context.

Another participant noted that the current state of public defense in Indian Country is based on the history of tribes and criminal justice. Historically, tribes' justice processes were restorative or restitution based. The current tribal court model is based more on a Western, adversarial model and consists of a judge (who may or may not be trained in law) and a prosecutor who is often an attorney, but rarely does it include a public defender. He noted that he is seeing a change among those tribes that are able to generate funds through economic development (because tribes do not have the ability to tax non-Indians and non-Indian businesses), but unfortunately many tribes are still in economically depressed areas. While it is important to require representation where incarceration might be ordered, it could be devastating to underresourced tribes to require public defense without providing funding.

He also suggested that special focus be placed on the availability of treatment for offenders including evidence-based research on treatment. Such research would assist the criminal justice system in Indian Country. He also suggested that the Department provide longer grant periods and fund the creation of centers of excellence.

Related Civil Issues

The EWG also discussed civil legal issues in tribal communities, which is an area where tribes have more control over their communities than in the criminal context.

In Indian Country, a number of tribal courts have strong civil legal systems. One participant expressed the belief that this empowers tribal governments to resolve problems for their community. However, the problem is that as in the criminal context, invoking civil jurisdiction is complicated. This can be traced to a line of decisions of the U.S. Supreme Court, which have weakened tribal authority. In *Oliphant v. Suquamish Indian Tribe*,[119] the Court held that non-Indians involved in criminal conduct in Indian Country cannot be prosecuted by tribal courts. Thus, tribes are dependent upon federal or state prosecutors to pursue many criminal cases in Indian County, which is an infrequent occurrence.[120] Consequently, Tribal courts have become very creative using quasi-civil procedures in criminal matters. For example, if a non-Indian commits a crime in Indian Country, tribes may pursue civil actions and seek to confiscate property or impose fines. These processes can empower tribal governments and create a sense of satisfaction among tribal leaders that they can administer justice within their communities.

Another participant felt that one area where tribal jurisdiction is particularly strong is in intramural matters, or internal disputes between tribal or family members, because tribal courts often have strong traditional justice options such as peacemaker courts, mediator courts and elder panels. One participant described a similar program in rural Nicaragua where judges work with lay people in isolated communities to resolve civil, legal problems.[121] Laypersons serve as facilitators for the court system by filing documents and managing the front office. He found that these individuals become important agents of justice within their communities. These processes empowered local communities by training local community members in how to resolve disputes with their own resources.

Interestingly, the experience in Canada is different. One expert remarked that Canada's efforts to support Aboriginal courts and traditional justice have focused on criminal disputes because of the perception that civil matters are less important.

Tribal Juvenile Justice

It was remarked that in the area of tribal juvenile justice, many tribal courts are failing. Washington State tribal leaders met in April 2010 to discuss how to improve tribal juvenile justice. Among the various goals set out at the meeting, the tribes identified reforming tribal juvenile delinquency codes (many of which are modeled on an adult code) as a key priority.[122] Towards that end, the University of Washington's Native American Law Center is developing model juvenile delinquency, truancy and at-risk youth codes.[123]

Participants in that Washington State meeting also discussed enhancing the use of community accountability boards that invoke traditional processes to help reform delinquent youth, such as elder panels or tribal councils. These community accountability boards ask the children to discuss how their actions affect the community. One extremely successful program requires the children to construct their genealogy so that they can better understand how the community is interrelated. They are also taught the history of the tribe in an effort to instill pride.

Sometimes young offenders are diverted into restorative processes, such as conferencing or healing circles, but given that lawyers are absent in these types of efforts, due process concerns exist.

Tribes are anxious to intervene well before children are absorbed in the criminal justice system and endeavor to work with schools to stage interventions for students who are truant. Unfortunately, given restrictions imposed by federal education and privacy laws on who can obtain information about students, tribal leaders often find it difficult to learn which students are not attending school. Therefore, some tribes are working within their counties to create tribal truancy boards sanctioned by the county court so that they might obtain information on truant children more quickly and intervene.

Recommendations

The breakout group on indigenous communities provided the following recommendations:

1. Fund Tribal Public Defender Programs. The federal government should fund public defenders in tribal court so that tribes can take advantage of the enhanced sentencing authority in the Tribal Law and Order Act. At a minimum, the federal government

should fund support and technical assistance to existing tribal public defender programs. As a preliminary matter, an assessment of which tribes are providing public defense must be made.

2. Establish Centers of Support for Tribes at Law Schools. The federal government should help to increase the number of centers of support established in law schools, which have been successful in providing technical assistance.
3. Provide Evidence-Based Services. The federal government should provide funding for evidence-based services in Indian Country. There are many services available in state courts which have been demonstrated to prove effective in the criminal context; however, most of these services, if not all, are not provided in Indian Country.
4. Fund Research to Assess Successes in Tribal and Federal Partnerships. The federal government should fund research to assess criminal justice partnerships between the tribal and federal systems, especially in the pretrial and post-adjudication areas. Research should also be funded to assess reentry of Native Americans post-incarceration into tribal communities.
5. Evaluate the Benefits of Public Defense. The federal government should evaluate the benefits of public defense to tribal communities. This could prompt tribal councils to evaluate existing public defense models to measure their benefits, cost savings and outcomes.
6. *Extend Grant Periods.* The Department should extend the time period for tribes to submit grant applications to the Department. Given the extra time needed to clear grant applications through internal tribe processes, such as elder and tribe councils, an additional 30 days would ease the burden of submitting timely and complete grant applications from applicants in Indian Country.
7. *Study the Transferability of Gladue Courts.* The Department should study Gladue Courts in Canada to assess whether they might be transferrable to urban American cities, where the United States had relocation programs for Native Americans.
8. *Study the Transferability of Reintegration Programs.* The Department should study the Canadian model of employing local reintegration workers as case workers for individuals reentering the community to evaluate long-term treatment and to assist reintegration into the community.

Conclusion: The Way Forward

The workshop was a success. In addition to providing specific recommendations to ATJ and NIJ on how to focus efforts to improve the availability and quality of indigent defense, the convening facilitated new collaborations between domestic and international experts in criminal legal aid. Many of the domestic participants noted that the international dimension of the convening was a new approach to addressing the long-standing problems in indigent defense in the United States.

While the EWG provided 40 recommendations to ATJ and NIJ, including suggestions for a potential research agenda, four key themes emerged:

1. Increased *funding* for quality defender services is needed;
2. Enforceable federal indigent defense *standards* should be created and implemented;
3. *Evidence-based research* on the delivery of legal services to the poor should be funded; including the evaluation of successful domestic and international practices; and
4. *International human rights standards* should be adopted.

All agreed that while increased funding for defenders is critical, more must be done than simply find new money for an old problem. The EWG stressed that federally enforceable standards for indigent defendants are needed to deliver on the nation‘s constitutionally guaranteed promise to provide legal representation to people accused of crime regardless of their ability to pay. And evidence-based research that identifies solutions, including evaluations of successful programs from around the country and the world, could guide policymakers on how to meet those standards. Moreover, the EWG made clear that if solutions could be found from other countries‘ practice or from international human rights standards, there should not be a reluctance to adopt such practices and standards at home.

While funding is a key component of many of these recommendations, the EWG agreed that if implemented, these recommendations would ultimately save money—both by creating greater efficiencies in the system and, more importantly, by creating opportunities for individuals who come into contact with the criminal justice system to turn their lives around.

The EWG acknowledged the many challenges that exist, including the need to convince the public and policymakers of the need for effective criminal defense for the poor during a time of economic uncertainty. But through their thoughtful discussion and collaboration, the participants provided important recommendations for how the federal government can help alleviate many of these challenges and find a way forward to help improve indigent defense.

APPENDIX A: INTERNATIONAL PRACTICES

This appendix provides additional detail on the international practices discussed at the January 24–25, 2011 Expert Working Group on *International Perspectives on Indigent Defense*, jointly convened by the Department of Justice‘s Access to Justice Initiative and National Institute of Justice‘s International Center in Washington, DC. This is not an exhaustive list of international practices mentioned during the workshop, but rather includes those practices that were discussed most extensively. No effort has been made to assess whether these practices can or should be transferred to the United States. The authors hope that assessments of the transferability of some of these practices can be produced in the future.

South African Ombudsman Model

In South Africa, the Office of the Public Protector was created to investigate any conduct in state affairs, or in the public administration in any sphere of government, that is alleged or suspected to be improper or to result in any impropriety or prejudice.[124]

This ombudsman office was established by the interim South African Constitution of 1993 and confirmed as a permanent institution by the final Constitution in 1996. Launched in October 1995, the office of the Public Protector affects jurisdiction over all state bodies, as well as institutions and public entities where the state is the majority owner.

During an investigation, the Public Protector has the discretion to:

- Compel an individual to appear before her to give evidence or to produce any document in his possession or under his control that has a bearing on the matter being investigated and may examine such person for that purpose;
- Request any person at any level of government, or performing a public function, or otherwise subject to her jurisdiction, to assist her in the performance of her duties with regard to a specific investigation; and
- Make recommendations and take appropriate remedial action.

The Public Protector is accountable to the South African National Assembly and must report on her activities and the performance of her functions at least once a year. Any report issued by the Public Protector must be open to the public unless exceptional circumstances require that it be kept confidential.

This ombudsman model has been hailed by many jurisdictions and most recently has influenced the development of similar offices in Eastern Europe.[125]

Community-based Paralegals in Africa

Several countries with limited financial resources and a limited number of trained lawyers have turned to non-lawyers to assist in the provision of criminal legal aid for the poor. Community-based paralegals or —barefoot lawyers" are non-lawyers trained by civil society organizations with local partners in the formal justice system. The role of community-based paralegals varies depending on the needs of a particular country.[126]

Community-based paralegals may represent indigent clients in local courts, in mediation, or in the formal justice system. They may also educate the community about their legal rights, which can increase citizens‘ ability to demand change from government and cultivate democratic culture. The legal services provided by a community paralegal may be combined with other social services in the community to add legitimacy to the legal representation. In some countries there are specialized paralegals that focus on criminal justice issues and mainly engage with police stations, prisons and courts.

They can also provide individuals living in rural communities without access to a formal legal system or representation, an opportunity to vindicate their rights. Community-based paralegals can provide representation for indigent defendants in local traditional courts and because they are members of the same community, they often have unique access and knowledge about the needs of all stakeholders in the community. First started in Africa, these programs have spread throughout the continent and to Ukraine and Indonesia.

Community-based paralegals are often used in countries with a shortage of trained lawyers. In *Sierra Leone*, there are an estimated 10 judges and 100 lawyers for a population of about 5 million individuals.[127] Timap for Justice, a local non-governmental organization, partnered with the Open Society Justice Initiative to establish thirteen paralegal offices to help meet the legal needs in the country.[128] The paralegal program combines training, education, mediation, negotiation, community organizing and advocacy.[129] The paralegals negotiate divorce settlements, resolve land disputes and can help hold government officials accountable for their actions in the community.[130] Specialized teams of criminal justice paralegals in three offices assist detainees to secure bail at police stations and through magistrates.

Additionally, Sierra Leone operates a dual system, recognizing both formal legal and traditional processes. The community-based paralegals are trained in both formal law and community-based dispute resolution.[131] This enables the paralegals to assist clients in the traditional system with the added knowledge of the defendant‘s rights under the formal legal system and the ability to assess conflict-of-law issues in the dual system.

In *Malawi*, the Paralegal Advisory Service was initially started to reach prison populations without access to lawyers. Paralegal training courses include criminal law and procedure, interviewing skills and information management.[132] The paralegals provide legal advice and ―know your rights‖ trainings for individuals who proceed pro se.[133] The paralegals also work with different criminal justice agencies in an effort to improve coordination and cooperation between them.[134] The program in Malawi has been adapted and applied in *Benin, Kenya* and *Uganda.*

The Malawi program has recently expanded its use of paralegals into other parts of the criminal justice system due to their success in the prison context. Paralegal services are now available in thirteen prisons, covering 84% of the prison population, four court rooms and eight police stations.[135]

Alternative Practices Related to Immigration and Criminal Defense

The EWG learned of alternative approaches in immigration policy when immigrants come into contact with the criminal justice system. In particular, the EWG learned about the European regional human rights system and the safeguards provided to immigrants by the European Convention on Human Rights, as developed through decisions of the European Court of Human Rights, and the practice of one of its member-states, Sweden.

The European Human Rights System

The European Convention on Human Rights (European Convention) contains very few explicit references to non-citizens.[136] As the European Court of Human Rights (ECHR) has made clear on many occasions, the European Convention‘s obligations on the treatment of aliens do not restrict a state‘s right to regulate immigration.

Nonetheless, the ECHR‘s case law has developed substantive rights pertaining to aliens under the following articles:

- Article 2 – providing for the right to life;
- Article 3 – prohibiting torture and inhuman or degrading treatment or punishment; and
- Article 8 – providing for the right to private and family life.

As a result of the special character of the protections afforded under Article 3, the ECHR has rarely needed to examine a case under Article 2.

The prohibition on torture and inhuman or degrading treatment or punishment found in Article 3 is not confined to the territory of the contracting state. It also applies in cases of deportation, extradition or expulsion —where substantial grounds have been shown for believing that the person concerned, if extradited, faces a real risk of being subjected" to treatment contrary to Article 3 in the receiving country.[137] This is an absolute rule and does not allow for a weighing of the state‘s interests against those of the individual. Thus, if the ECHR finds that an expulsion order would violate Article 3, there is an implied obligation of the state to not expel the alien. This is true even when an alien is found guilty of a serious offense or when national security considerations like terrorism are involvei[138] Moreover, this prohibition extends to exceptional circumstances such as in cases where the alien might face the United States‘ —death row phenomenon"[139] or when an alien has been diagnosed with AIDS.[140]

Article 8 of the European Convention protects the rights of everyone to private life and in particular family life. In cases involving Article 8, the issue is whether a fair balance has been struck between the individual‘s private or family life and the state‘s interest in preventing disorder or crime. The ECHR has established certain criteria for the balancing of these interests; however, it has not indicated the relative weight to be given to each. It will consider the nature and seriousness of the offense, the length of stay in the expelling country, the time that has passed since the offense was committed, the best interests of children and the strength of social, cultural and family ties both within the host country and the country of destination. The criteria that usually favor individuals the most are family situation and length of stay in the country.

Nevertheless, the ECHR has made clear that there is no absolute right for immigrants —not to be expelled."[141]

Swedish Law and Practice

The Swedish rules governing the expulsion of convicted immigrants are found in the Aliens Act of 2005, as amended in 2009.[142]

The decision whether to issue a removal order of an immigrant convicted of a crime rests with the criminal court. Under Swedish law, such an order is not characterized as a criminal penalty but is a —special legal consequence" of the crime.[143] The court takes into account the consequences of an expulsion and can reduce the penalty accordingly. Generally, an expulsion order is combined with a prohibition of the non-citizen‘s return to Sweden, either for a limited duration (normally five or ten years) or indefinitely.

The Aliens Act also sets conditions for expulsion of a convicted immigrant.[144] First, the immigrant must have committed a crime of such seriousness that it could lead to imprisonment. Second, either there should be reason to assume that the immigrant will continue his criminal activities in the country or the crime should be so serious that he could not be allowed to remain. For the court to conclude that an immigrant has the propensity to commit additional crimes, a prior criminal record is usually a prerequisite. Serious crimes of violence, sex crimes and drug offenses are grounds for expulsion without a prior record. In fact, under Swedish practice, an offense that warrants imprisonment for at least one year will normally justify the expulsion of the offender.

The Swedish courts weigh the conflicting interests of the state and the individual in a manner similar to the balancing test performed by the ECHR under Article 8 of the European Convention. The Aliens Act stipulates that the court shall consider the immigrant‘s general life situation, including whether she has children in Sweden who need her, her other family ties and her length of stay in Sweden.[145] Other factors include the immigrant‘s housing and work situation and other signs of integration into Swedish society, such as knowledge of the Swedish language. Family ties carry great weight, especially if a spouse or a child is a Swedish citizen.

The immigrant‘s length of stay is a particularly important factor under Swedish law. If she has been in Sweden legally for five or more years – or four years since being granted permanent residency – she can only be expelled for exceptional reasons.[146] But a child who has come to Sweden before turning 15 and who has lived in Sweden for at least five years cannot be expelled at all.[147]

Law School Clinics in South Africa

Law school clinics can help fill a need for defender services, while also providing law students with practical legal skills. Student engagement in criminal defense clinics may also encourage law students to pursue careers in criminal defense or at least have an appreciation for the importance of effective criminal defense in the legal system.

In *South Africa,* there are several law school clinics operating with a variety of important partners. The University of Witwatersrand‘s Wits Law Clinic was created approximately twenty years ago and is one of the biggest law school clinics in South Africa. In 1994, the Wits Law Clinic entered into a partnership agreement with the South African Legal Aid Board.[148]

The University of Johannesburg‘s law school also has a clinical program. It operates a variety of clinics, including the Johannesburg Courts Clinic, which exists through a partnership with the South African Department of Justice. In exchange for alleviating caseloads and improving legal services to the general public, the clinic has access to the Department of Justice‘s facilities.[149] The clinic has four locations in the Central Divorce Court, the Inquests Court, the Centre for Juvenile Offenders in the Johannesburg Magistrate‘s Court and the Office for Family Violence.[150] Students at these clinics provide advice to clients and also draft case pleadings, notices and other documents.[151]

The law school clinic at University of KwaZulu-Natal also has an established legal clinic. The clinic operates a version of the popular American Street Law program developed by Professor David McQuoid-Mason.[152] In the program law school students volunteer their time, sometimes for school credit, to teach school children, prisoners and communities about their legal rights.[153] Another component of the clinic is to provide legal aid, which is primarily civil and juvenilerelated.[154] This opportunity provides law students with practical experience and also provides indigent clients with an additional resource in the community.

Restorative Justice for Aboriginal Communities in Canada

For traditional and Aboriginal communities, western notions of criminal justice may not be the best fit. Instead, communities might be strengthened by adopting alternative methods of seeking to restore justice by more directly focusing on the victim and the harm done to the community while protecting the rights of the accused. While no formal definition of restorative justice exists, NIJ held a series of symposia in the late 1990s that offered a variety of working definitions.[155]

Based on these symposia, NIJ has characterized the concept as follows:

> Restorative justice principles offer more inclusive processes and reorient the goals of justice. Restorative justice has been finding a receptive audience, as it creates common ground which accommodates the goals of many constituencies and provides a collective focus. The guiding principles of restorative justice are:
>
> - Crime is an offense against human relationships;
> - Victims and the community are central to justice processes;
> - The first priority of justice processes is to assist victims;
> - The second priority is to restore the community, to the degree possible;
> - The offender has personal responsibility to victims and to the community for crimes committed;
> - Stakeholders share responsibilities for restorative justice through partnerships for action;
> - The offender will develop improved competency and understanding as a result of the restorative justice experience.[156]

Canada has invoked restorative justice processes with its Aboriginal communities. Two of these processes that have received considerable attention are Sentencing Circles and Gladue Courts.

The more common of the two is alternative sentencing known as *Sentencing Circles,* which allows communities to intervene in criminal justice matters.[157] In order to access this alternative sentencing process, the accused must plead guilty to an offense. Sentencing Circles may also require offenders to confess to other crimes that were not the focus of the particular investigation, which can create due process violations. For example, if a Sentencing Circle can be accessed by an individual accused of child sex abuse, not only must the individual plead guilty to the offense that has brought him or her to the attention of the authorities, but the defendant must also plead guilty to all other unreported and detected incidents against a child.[158]

Sentencing Circles are essentially conversations between the victim, offender and their families with members of the community present as facilitators. They proceed without the presence of a judge, prosecutor, defense attorney or other court personnel in the room. The primary objectives are to initiate a healing process between the victim and offender so they can move on from the offense and continue to live in the same community and to produce a more relevant and culturally informed sentence for the offender.

Researchers find that in these types of processes, the primary motive for defense lawyers to encourage their clients to enter into a Sentencing Circle process is to avoid incarceration. This often creates a conflict for the lawyer as they ask their clients to give up important due process rights for the opportunity to receive a potentially non-incarcerative sentence. However, often after the offender enters into the Sentencing Circle process, the risk-need profile presented by the offender through his or her own testimony is not conducive to a non-incarcerative sentence. Thus, the offender will have to be sentenced to a program outside of the community given that only a few Aboriginal communities have services to support community-based sentencing, such as drug and alcohol treatment or other health or social services.

Measuring the effectiveness of these Sentencing Circles is somewhat difficult. One Sentencing Circle in Canada claimed that it reduced recidivism by 80%.[159] However, the Canadian government has not formally evaluated these processes so far. The Australian Institute of Criminology (AIC) has conducted an evaluation of Sentencing Circles in *Australia* and found that they have not made an impact on recidivism.[160] Instead, AIC found that the best predictor of an offender's future behavior is past behavior.

Other researchers have found that Sentencing Circles probably benefit offenders more than victims. An unfortunate, but frequent result is re-victimization of the injured. Moreover, while the community members often report feeling empowered at the start of the process, the end result is often one in which promises are not fully kept and follow-up is difficult to conduct.[161]

Another restorative justice model used in Canada for Aboriginal communities is problem-solving courts staffed with Aboriginal community members. The most common problem-solving court in Canada is the *Gladue Court.*[162] In Gladue Courts, court-personnel obtain extensive training on Aboriginal communities and the possible reasons why individuals from these communities are overrepresented in the criminal justice system. The Gladue workers create a comprehensive pre-sentencing report, which includes information obtained through meetings conducted with family and community members. They then work with offenders to help resolve problems and to prevent recidivism. The pre-sentencing report includes a risk-needs assessment to consider the resources the individuals need to overcome their problems. To date, evaluations of Gladue Courts indicate that they work well and are cost effective.[163]

APPENDIX B: AGENDA

Monday, January 24, 2011

8:30 –9:00 Registration, Networking Coffee and Continental Breakfast
9:00 –9:15 Opening Remarks

National Institute of Justice Director Dr. John H. Laub Associate Attorney General Thomas Perrelli

9:15 – 9:25 Workshop Goals and Outcomes

Ed Connors, President, Institute for Law and Justice, Workshop Facilitator

The facilitator will provide instruction on the roundtable format and the direction, goals, and outcomes of the workshop.

9:25 – 11:00 Framing the Issue: Indigent Defense in the United States

Presentations

- Prof. Randolph Stone, University of Chicago School of Law
- Jo-Ann Wallace, President & CEO, NLADA
- Christina Swarns, Director of Criminal Justice Practice, NAACP – LDF
- Virginia Sloan, President & Founder, The Constitution Project

Facilitated Roundtable Discussion

Participants will have an opportunity to discuss their goals for the workshop and the questions they would like to explore over the course of the day and a half.

11:00 – 11:15 Break

11:15 – 12:45 Costs Associated with Being Indigent in the Criminal Justice System

Presentations

- Tapio Lappi-Seppala, Director, National Research Institute of Legal Policy – Finland
- Brian Ostrom, Principal Court Research Consultant, National Center for State Courts
- Nicholas Green, QC, Immediate Past Chairman, English Bar Council
- Prof. David Bruck, Washington & Lee School of Law

Facilitated Roundtable Discussion

This panel will explore the economic and non-economic costs associated with incarcerating and sentencing low-income individuals convicted of crimes across a variety of jurisdictions. Discussion will focus on how poverty amplifies such issues as the rate of incarceration in different jurisdictions and the costs associated with incarceration and sentences such as the death penalty.

12:45 – 2:00 Lunch

Lynn Overmann, Deputy Counselor for Access to Justice Assistant Attorney General Laurie Robinson

Keynote Speaker: Chief Justice Margaret Marshall (ret.)

2:00 – 3:30 Improvements to the Provision of Defender Services for the Poor

Presentations

- Prof. Norm Lefstein, Indiana University School of Law-Indianapolis
- Zaza Namoradze, Director of Budapest Office, Open Society Justice Initiative
- Thomas Giovanni, Director, Community Oriented Defender Network, Brennan Center for Justice
- Michael Karnavas, International Criminal Defense Lawyer

Facilitated Roundtable Discussion

Panelists will discuss innovations that have improved the provision of defender services to low-income individuals both domestically and abroad.

3:30 –3:45 Break

3:45 –5:00 The Intersection of Indigent Defense and Immigration

Presentations

- Prof. John Rubin, UNC-Chapel Hill School of Government
- Anders Mansson, Head of Division, European Court of Human Rights

Facilitated Roundtable Discussion

This panel will discuss the effects of the intersection of immigration and criminal law on indigent defense, both domestically and abroad.

5:00 – 5:30 Highlights from the Day

In this facilitated roundtable, participants will have a chance to comment on the day's highlights and discuss the research questions raised in presentations and discussions.

5:30 Adjourn Day 1

Tuesday, January 25, 2011

8:00 – 8:25 Networking Coffee and Continental Breakfast

8:25 – 8:30 Welcome

Deborah Leff, Deputy Counselor for Access to Justice

8:30 – 10:00 I mprovements for Juveniles

Presentations

- Robert Schwartz, Executive Director, Juvenile Law Center
- Prof. Ton L iefaard, University of Utrecht
- Prof. Thomas Geraghty, B l uhm Legal Clinic, Northwestern University School of Law
- Patricia Puritz, Executive Director, National Juvenile Defender Center

Facilitated Roundtable Discussion

This panel will discuss the special problems chi l dren of l ow-i ncome fami l i es encounter when they are involved i n the criminal justice system and alternative international practices to address juveni le justice.

10:00 – 10:10 Break
10:10 – 11:30 Indigent Defense in Indigenous Communities

Presentations

- John Harte, Partner, Mapetsi Policy Group
- Prof. Ron Whitener, Director, Tribal Court Criminal Defense Clinic, University of Washington School of Law
- Prof. Jane Dickson-Gilmore, Carleton University- Ottawa

Facilitated Roundtable Discussion

Panelists will discuss the unique situations faced by indigenous communities in providing access to justice for the accused in tribal and national criminal justice systems. The panel will also cover informal or traditional justice mechanisms.

11:30 – 11:40 Facilitator Review of Panels and Discussion Highlights
11:40 – 11:55 Break
11:55 – 1:15 What Research is Needed?

Breakout Sessions

Participants will be divided into moderated roundtable discussions to discuss highlights and research needs.

Facilitated Review of Breakout Sessions

The groups will come together to discuss major points of interest to explore in research and to propose a new research agenda.

1:15 Adjourn Day 2

APPENDIX C: LIST OF PARTICIPANTS

Duren Banks
Chief, Prosecution and Adjudication Statistics Unit
Bureau of Justice Statistics
U.S. Department of Justice Washington, DC

Marlene Beckman
Counselor, Office of the Assistant Attorney General
Office of Justice Programs U.S. Department of Justice Washington, DC

Ira Belkin
Program Officer, Law and Rights The Ford Foundation, Beijing Office
Beijing, China

David Bruck
Professor
Washington and Lee University
School of Law, Lexington, VA
Melanca Clark Senior Counsel
Access to Justice Initiative
U.S. Department of Justice Washington, DC

Cait Clarke
Director, Federal Programs Equal Justice Works
Washington, DC
Edward Connors President
Institute for Law and Justice
A l exandri a, VA

Robin Dahlberg
Senior Staff Attorney, Racial Justice Program/National Legal Staff American Civil Liberties Union New York, NY

Jane Dikson-Gilmore
Associate Professor
Carleton University Ottawa, Canada

Joshua Dohan Director
Youth Advocacy Department Roxbury, MA

Donald Farole
Statistician, Prosecution and Adjudication Statistics Unit Bureau of Justice Statistics U.S. Department of Justice Washington, DC

Nadine Frederique
Social Science Analyst
National Institute of Justice U.S. Department of Justice Washington, DC

Thomas Geraghty
Associate Dean for Clinical Education, Professor of Law Director, Bluhm Legal Clinic
Northwestern University School of Law
Chicago, IL

Thomas Giovanni
Director of the Community Oriented
Defender Network

Brennan Center for Justice
New York, NY

Jon Gould
Director, Washington Public Policy
Research Institute
American University
Washington, DC
Martin Gramatikov
Assistant Professor Tilburg University Tilburg, The Netherlands

Kathi Grasso
Senior Juvenile Justice Policy and Legal Advisor, Office of Juvenile Justice and Delinquency Prevention U.S. Department of Justice Washington, DC

Nicholas Green
Immediate Past Chairman of the Bar English Bar Council
London, United Kingdom

Mary Greer
Senior Criminal Law Advisor ABA Rule of Law Initiative Washington, DC

John Harte
Partner
Mapetsi Policy Group Washington, DC

Sam Hirsch
Deputy Associate Attorney General Office of the Assistant Attorney General
U.S. Department of Justice Washington, DC

Benita Jain
Co-Director
Immigrant Defense Project
New York, NY

Miranda Jolicoeur
International Liaison and Research Analyst (MetaMetrics, Inc. Contractor)
International Center
National Institute of Justice U.S. Department of Justice Washington, DC

Joseph Jones
Senior Counsel for Rule of Law Office of the Deputy Attorney General
U.S. Department of Justice Washington, DC

Maha Jweied
Senior Counsel
Access to Justice Initiative U.S. Department of Justice Washington, DC

Michael Karnavas
International Criminal Defense Lawyer
The Hague, The Netherlands

Tapio Lappi-Seppala
Director
National Research Institute of Legal
Policy - Finland
Helsinki, Finland

Steven Lang
Coordinator, Legal Orientation and Pro Bono Program
Executive Office for Immigration Review
Falls Church, VA

Karen Lash
Senior Counsel
Access to Justice Initiative U.S. Department of Justice Washington, DC

Deborah Leff
Deputy Counselor for Access to Justice
Access to Justice Initiative U.S. Department of Justice Washington, DC

Norman Lefstein Professor of Law and Dean Emeritus
Indiana University School of Law - Indianapolis
Indianapolis, IN

Kirsten Levingston
Program Officer, Reforming Civil and Criminal Justice Systems
The Ford Foundation New York, NY

Ton Liefaard
Assistant Professor
University of Utrecht Willem Pompe Institute for Criminal Law and Criminology Utrecht, The Netherlands
Katayoon Majd
Program Officer for Criminal and Juvenile Justice Public Welfare Foundation Washington, DC

Anders Mansson Head of Division,
Human Rights Chamber
European Court of Human Rights Strasbourg, France

Chief Justice Margaret Marshall (ret.)
Supreme Judicial Court of Massachusetts
Boston, MA

Vivek Maru
Senior Counsel, Justice Reform
Practice Group
The World Bank
Washington, DC

Mary Meg McCarthy
Executive Director
Heartland Alliance's National Immigrant Justice Center Chicago, IL

Maureen McGough
Outreach Coordinator
National Institute of Justice U.S. Department of Justice Washington, DC

Liz McGrail
Legal Director
Capital Area Immigrants Rights
Coalition
Washington, DC

Joanne Moore
Director
Washington State Office of Public
Defense
Olympia, WA

Zaza Namoradze Director, Budapest Office
Open Society Justice Institute Budapest, Hungary
Daniel Olmos Senior Counsel
Access to Justice Initiative
U.S. Department of Justice Washington, DC

Brian Ostrom
Principal Court Research Consultant National Center for State Courts Williamsburg, VA

Lynn Overmann
Deputy Counselor for Access to Justice, Access to Justice Initiative U.S. Department of Justice Washington, DC

Patricia Puritz
Executive Director National Juvenile Defender Center Washington, DC

JoAnne Richardson
Senior Program Manager
National Center for State Courts Arlington, VA

Jane L. Ross
Director, Committee on Law and Justice
The National Research Council Washington, DC

John Rubin
Professor of Public Law and Government, School of Government University of North Carolina-Chapel Hill

Chapel Hill, NC
Robert Schwartz Executive Director Juvenile Law Center Philadelphia, PA

Virginia Sloan
President & Founder
The Constitution Project Washington, DC

Robin Steinberg
Executive Director
The Bronx Defenders Bronx, NY

Randolph Stone
Clinical Professor of Law University of Chicago
School of Law Chicago, IL

Christina Swarns
Director of the Criminal Justice Practice
NAACP Legal Defense Fund New York, NY

Danica Szarvas-Kidd
Policy Advisor for Adjudication Bureau of Justice Assistance U.S. Department of Justice Washington, DC

Jo-Ann Wallace
President & Chief Operating Officer National Legal Aid & Defender Association Washington, DC

Ron Whitener
Director, Tribal Court Public Defense Clinic University of Washington School of Law Seattle, WA

Wendy Young
Executive Director Kids in Need of Defense Washington, DC

Lin Zhu
China University of Political Science and Law
International Visiting Scholar American University
Washington College of Law Washington, DC

APPENDIX D: RECENT DOJ EFFORTS AND FUNDED RESEARCH ON INDIGENT DEFENSE

Access to Justice Initiative (ATJ) http://www.justice.gov/atj/

- Indigent Defense

A key priority of the Access to Justice Initiative is working with national indigent-defense advocacy groups and public defenders from across the country to address the crisis in the provision of indigent legal defense. The Initiative's strategic goals in this area include expanding research on the delivery of indigent defense, encouraging comprehensive planning and reform, increasing training and technical assistance for defender programs, strengthening juvenile justice and supporting tribal courts. For more information on the Access to Justice Initiative, visit http://www.justice. gov/atj/.

Office of Justice Programs (OJP) http://www.ojp.usdoj.gov/

- *DOJ National Symposium on Indigent Defense held February 18-19, 2010* Symposium Materials available at: http://www.ojp.usdoj.gov/ BJA/topics/inddef index.html

National Institute of Justice (NIJ) http://www.ojp.usdoj.gov/nij/

- *NIJ 2010 Conference, Keynote Address by Laurence Tribe, former Senior Counselor for Access to Justice.* Discussing indigent defense in the United States. Video of Keynote Speech available at: http://nij.ncjrs.gov/multimedia/video-nijconf2010-keynote-tribe.htm
- *International Perspectives on Wrongful Convictions Report (Sept. 2010)* This report provides an overview of the participants' discussions at the International Perspectives on Wrongful Convictions Workshop held in September 2010. Report available at: http://www.nij.gov /topics/ courts/sentencing/internationalperspective-on-wrongful-convictions.pdf
- *Implementation and Impact of Indigent Defense Standards. (Dec. 2003)* (NIJ grant recipient: National Legal Aid and Defender Association) This report discusses the impact of indigent defense standards in assessing the need for standardization of this constitutionally mandated governmental service. Report available at: http://www.ncjrs.gov/pdffiles1/nij/grants/205023.pdf

Bureau of Justice Assistance (BJA) http://www.ojp.usdoj.gov/ BJA/

- BJA Projects and Programs on Indigent Defense http://www. ojp.usdoj.gov/BJA/ topics/IndigentDefense.pdf
- Public Defense Reform Since Gideon: Improving the Administration of Justice By Building On Our Successes and Learning From Our Failures: A Public Defense Leadership Focus Group (2008) (BJA grant recipient: American University Criminal Courts Technical Assistance Project and American University Criminal Courts Technical Assistance Project). This report provides a summary of focus group discussions held to review the successes and failures in the delivery of public defense services and assess the lessons learned resulting in recommendations for the future. Report available at: http://www.ojp.usdoj.gov/BJA/pdf/NLADA PubDefLeadership. pdf
- *What Policymakers Need To Know To Improve Public Defense Systems (Dec. 2001)* (BJA grant recipient: Harvard University, John F. Kennedy School of Government). One in a series of papers developed by the Executive Session on Public Defense, a 30-member effort with leading figures in public defense. In This paper sets out questions to aid policymakers in assessing the value and effectiveness of their public defense systems. Paper available at: http://www.ncjrs. gov/pdffiles1/bja/190725.pdf
- *Keeping Defender Workloads Manageable (2001)* (BJA grant recipient: The Spangenberg Group) This report discusses approaches developed by public defender organizations, state legislatures, state courts and other entities to managing the workloads of attorneys who represent indigent defendants. Report available at: http://www.ncjrs.gov/ pdffiles1/ bja/185632.pdf
- *Contracting for Indigent Defense: Special Report (2000)* (BJA grant recipient: The Spangenberg Group) Written for individuals in the justice system who are using, considering or implementing an indigent defense contract system, this report presents the major judicial and legislative attempts to deal with those systems, examines the best and worst features of contract systems and discusses the national standards that govern contract systems. Report available at: http://www.ncjrs.gov/ pdffiles1/bja/ 181160.pdf
- *Indigent Defense and Technology: A Progress Report (1999)* (BJA grant recipient: The Spangenberg Group)
- This report looks at how technology is changing the way attorneys and staff work in public defender offices. Report available at: http://www.ncjrs.gov/pdffiles1/bja/ 179003.pdf

Bureau of Justice Statistics (BJS) http://bjs.ojp.usdoj.gov/

- County-based and Local Public Defender Offices (2007) This BJS produced report examines the provision of public defender services in the 27 states and the District of Columbia in which indigent defense services were funded and administered by counties or local jurisdictions in 2007. Report available at: http://bjs.ojp.usdoj.gov /index.cfm?ty=pbdetail&iid=2211

- State Public Defender Programs (2007) This BJS produced report examines the provision of public defender services in the 22 States that had an entirely State-funded and State-administered indigent defense program in 2007. Report available at: http://bjs.ojp.usdoj. gov/index.cfm?ty=pbdetail&iid=2242

Office of Juvenile Delinquency and Prevention (OJJDP) http://www.ojjdp.gov/

- OJJDP FY 10 Juvenile Indigent Defense National Clearinghouse. The National Juvenile Defender Center was awarded OJJDP funding to operate this clearinghouse: http://www.njdc.info
- OJJDP News At A Glance Article (March/April 2010)
  Summary of juvenile defender topics addressed at the 2010 DOJ National Symposium on Indigent Defense. Available at: http://www.ncjrs.gov/html/ojjdp/ news at glance/229711/topstory.html

National Institute of Corrections, Federal Bureau of Prisons (NIC) http://nicic.gov/

- Evidence-Based Practices and Criminal Defense: Opportunities, Challenges, and Practical Considerations (Aug. 2008)
- One in a set of papers focused on the role of system stakeholders in reducing offender recidivism through the use of evidence-based practices in corrections.
- Available at: http://nicic.gov/library/files/023356.pdf

End Notes

1 Andrea Estes, —Call for Public Defender Overhaul,|| *The Boston Globe,* Jan. 24, 2011.

2 Participants came from Bulgaria, Canada, China, Finland, Hungary, the Netherlands, Sweden, the United Kingdom, and the United States. The list of participants for this workshop can be found at Appendix C.

3 The Workshop Agenda can be found at Appendix B.

4 *See* Appendix A, International Practices.

5 On wrongful convictions, see Miranda Jolicoeur, "International Perspectives on Wrongful Convictions: Workshop Report," September 2010, U.S. Department of Justice, National Institute of Justice, International Center, *available at* http://www.nij.gov/topics/courts/sentencing/international-perspective-on-wrongful-convictions. pdf.

6 *See* Carrie Geer Thevenot, —Settlement Ends Ex-Inmate's Saga, County Insurance to Pay Miranda, Who Spent Years on State's Death Row," *Las Vegas Review-Journal,* June 30, 2004.

7 *See* written testimony of Dawn Van Hoek, Chief Deputy Director, State Appellate Defender Office, Detroit, Michigan, to U.S. House of Representatives Committee on the Judiciary, House Subcommittee on Crime, Terrorism and Homeland Security, Congressman Robert Scott, Chairman, —Penny-Wise and Pound-Foolish: Waste in Michigan Public Defense Spending," Mar. 26, 2009, *available at* http://www.michigan campaignforjustice.org/ docs/DVH%20written%20testimony%203-26-09.pdf.

8 David Carroll and Scott Wallace, —Implementation and Impact of Indigent Defense Standards," (Dec. 2003), Award No. 1999-IJ-CX-0049, National Institute of Justice, Office of Justice Programs, U.S. Department of Justice, *available at* http://www. ncjrs.gov/pdffiles1/nij/grants/205023.pdf.

[9] Bill Luchansky, Ph.D., *Looking Glass Analytics,* The Public Defense Pilot Projects Washington State Office of Public Defense (June 2010), *available at* http://www.opd.wa.gov /Reports/TrialLevelServices/1006 PilotProject.pdf. The Washington State Office of Public Defense has also run Pilot Projects Providing Parental Representation in Dependency Proceedings. Evaluations of those projects can be found at http://www. opd.wa.gov/ Reports/DTReports.htm.

[10] *Id.*

[11] An ombudsman is —[a]n official appointed to receive, investigate, and report on private citizens' complaints about the government," Bryan A. Garner, ed., *Black's Law Dictionary,* 9th ed. (2009).

[12] The American Bar Association (ABA) has a longstanding tradition of supporting the creation of ombudsman offices in the federal government, dating back to 1969. The most recent ombudsman-related ABA policy was adopted in August 2001 and states that the ABA —[(1) s]upports the greater use of ‗ombuds' to receive, review and resolve complaints involving public or private entities and [(2)] endorses the Standards for the Establishment and Operation of Ombuds Offices." *See* ABA's Section of Administrative Law and Regulatory Practice Policy page, *available at* http://www. americanbar.org/groups/ administrative law/policy.html.

[13] *Argersinger v. Hamlin*, 407 U.S. 25 (1972).

[14] *See* Donald J. Farole, Jr., Ph.D., & Lynn Langton, U.S. Department of Justice, Bureau of Justice Statistics, *Census of Public Defender Offices: County-based and Local Public Defender Offices, 2007,* NCJ 231175 (Sept. 2010); Lynn Langton & Donald Farole, Jr., Ph.D., U.S. Department of Justice, Bureau of Justice Statistics, *Census of Public Defender Offices: State Public Defender Programs, 2007,* NCJ 228229 (Sept. 2010).

[15] Farole & Langton, U.S. Department of Justice, Bureau of Justice Statistics, *Census of Public Defender Offices: County-based and Local Public Defender Offices, 2007,* NCJ 231175 (Sept. 2010) at 1.

[16] Langton & Farole, U.S. Department of Justice, Bureau of Justice Statistics, *Census of Public Defender Offices: State Public Defender Programs, 2007,* NCJ 228229 (Sept. 2010) at 18.

[17] Farole & Langton, U.S. Department of Justice, Bureau of Justice Statistics, *Census of Public Defender Offices: County-based and Local Public Defender Offices, 2007,* NCJ 231175 (Sept. 2010) at 1; Langton & Farole, U.S. Department of Justice, Bureau of Justice Statistics, *Census of Public Defender Offices: State Public Defender Programs, 2007,* NCJ 228229 (Sept. 2010) at 1.

[18] West, Sabol, & Greenman, U.S. Department of Justice, Bureau of Justice Statistics, *Prisoners in 2009,* NCJ 231675 (Dec. 2010); *see also* The Sentencing Project, —Facts About Prisons and Prisoners," June 2011, *available at* http://www.sentencingproject.org/ doc/publications /publications/inc factsAboutPrisons Jun2011.pdf.

[19] Peter Wagner, —Incarceration Is Not an Equal Opportunity Punishment," Prison Policy Initiative, http://www.prisonpolicy.org/articles/notequal.html (last updated June 28, 2005).

[20] Alice King, Justice Action Center, *Collateral Consequences of Criminal Conviction: Five-State Resource Guide* (2007) at 14-18.

[21] *See* Randolph Stone, —The Role of State Funded Programs in Legal Representation of Indigent Defendants in Criminal Cases,|| 17 *Am. J. Trial Advocacy* 205, 217-18 (1993) (describing the creation of the Criminal Defense Consortium of Cook County).

[22] *See* Burge Archive on the *Chicago Tribune* website: http://articles.chicagotribune.com/ keyword/jon-burge

[23] *See* University of Chicago Human Rights Program, Human Rights at Home: The Chicago Police Torture Archive, Timeline, *available at* http://humanrights.uchicago.edu/ chicagotorture/timeline.shtml.

[24] The Byrne JAG Program, administered by the Department's Bureau of Justice Assistance (BJA), is the leading source of federal justice funding to state and local jurisdictions. The Byrne JAG Program provides states, tribes and local governments with critical funding necessary to support a range of program areas including law enforcement, prosecution and court, prevention and education, corrections and community corrections, drug treatment and enforcement, planning, evaluation and technology improvement, and crime victim and witness initiatives. For more information on this program, visit: http://www.ojp.usdoj. gov/BJA/grant/jag.html.

[25] Justice for All Reauthorization Act of 2010, S. 3842, 111th Cong. (2010).

[26] *See* National Advisory Commission on Criminal Justice Standards and Goals United States, Report of the National Advisory Commission on Criminal Justice Standards and Goals, NCJ 010865 (1973), *abstract available at* http://www.ncjrs.gov/App/ Publications/ abstract.aspx?ID=10865.

[27] Tapio Lappi-Seppa, —Exploring the Differences in Incarceration Rates" (Jan. 2011) at 1, unpublished manuscript (on file with the National Institute of Legal Policy, Finland).

[28] Tapio Lappi-Seppa, —Trust, Welfare, and Political Culture: Explaining Differences in National Penal Policies," 37 *Crime & Just.* 313, 316 (2008).

[29] *Id.*

[30] Interview with Tapio Lappi-Seppa, Director General of the National Research Institute of Legal Policy. Finland, International Juvenile Justice Observatory (July 21, 2010); *see also* Justice Policy Institute, *Finding Direction: Expanding Criminal Justice Options by Considering Policies of Other Nations*, at 46 (Apr. 2011) (indicating that 6 children in Finland were in secure confinement in 2008).

[31] Plan International, The Netherlands, —Kids Behind Bars," at 78 (Stan Meuwese, 2003).

[32] The expert also noted that the United Kingdom‘s Ministry of Justice has also begun to look into private involvement in noncustodial sentences to reduce prison populations (i.e., sending prisoners to perform community service instead of serving prison time).

[33] Catherine T. Clarke, —Message in a Bottle for Unknowing Defenders: Strategic Plea Negotiations Persist in South African Criminal Courts," 32 *Comp. Int'l. L.J. S.Afr.* 141, 142 (1999).

[34] *See, e.g.*, Open Society Justice Initiative, Global Campaign for Pretrial Justice Report, *The Socioeconomic Impact of Pretrial Detention* (Feb. 2011), *available at* http://www. soros.org/initiatives/justice/focus/criminal justice/articles publications/publications/ socioeconomicimpact-detention-20110201/socioeconomic-impact-pretrial-detention-02012011.pdf.

[35] *See* Open Society Justice Initiative, —Legal Empowerment for the Poor" webpage at http://www.soros.org/initiatives/justice/focus/legal capacity/projects/lep.

[36] Vivek Maru, Open Society Justice Initiative, —Between Law and Society: Paralegals and the Provision of Primary Justice Services in Sierra Leone," at 28 (Mar. 2010), *available at* http://www.soros.org /initiatives/justice/articles publications/publications/between-law-and-society-20100310.

[37] *Id.* at 4.

[38] Martin Gramatikov, Maurits Barendrecht, Malini Laxminarayan, Jin Ho Verdonschot, Laura Klaming, & Corry van Zeeland, *A Handbook for Measuring the Costs and Quality of Access to Justice* (2010), Maklu: Apeldoorn, Antwerpen, Portland.

[39] Brian J. Ostrom, Matthew Kleiman, & Christopher Ryan, *Maryland Attorney and Staff Workload Assessment, 2005*, Maryland Office of the Public Defender, National Center for State Courts, (2005), at 7, *available at* http://www.ncsconline.org/ WC/ Publications/Res WorkLd MDAtty&StaffWkLdAs05Pub.pdf.

[40] *See id.* at 7.

[41] *Id.* at 8-9.

[42] *Id.* at 7-8.

[43] *Id.*

[44] *Id.* at 8.

[45] *See* Maryland Office of the Public Defender, FY 2008 Annual Report, at 18, *available at* http://www.opd.state.md.us/News%20Assets/annual%20report%202008.pdf.

[46] Holly R. Stevens et al., The Spangenberg Project, "State, County and Local Expenditures for Indigent Defense Services: Fiscal Year 2008," at 9-68 (2010).

[47] In the United Kingdom, the legal aid schemes for Scotland and Northern Ireland are run independently of the system in England and Wales. For a comparison of the criminal defense systems in England and the United States, *see* Norman Lefstein, —Criminal Defense Representation in England and the United States," International Legal Aid Group Conference Paper (June 2005), *available at* http://www.ilagnet.org/jscripts/tiny mce/plugins/filemanager/files/Killarney 2005/Additional Papers/6.1 Norman Lefstein. pdf.

[48] *Id.* at 3.

[49] *See* Eurojustice Prosecution in the European Union, Country Report for England and Wales, —The Role of the Public Prosecutor in Court" webpage, *available at* http://www.eurojustice.com/member states/england wales/country report/451/.

[50] For a description of the funding scheme for legal aid in England Wales from the 1940s until today, *see* Roger Smith, —Legal Aid in England and Wales: Entering the Endgame," *International Legal Aid Group Newsletter* (May 5, 2011), *available at* http://www. ilagnet.org/newsletterstories.php?id=37.

[51] European Convention on Human Rights, Council of Europe, § I, art. 6, Nov. 4, 1950, E.T.S., at 5, *available at* http://www.conventions.coe.int/Treaty/ Commun/QueVoulez Vous.asp? NT=005&CM=8&DF=14/06/2011&CL=EN G.

[52] *See* Legal Services Commission, —What is Legal Aid?" page, *available at* http://www.legalservices.gov.uk/public/what legal aid.asp (last updated April 1, 2011). Note that the Legal Services Commission also runs the civil legal aid scheme in England and Wales.

[53] *See* Ministry of Justice, —Proposals for the Reform of Legal Aid in England and Wales," Consultation Paper CP12/10 at 31 (Nov. 2010), *available at* http://www.justice.gov. uk/consultations/legal-aid-reform.htm.

[54] *Id.*

[55] *See* Ministry of Justice, —Breaking the Cycle: Effective Punishment, Rehabilitation and Sentencing of Offenders," Cm 7972 (Dec. 2010); *see also* Ministry of Justice, —Breaking the Cycle: Effective Punishment, Rehabilitation and Sentencing of Offenders," Green Paper Evidence Report, (Dec. 2010); both *available at* http:// www.justice.gov.uk/ consultations /consultation-040311.htm.

[56] Alan Travis, —Kenneth Clarke Down, Prison Population Up," *The Guardian* (June 21, 2011).

[57] *See* Ministry of Justice, "Proposals for Reform of Civil Litigation Funding and Costs in England and Wales Implementation of Lord Justice Jackson's Recommendations," Consultation Paper CP 13/10 (Nov. 2010); *see also*, Ministry of Justice, "Reforming Civil Litigation Funding and Costs in England and Wales – Implementation of Lord Justice Jackson's Recommendations – The Government Response," Cm 8041 (Mar. 2011); *both available at* http://www.justice.gov.uk/consultations/jackson-review.htm.

[58] *See* Suzi Ring, "Government Confirms Jackson Civil Litigation Reforms and Legal Aid Cuts," June 21, 2011, *Legalweek.com*.

[59] Rhonda Cook & Steve Visser, "Murderer Nichols' Tab: $3 Million and Growing," *The Atlanta-Journal Constitution,* July 21, 2009.

[60] Jon B. Gould & Lisa Greenman, Report to the Committee on Defender Services, Judicial Conference of the United States, *Update on the Cost and Quality of Defense Representation in Federal Death Penalty Cases* 25, 44 (2010).

[61] The Spangenberg Group, "Rates of Compensation for Court-Appointed Counsel in Capital Cases at Trial: A StateBy-State Overview" (June 2007), *available at* http://www.americanbar.org/content/dam/ aba/migrated/legalservices/sclaid/defender/downloads/2007FelonyCompR atesUpdate Capital.authcheckdam. pdf.

[62] Virginia Capital Litigation Data Excel Spreadsheet, Virginia Capital Case Clearinghouse, http://www.vc3. org/resources/page.asp?pageid=561.

[63] *See generally*, Virginia Indigent Defense Commission, Annual Report 2008 6-14 (2008) (describing the creation, purpose and operation of the Commission).

[64] ABA Standing Committee on Legal Aid and Indigent Defendants, —ABA Ten Principles of a Public Defense Delivery System, Principle 1 (note commentary at p. 2) (Feb. 2002); *see also* ABA Standards for Criminal Justice: Providing Defense Services (3d ed., 1992) at 5-1.3.

[65] *Strickland v. Washington*, 466 U.S. 668, 686 (1984).

[66] ABA Standing Committee on Legal Aid and Indigent Defendants, —ABA Ten Principles of a Public Defense Delivery System, Principle 2 (note commentary at p. 2) (Feb. 2002).

[67] *See* Norman Lefstein, —In Search of Gideon's Promise: Lessons from England and the Need for Federal Help,|| 55 *Hastings L.J.* 835, 861-920 (Mar. 2004).

[68] *See* San Mateo County Bar Association's Private Defender Program description, *available at* https://www.smcba.org/News/NewsDetail.aspx?NewsId=3

[69] European Commission, *Procedural Safeguards for Suspects and Defendants in Criminal Proceedings Throughout the European Union*, Green Paper from the Commission, Brussels, Belgium, 19 February 2003, COM(2003) 75 final, para. 2.5.

[70] Ed Cape, Zaza Namoradze, Roger Smith & Taru Spronken, *Effective Criminal Defence in Europe* (Antwerp: Intersentia, 2010), at 613.

[71] *Id.*

[72] *Salduz v. Turkey*, 49 EHRR 19 (2009), (holding that access to a lawyer should be provided, as a rule, from the first police interview of a suspect, unless it could be demonstrated, in light of the particular circumstances of a given case, that there had been compelling reasons to restrict this right), *available at* http://www.bailii. org/eu/cases/ECHR/2008/ 1542.html).

[73] *See, e.g.*, European Commission Press Release, —European Commission to Guarantee Suspects' Rights to Speak With a Lawyer, Inform Family of Arrest" (June 8, 2011), *available at* http://europa.eu/rapid/press ReleasesAction.do? reference=IP/11/ 689&format =HTML&aged=0&language=EN&guiL anguage=en; *see also*, European Commission's Criminal Justice page, —Rights of Suspect and Accused," *available at* http://ec. europa.eu/justice/criminal/criminal-rights/index en.htm.

[74] See Melanca Clark & Emily Savner, *Community Oriented Defense: Stronger Public Defenders*, Brennan Center for Justice, p. 14 fn. 13 (2010) (listing studies demonstrating reductions in incarceration and recidivism rates), *available at* http:// www. brennancenter.org/content/resource/CODrcport/.

[75] For information on the International Criminal Defence Attorneys Association, see http://www.aiad-icdaa.org/index.php?section=1.

[76] *See* International Criminal Tribunal for the Former Yugoslavia's Defence page, http://www.icty. org/sections/AbouttheICTY/Defence; *see also* International Criminal Tribunal for Rwanda, Defence Counsel

and Detention Management Section page, http://www.unictr.org/tabid/107/default.aspx; *see also* Association of Defence Counsel Practising Before the International Criminal Tribunal for the Former Yugoslavia, http://adc-icty.org/.

[77] *See* International Criminal Court Defence webpage, http://www.icccpi.int/Menus/ ICC/ Structure+of+the+Court/Defence/.

[78] *See* The Special Court for Sierra Leone Registry webpage, http://www.scsl.org/ABOUT/ CourtOrganization/TheRegistry/tabid/79/Default.aspx.

[79] *See* The Extraordinary Chambers in the Courts of Cambodia Defence Support Section webpage, http://www.eccc.gov.kh/en/dss/defence-support-section-dss/.

[80] *See* Special Tribunal for Lebanon, Defence Office description, http://www.stl-tsl.org/sid/28.

[81] *Padilla v. Kentucky*, 130 S. Ct. 1473 (2010).

[82] *See, e.g.*, Immigrant Defense Project, *A Defending Immigrants Partnership Practice Advisory: Duty of Criminal Defense Counsel Representing an Immigrant Defendant after Padilla v. Kentucky* (Apr. 6, 2010), *available at* http://txe.fd.org/PDF% 20files/ PadillaPractice Advisory.pdf.

[83] Collateral consequences are consequences that are not part of the criminal sentence but arise or are imposed as a result of a conviction.

[84] *See* ABA Criminal Justice Section, Adult Collateral Consequences Project Site, *available at* http://isrweb.isr.temple.edu/projects/accproject/blog.cfm?RecordID=1.

[85] *See* ABA Criminal Justice Section, Adult Collateral Consequences Statute Demonstration Site, *available at* http://isrweb.isr.temple.edu/projects/accproject/. As of August 1, 2011, the project catalogued 38,012 collateral consequences statutes, an average of 700 collateral consequences per state.

[86] *See* Letter from Attorney General Eric Holder to State Attorneys General, April 18, 2011, *available at* http://www.nationalreentryresourcecenter. org/documents/0000/1088/ Reentry Council AG Letter.pdf.

[87] *See* Laura Abel, Brennan Center for Justice, *Language Access in State Courts* at 16 (2009) (describing the practice of court systems that charge interpreter costs and the steps the Department of Justice takes to combat these bad practices). For recent Department efforts on this issue, *see* Letter from Assistant Attorney General Thomas E. Perez to Chief Justices and State Court Administrators, providing guidance to state courts on the requirement to provide meaningful access for limited-English-proficient individuals (Aug. 16, 2010), *available at* http://www.lep.gov/final courts ltr 081610. pdf.

[88] Exceptional circumstances include an offence that entails serious danger to public order and security, including a danger to national security. *See* Swedish Aliens Act of 2005, SFS 2005:716, chapter 8, §11 (Sept. 29, 2005) and Act amending the Aliens Act 2009, SFS 2009:1542, chapter 8 (Dec. 30, 2009). For an English summary of the 2005 Act and 2009 Amendments, visit this Government of Sweden site: http://www.sweden.gov.se/sb/d/5805/a/66122.

[89] *See* Illegal Immigration Reform and Immigrant Responsibility Act of 1996, Pub. L. 104-208, 110 Stat. 3009-546 (codified in scattered sections of 8 U.S.C.).

[90] Juvenile Law Center, —Luzerne County Kids for Cash‘ Scandal" (2009), *available at* http://www.jlc.org/luzerne/.

[91] *See, e.g.,* Pennsylvania Juvenile Court Judges‘ Commission, Pennsylvania Juvenile Court Dispositions at 41-46 (2007) (reporting that in 2007 for all delinquency dispositions in Luzerne County, approximately 64% concerned juveniles were white, 19% concerned juveniles were Latino, and 16% concerned juveniles were African American).

[92] National Juvenile Defender Center and National Legal Aid & Defender Association, —Ten Core Principles for Providing Quality Delinquency Representation Through Public Defense Delivery Systems," Principle 1 (July 2008).

[93] Convention on the Rights of the Child, G.A. Res 44/25, *opened for signature* Nov. 20, 1989 (entered into force on Sept. 2,1990), *available at* http://www2.ohchr.org/english/ law/crc.htm.

[94] For more information on the Juvenile Indigent Defense Action Network, *see* http://www. modelsforchange.net/about/Action-networks/Juvenile-indigent-defense.html.

[95] *Id.*

[96] The states in JIDAN are California, Florida, Illinois, Louisiana, Massachusetts, New Jersey, Pennsylvania and Washington.

[97] *See* Convention on the Rights of the Child, Art. 37 (emphasis added), *available at* http:// www2.ohchr.org/english/law/crc.htm#art37.

[98] *Id.*

[99] *See Muskhadzhiyeva et autres c. Belgique,* Requête 41442/07, Council of Europe: European Court of Human Rights, Jan. 19, 2010, *available at* http://www.unhcr.org/refworld/ docid/4bd55f202.html; *Mubilanzila*

Mayeka et Kaniki Mitunga c. Belgique, 13178/03, Council of Europe: European Court of Human Rights, Oct. 12, 2006, *available at* http://www. unhcr. org/refworld/docid/4533718d4.html.

[100] *See* American Bar Association Rule of Law Initiative, Detention Procedures Assessment Tool, http://apps. americanbar.org/rol/publications/detention procedure assessment tool.shtml.

[101] These reports and assessments are available at http://apps.americanbar.org/ rol/publications. shtml.

[102] The United States signed the convention on February 16, 1995, but has not ratified it. The United States remains one of only two countries that have not ratified the convention — the other is Somalia.

[103] *See* Inter-American Commission on Human Rights, —Report on Immigration in the United States: Detention and Due Process," page 131, Section 379 (stating that the rural location of U.S. detention centers creates significant barriers to legal representation); *see also* Wendy Young & Megan McKenna, —The Measure of a Society: The Treatment of Unaccompanied Refugee and Immigrant Children in the United States," 45 *Harvard Civil Rights-Civil Liberties Law Review* 247 (2010).

[104] For an interesting review of the use of non-lawyers in the legal aid scheme in England and Wales, *see* Richard Moorehead, Avrom Sherr, & Alan Paterson, "Contesting Professionalism: Legal Aid and Nonlawyers in England and Wales," 37 *Law & Soc'y Rev.* 765 (Dec. 2003).

[105] European Network of Ombudspersons for Children (ENOC), http://www.crin.org/enoc/.

[106] Tribal Law and Order Act of 2010, Pub.L. No. 111-211, 124 Stat. 2258 (codified in scattered sections of 25 U.S.C.).

[107] 25 U.S.C § 1302(c) (2) requires that an Indian tribe "at the expense of the tribal government, provide an indigent defendant the assistance of a defense attorney licensed to practice law by any jurisdiction in the United States that applies appropriate professional licensing standards and effectively ensures the competence and professional responsibility of its licensed attorneys."

[108] *Id.* § 1302(c)(1).

[109] *Id.* § 1302(c)(3).

[110] *Id.* § 1302(c)(4).

[111] *Id.* § 1302(c)(5).

[112] In Canada, defendants apply for legal aid and, if they qualify, they receive a certificate for legal aid and can then find their own lawyer.

[113] In Gladue courts, court-personnel obtain extensive training on Aboriginal communities and the reasons why Aboriginal people are overrepresented in the criminal justice system. The Gladue workers create a comprehensive pre-sentencing report, which includes information obtained through meetings with family members and community members, and work with offenders to resolve their problems to prevent recidivism. For more information on the Gladue Courts, *see* Appendix A, International Practices, Restorative Justice in Canada.

[114] Indigenized courts function like other Canadian courts but are staffed entirely by Aboriginal people.

[115] Itinerant courts are mobile and can go into communities, such as the Aboriginal communities.

[116] *See* Wendy Church, —Why Does the Tribe Use the UW Tribal Court Public Defense Clinic?|| (2009), *available at* http://www.tulaliptribes-nsn.gov/Portals/0/pdf/ departments/tribal court/Why-Does-the-Tribe-Use-the-UW-TribalCourt-Public-De fense-Clinic.pdf.

[117] *See* University of Washington, School of Law, Tribal Court Public Defense Clinic website, *available at* http://www.law.washington.edu/Clinics/Tribal/.

[118] *Id.*

[119] *Oliphant v. Suquamish Indian Tribe*, 435 U.S. 191 (1978).

[120] *See, e.g.,* GAO Report, U.S. Department of Justice Declinations of Indian Country Criminal Matters, Dec. 13, 2010, *available at* http://www.gao.gov/new.items/d11167r.pdf.

[121] See Edward Quintanilla, —Support for the Administration of Justice in Nicaragua — The Rural Judicial Facilitators Program," Scaling Up Poverty Reduction: A Global Learning Process and Conference, Shanghai, China, May 25-27, 2004, *available at* http:// siteresources.worldbank.org/EXTGOVAN TICORR/ Resources/3035863- 1291223960989/Nicaragua Rural Judicial1.pdf

[122] *See* University of Washington School of Law, Native American Law Center, —Washington State Tribal Gathering: Tribal Juvenile Justice Enhancement" (Dec. 31, 2010).

[123] *Id.* at 23.

[124] *See* Public Protector of South Africa website, *available at* http://www.pprotect.org/. For a description of the constitutional considerations in creating this office, *see* Jeremy Sarkin, —The Drafting of South Africa's Final Constitution From a Human-Rights Perspective," 47 *Am. J. Comp. L.* 67 (1999).

[125] *See* United Nations Development Programme, Human Rights and Justice in Europe & CIS, —Support to Ombudsman Institutions," *available at* http://europeandcis.undp. org/ governance/hrj/show/D468315E-F203-

1EE9- B48913F1882228DE; *see also* United Nations Development Programme, Human Rights and Justice in Europe & CIS, Ombudsman Creation Acts, *available at* http://europeandcis.undp. org/governance/ hrj/show/D4DBEA27-F203- 1EE9-B982684BD0814688.

[126] Open Society Justice Institute has created a guide to creating a paralegal program: *Community-Based Paralegals: A Practitioners Guide* (2010), *available at* http://www._soros.org/initiatives/justice/focus/legal capacity/articles publications/ publications/ paralegals-manual20101208.

[127] Timap for Justice, www.timapforjustice.org; *see also* Vivek Maru, —Between Law and Society: Paralegals and the Provision of Primary Justice Services in Sierra Leone," Open Society Justice Initiative (2006).

[128] *Id.*

[129] *Id.*

[130] *Id.*

[131] *Id.*

[132] *Access to Justice in Africa and Beyond: Making the Rule of Law a Reality* (2007), Penal Reform International and the Bluhm Legal Clinic of the Northwestern University School of Law, p. 147; full text *available at* http://www.penalreform.org/files/rep-2007-access-africa-and-beyond-en.pdf.

[133] *Id.*

[134] *Id.*

[135] *Id.*

[136] European Convention on Human Rights, Council of Europe, Nov. 4, 1950, E.T.S. at 5, *available at* http://www.conventions.coe.int/Treaty/ Commun/QueVoulezVous.asp ?NT=005&CM=8&DF=14/06/ 2011& CL=EN G.

[137] *Soering v. the United Kingdom*, 11 EHRR 439, §91 (1989), *available at* http://www. bailii.org /eu/cases/ECHR/1989/14.html.

[138] *See, e.g., Chahal v. the United Kingdom*, 23 EHRR 413, §80 (1997) (holding —The prohibition provided by Article 3 (art. 3) against ill-treatment is equally absolute in expulsion cases. Thus, whenever substantial grounds have been shown for believing that an individual would face a real risk of being subjected to treatment contrary to Article 3 (art. 3) if removed to another State, the responsibility of the Contracting State to safeguard him or her against such treatment is engaged in the event of expulsion [...]. In these circumstances, the activities of the individual in question, however undesirable or dangerous, cannot be a material consideration. The protection afforded by Article 3 (art. 3) is thus wider than that provided by Articles 32 and 33 of the United Nations 1951 Convention on the Status of Refugees [...],"*available at* http://www.bailii.org/eu/cases/ECHR/1996/54.html.

[139] *Soering v. the United Kingdom*, 11 EHRR 439, §111 (holding —[I]n the Court's view, having regard to the very long period of time spent on death row in such extreme conditions, with the ever present and mounting anguish of awaiting execution of the death penalty, and to the personal circumstances of the applicant, especially his age and mental state at the time of the offence, the applicant's extradition to the United States would expose him to a real risk of treatment going beyond the threshold set by Article 3 (art. 3). A further consideration of relevance is that in the particular instance the legitimate purpose of extradition could be achieved by another means which would not involve suffering of such exceptional intensity or duration. Accordingly, the [United Kingdom‘s] Secretary of State's decision to extradite the applicant to the United States would, if implemented, give rise to a breach of Article 3 (art. 3)," *available at* http://www.bailii.org/eu/ cases/ ECHR/ 1989/14.html.

[140] *D. v. the United Kingdom*, 24 EHRR 423 (1997) (holding that the United Kingdom‘s deportation order violated Article 3 of the European Convention on Human Rights because the applicant was diagnosed with AIDS and would receive inferior medical treatment in his home country of St. Kitts), *available at* http://www.bailii.org/eu/cases/ECHR/1997/25.html.

[141] *Üner v. the Netherlands*, 45 EHRR 14, §5 (2007), *available at* http://www.bailii.org/ eu/cases/ ECHR/2006/873.html (holding —While a number of Contracting States have enacted legislation or adopted policy rules to the effect that long-term immigrants who were born in those States or who arrived there during early childhood cannot be expelled on the basis of their criminal record (see paragraph 39 above), such an absolute right not to be expelled cannot, however, be derived from Article 8 of the Convention, couched, as paragraph 2 of that provision is, in terms which clearly allow for exceptions to be made to the general rights guaranteed in the first paragraph.").

[142] Swedish Aliens Act of 2005, SFS 2005:716 (Sept. 29, 2005) and Act amending the Aliens Act, 2009, SFS 2009:1542 (Dec. 30, 2009). For an English summary of the 2005 Act and its 2009 Amendments, visit the Government of Sweden website: http://www.sweden. gov.se/ sb/d/5805/a/66122.

[143] Swedish Penal Code, Chapter 29, § 5(4).

[144] Swedish Aliens Act, Ch. 8, § 8.

[145]*Id.* Ch. 8, §11(1).

[146] *Id.* Ch. 8, § 12. Exceptional circumstances include an offence that entails serious danger to public order and security, including a danger to national security. *See id.* at § 11.

[147] *Id.*

[148] University of Witwatersrand, Johannesburg, Wits Law Clinic, *available at* http://www.wits. ac.za/lawclinic/ 11045/witslawclinic.html.

[149] University of Johannesburg Law Clinic, http://www.uj.ac.za/EN/Faculties /law/about/ Pages/LawClinic.aspx.

[150] *Id.*

[151] *Id.*

[152] For more information on the Street Law model, visit http://www.streetlaw.org/en/index.aspx.

[153] University of KwaZulu-Natal, Street Law Program webpage, *available at* http://law.ukzn.ac. za/StreetLaw Programme.aspx.

[154] University of KwaZulu-Natal, Law Clinic webpage, *available at* http://law.ukzn.ac.za/ LawClinic.aspx.

[155] *See* National Institute of Justice, Working Definition of Restorative Justice webpage, *available at* http://www.ojp.usdoj.gov/nij/topics/courts/restorative-justice/ definitions 1. htm.

[156] *See* National Institute of Justice, Restorative Justice webpage, *available at* http://www.ojp. usdoj.gov/nij/ topics/courts/restorative-justice/welcome.htm.

[157] For more information on Sentencing Circles in Canada, *see* Jane Dickson-Gilmore & Carol LaPrairie, *Will the Circle Be Unbroken?: Aboriginal Communities, Restorative Justice, and the Challenges of Conflict and Change* (2005).

[158] This is the experience reported out of the —Community Holistic Circle Healing" program being administered in the community of Hollow Water, Manitoba. *See* Therese Lajeunesse, *Evaluation of the Hollow Water Community Holistic Circle Healing Project,* Ottawa: Solicitor General Canada, 1996; Native Counselling Services of Alberta, *A Cost-Benefit Analysis of Hollow Water's Community Holistic Circle Healing Process* (Ottawa: Solicitor General, Aboriginal Peoples' Collection no. 20, 2001).

[159] Robin J. Wilson, Franca Cortoni, & Andrew J. McWhinnie, —Circles of Support & Accountability: A Canadian National Replication of Outcome Findings," 21(4) *Sex Abuse* (2009), 412-430.

[160] Jacqueline Fitzgerald, —Does Circle Sentencing Reduce Aboriginal Offending?" 115 *Crime and Justice Bulletin* (May 2008), 1-2.

[161] *See* Jane Dickson-Gilmore & Carol LaPrairie, *Will the Circle Be Unbroken?: Aboriginal Communities, Restorative Justice, and the Challenges of Conflict and Change* (2005) at 133-153.

[162] For more information on Gladue Courts, visit this page administered by the Community Legal Education Ontario http://www.cleonet.ca/resources/1042; *also* visit the Aboriginal Legal Services of Toronto website at http://www.web.net/~alst/.

[163] For example, in Toronto, the Gladue Court costs only $500,000 over three years. *See* Aboriginal Legal Services of Toronto (ALST) Evaluation of Gladue Courts (Years 1, 2, 3), *available at* http://www.aboriginallegal. ca/gladue.php.

INDEX

#

A

B

C

D

E

F

G

H

N

O

P

Q

R

S